Protecting Plants:

[10—0]
With chicken wire fence against rabbits

[10—0a]
From excessively strong light by green-tinted shade applied to greenhouse

[10—0b]
By mulching

[10—0c]
By keeping them in a cold frame

[10—1]
Flowering Peach
(Prunus Persica variety)

[10—1a]
Flowering Cherry
(Prunus serrulata variety)

NEW ILLUSTRATED ENCYCLOPEDIA

OF GARDENING

UNABRIDGED

EDITED BY T. H. Everett

Assistant Director (Horticulture) and Curator of Education
The New York Botanical Garden

WITH CONTRIBUTIONS FROM

TWENTY HORTICULTURISTS AND AUTHORITIES IN THE UNITED STATES AND CANADA

Growers, Breeders, Exhibitors, Plantsmen, Writers, Lecturers, Professors, Editors and Superintendents of Famous Estates, who are Experts in all Fields of Horticulture, including Pests and Their Control.

VOLUME TEN—Pro-Root

GREYSTONE PRESS · NEW YORK

This cold frame has an outer framework of wood built around it with the space between packed with straw to give added protection against winter cold.

Frames will need attention in the matters of ventilating on favorable occasions and protecting during very cold weather with mats or other special insulation. Sometimes additional protection for cold frames is provided by banking their outside walls with earth or by erecting around them a supplementary wooden framework and stuffing the space between it and the sides of the frame with straw, hay, dry leaves or other insulating material. This may, with advantage, be

Mats may be rolled over cold frames at night to protect the plants they contain from extreme cold.

topped off with a layer of waterproof paper or plastic film.

A favorite method of protecting young rock-garden plants, shrubs, perennials, etc., that are hardy or nearly so and that are in small pots, is to plunge (bury to the rims of the pots) them in a bed of sand, sand and peat moss, or fine coal ashes in a cold frame. This keeps them from drying too quickly and reduces the danger of the pots being broken by the expansion of the soil as it freezes.

Many tender, summer-flowering bulbs, corms and tubers such as Dahlia, Gladiolus, Montbretia, Fancy-leaved Caladium, Tuberous Begonia, Ismene and Tuberose are dug up in fall before severe frost and are stored in a frost-free room or cellar where they will not shrivel by being subjected to a too dry and warm environment. Often the bulbs, corms and tubers are stored in peat moss or sand to keep them from drying.

Cold frames are used in spring to harden off plants that have been grown in greenhouses and later are to be planted outdoors. They are also used to raise early plants that are sown directly in them. In both cases the purpose is to protect the plants from low temperatures and other unfavorable conditions, such as wind and too-strong sunshine.

Plants cared for in cold frames in spring should be gradually accustomed to air and sun as the date for their removal from the frames to the outside approaches. This process is known as hardening off.

Hotcaps, Hottents and Cloches. Hotcaps and Hottents are manufactured devices of translucent paper that are inverted over seedlings or small plants, newly set out in the garden, to protect them from cold and wind for a few days or even two or three weeks. They are used in spring, especially for such crops as Melons, Cucumbers and others that are notoriously sensitive to cold.

Cloches are made of wire and glass or wire and transparent plastic and are designed to protect young plants in the garden much in the same manner as Hotcaps and Hottents do. They may be of a size to cover a small area or a continuous row of plants.

Snow, Ice and Water. There is no better

Tying evergreens to prevent snow injury. *(Left to right)* Snow on branches causes drooping and breaking. Winding the tree with twine keeps the branches from spreading when loaded with snow.

winter protective mulch for plants than snow. Where it remains on the ground throughout the winter, mulches for protection from cold are unnecessary.

Snow rarely does damage to plants unless it lies so heavily on branches that it breaks them by its weight. Heavy snow can be harmful to evergreens. Boxwood is especially vulnerable. A heavy, wet snow is naturally more likely to do damage than snow that is light and fluffy. When removing snow, disturb the branches with an upward push of a rake or broom rather than push downwards and increase the weight they already bear. This should be done as soon as

To prevent breakage, snow should be removed from evergreens before it becomes wet and heavy or freezes hard. The snow should be removed from the lower part of the bushes or shrubs first.

possible after the snow has fallen, before it freezes or becomes wet and heavy.

Snow falling from roofs on to foundation plantings can cause a lot of breakage. The installation of snow guards on the roof will do much to prevent this. Small evergreens may be protected by inverting bushel baskets or large boxes over them.

Ice storms are very damaging; unfortunately little can be done to prevent the harm they do. Good pruning practices build trees and shrubs with stout, strong frames; such specimens are less likely to suffer damage than are others.

Ice and water lying around the crowns and bases of plants cause much loss. Adequate soil drainage is the surest preventative of these happenings. Water in poorly drained ground is responsible for poor growth and rotting of roots and other underground plant parts. Attention to drainage takes care of this. On sloping land, surface drainage not properly controlled can wash out newly planted areas, causing gulleys and surface erosion. Careful grading, draining and planting to prevent washing of the surface soil is a first responsibility of every gardener.

PROTHALLUS. The prothallus or prothallium represents an essential stage in the life history of a number of plants such as the Fern, Lycopodium (Club Moss), Selaginella and Equisetum. In all these the prothallus is formed by the germination and development of the spores. For example, Fern spores, when they come in contact with moisture, give rise to a prothallus. This is a thin, green, heart-shaped structure bearing a number of root hairs which fix it to the soil and extract the nourishment.

On the underside small male and female organs are produced. The male organ is a small roundish body with two cilia (hairs) which propel it through a film of moisture to the female and fertilization is effected. When the female organ has been fertilized it develops into a young Fern plant, which at first has a single Fern-shaped leaf and finally grows into a complete Fern plant.

In Lycopodium the prothalli are mostly cylindrical, the upper part lobed and green, and the lower part more solid and sunk into the soil. They take several years to mature, but finally produce sexual organs, and after fertilization, new Lycopodiums (Club Mosses) are produced.

The prothalli in Selaginella are very minute and remain practically enclosed in the spores. There are two types, the male and female prothalli. Therefore the two kinds of spores must be sown to produce fertilization. The Horsetails (Equisetum) also produce two types of prothalli.

There is a danger of confusing the prothallus of a Fern with the thallus of a Liverwort, which is similar in appearance but much larger and of altogether coarser texture.

PROVENCE ROSE. Rosa centifolia, which see.

PRUMNOPITYS ELEGANS. Podocarpus andina, which see.

PRUNE. This name is applied to varieties of Plums which have firm flesh and a high content of sugar and thus are especially well adapted for drying. They are much grown for drying on the Pacific coast, and in the East are often grown and sold to be consumed in a fresh state, as are other Plums. See Plum.

PRUNE. See Pruning.

PRUNELLA—*Selfheal* (Prunel'la). Dwarf, hardy, herbaceous plants which belong to the family Labiatae. They grow wild in most of northern Europe and northern Asia and North America.

The Prunellas form tufts of foliage close to the soil, and the leaves are stalked, ovate, crinkled, green or purplish-green. The flowers, which are purple, red or white, are formed in dense upright spikes in summer.

The name Prunella, which has been altered from Brunella, is derived from the German *die Braune*, quinsy, for which this plant was supposed to be a remedy.

The most showy kind is P. Webbiana, 9 in., bright rosy-purple. P. grandiflora grows about 6 in. in height and has large spikes of purple flowers. The varieties alba (white) and rubra (red) are also free-flowering and ornamental. They are used for furnishing the rock garden and will flourish in almost any soil or position. They do best, however, in light soil and require shading from the midday sun.

The rose-purple Prunella Webbiana.

Planting and Propagation. Planting is done in September–October, or spring, the plants being set about 6 in. apart and the soil made firm around the roots. The soil is kept moist by watering in dry weather and a mulch of decayed manure or rich compost is applied in April. The plants should not be disturbed for several years, but, when they show signs of deterioration, they are lifted in spring or autumn, divided and replanted in fresh soil. This is the chief method of propagation.

PRUNING: AN IMPORTANT ART
How to Prune Trees, Shrubs and Vines

Pruning is an old, important and much misunderstood garden art. Many amateurs make the mistake of supposing that all, or nearly all, trees and shrubs need this attention regularly and so cut out branches and shorten them back indiscriminately. These are serious errors. No cut

A pole pruner enables the operator to cut off small high branches while standing on the ground.

should ever be made without good reason and without an understanding of what the results are likely to be.

The extent to which pruning is advisable may depend not only upon the kind of plant but also upon the purposes for which it is being grown. A tree espaliered against a wall or fence is obviously pruned differently from one allowed to develop its natural shape in the open; evergreens used as hedges are closely and regularly sheared, but those grown as solitary lawn specimens are left unpruned.

The kind and amount of pruning required may vary, too, at different periods in the life of a plant. Young trees, shrubs and vines often need formative or developmental pruning to encourage them to grow in desired patterns and to develop into satisfactory mature specimens. In middle age the pruning required will be of a kind designed to maintain them in good health and productive of flowers, fruits and foliage. Later, pruning may need to be done with especial emphasis on prolonging the life of valued specimens.

One type of pruning that can be done without fear of making a mistake, and that can be done at any time, is the removal of dead and seriously diseased wood. This should be done promptly and effectively. Besides being unsightly, dead branches harbor destructive pests and diseases and, in the case of trees, may be a danger to property and people.

Tools and Implements. The chief tools used by the pruner are saws, shears and knives. To these may be added ladders and, if cuts more than an inch in diameter are to be made, some type of dressing to apply to the wounds.

Tools should be sharp, of good quality, and adapted to the type of pruning that is to be done. They should be handled with care and respect. Serious accidents can occur from the careless employment of pruning tools. Particular

The upper end of the pole pruner is hooked around the branch to be severed.

A downward pull of the rope produces a scissors-like action which cuts off the branch.

Ladders must be carefully placed to avoid slipping. They should be strong and in good condition. It is always advisable to have someone standing on the lowest rung when pruning from a ladder. When doing such work, it is wise to wear shoes with rubber or composition soles rather than leather. If wet, leather-soled shoes are very likely to slip.

Special tree-wound paints are procurable from

A pole saw is admirable for removing out-of-reach branches.

A pole saw cuts on the pull or downward stroke.

caution should be exercised when using electrically driven implements such as hedge shears. As a safety measure it is well to wear rubbers or stand on a dry plank when using these. Wooden ladders are safer to stand on when using electric tools than are metal ones. Always disconnect power pruners from the source of power when they are not in use.

To make tree-wound paint, take some white lead.

Mix with the white lead an equal bulk of powdered sulphur.

Then add enough lampblack to give a desirable color.

Next, add sufficient linseed oil to make a thick paint.

Stir the ingredients thoroughly until a uniform mixture is obtained.

Margins of cut surfaces should first be painted with shellac to protect the cambium.

Next, tree-wound paint is applied to cover the entire cut surface.

Over large cuts the coat of tree-wound paint is renewed periodically.

Protective callus tissue continues to grow from the cambium layer.

dealers in horticultural supplies and are very good. Equal parts by weight of Bordeaux mixture and boiled linseed oil or of fine sulphur and thin white lead-linseed oil paint are also satisfactory dressings for pruning cuts. To protect the cambium layer, the rim of the cut, for a distance of about half an inch from its outside circumference, should be painted with shellac dissolved in alcohol before the wound paint is applied. Large cuts should be repainted yearly until they have healed over.

Techniques. Every effort should be made not to damage trees or shrubs accidentally or carelessly when pruning. Damage may occur when placing ladders, or may be caused by branches being torn off as the result of faulty cuts, and in

Eventually, the wound heals completely and is covered with new bark.

branch will develop. The cut should be a sloping one.

When removing large, heavy limbs, the safest plan is to take them off in sections. To remove the last major section (or the entire branch, if it is small enough to be taken off in one piece), three distinct cuts should be made. This prevents the bark and wood of the trunk or portion of the branch that is to be retained from being torn when the cut-off portion falls. The first cut, an undercut, should be made about a foot from the trunk and extend through a quarter or a third of the diameter of the branch. Then the limb should be sawed through from the upper side, beginning 3-4 in. further from the trunk than the undercut and cutting straight through the branch (not towards the undercut) until the branch falls. The last cut is made from above and removes the stump that is left. Because the stump is light, the result will be a

other ways. Climbing irons or spikes such as telephone linemen use should never be worn when pruning valued trees.

When an entire limb is to be removed, the final cut should be made flush or nearly flush with the trunk. When a branch is to be shortened, it should be cut back to just above (beyond) a side branch or bud from which a side

When pruning, stubs such as this should never be left. They die, prevent healing and encourage decay.

When cutting off a branch, an undercut is made first.

Then saw through the branch completely with an overcut.

The falling branch does not tear off bark beyond the undercut.

The stub is removed by sawing it off close to the trunk.

Finally the edges of the cut surface are pared with a sharp knife prior to applying tree-wound paint.

clean wound without any tearing of the bark, if the cut is carefully made.

It is much better for inexperienced individuals to leave the pruning of big trees strictly to professional tree surgeons than to risk life and limb doing it themselves.

All cuts should be made cleanly without fraying the tissues. Saw cuts should be pared around their edges with a sharp knife to give them a smooth surface.

Formative Pruning. From their earliest stages the grower of trees, shrubs and woody vines

Unless they are needed to form new main branches, suckers like these, arising from the main trunks of this English Hawthorn, should be cut out while they are young.

So far as is practicable, unwanted growths, such as the thin sucker shoots shown here, should be removed early.

Young sucker shoots or water sprouts such as these, which spring from older branches of Apples and other trees, should be removed when quite small.

Crossing branches that are likely to cause interference as they develop should be cut out while they are yet young.

should have clearly in mind the purpose for which each is being grown and the ideal form the plant must have to satisfy this purpose. Clearly, specimens that are espaliers must be trained in one plane (flat), with their branches arranged in fan-form, gridiron or other suitable pattern. Trees, especially fruit trees, are often pruned so that they develop an open, more or less round top or head, with a number of main branches (scaffold branches) of approximately equal importance arising from different levels, instead of a single central trunk.

Single-Leader Pruning. Many shade trees are pruned "to a single leader"—that is, in such a manner that the central trunk is dominant throughout the life of the tree and no secondary trunks are permitted to develop. Not all shade trees lend themselves, however, to this mode of development. The American Elm, for example, naturally produces several trunks of approximately equal girth and size, a feature which is responsible for its beautiful vaselike form.

Modified-Leader Pruning. The modified leader form of tree is often preferred for Apples,

Apricots, Cherries, Peaches and some other fruits. The pruning required to produce modified leader trees consists of cutting off the top of the year-old tree to induce the formation of side branches and a new leader, the early removal of all branches that develop except those selected to be retained as scaffold branches (main framework limbs of the tree), the cutting back of the leader after two or three years to a point where a strong side branch grows from it and the prevention, by pruning, of the development of any dominant central leader.

Open-Center Pruning. Apples and other fruit trees are sometimes pruned to form open-center trees, vase-shaped specimens that branch low down and have no central leader. Pruning to develop this type of tree consists of cutting back a year-old specimen to a height of about 3 ft., selecting a limited number of side shoots to form scaffold branches, pruning out all others, and preventing the development of any new central leader by cutting out any shoots which arise that might develop into one.

Standards. Fuchsias, Geraniums, Heliotropes, Lantanas, Buddleias and other plants may be grown as "standards"—that is, with a single, erect stem that is unbranched for a distance of two or three feet or more and carries at its top a bushy head of branches. These and other plants may be pruned to other formal shapes.

Pruning to develop trees, shrubs and vines to required forms should begin early. Shoots not needed in the development of the trunk and branch system should be removed before they become large. The shoots retained should be, as far as is practicable, stout healthy ones and well placed. In most instances, and particularly in the case of fruit trees, the main branches should be disposed so that each receives plenty of light and good air circulation even when the foliage is fully out. Crossed branches are generally considered to be a defect, so formative pruning should aim to prevent these from developing.

Hedges. During their formative years hedges need special attention. They should be sheared regularly, one or more times each season, depending upon the amount of growth they make. Fast-growing kinds such as Privet and Barberry may need two or more clippings each year;

slower-growing items, such as Beech, Yew and Holly, only one.

A hedge should be clipped during its formative period in such a way that it increases in height and width a few inches only each year (perhaps as much as a foot in the case of vigorous-growing kinds), and always so that the base of the hedge is slightly wider than the top. This permits the lower foliage to receive good light and prevents it from being shaded by the upper part of the hedge.

Compensatory Pruning. It often happens that when a tree, shrub or other plant is transplanted, a considerable proportion of its roots is cut off. Those that remain are very likely to be insufficient to absorb enough moisture to provide for the needs of the normal leafage the plant has or will soon develop. To bring about a more assured balance of intake and outgo of water (moisture is lost through the leaves), it is common practice to prune back the tops of plants at transplanting time.

This is done with trees, shrubs, vines and Roses as well as with such plants as Geraniums, Fuchsias, Heliotropes, Lantanas and Begonias that are lifted from the outdoor flower beds in late summer or fall and are planted in pots for wintering indoors.

Whenever roots are seriously reduced or damaged, consideration should be given to the desirability of carrying out compensatory pruning of the branches. The extent to which the tops are cut back should depend upon the amount by which the roots have been reduced and upon the type of plant, as well as upon the season and purposes for which it is being grown. Often the top is reduced by as much as one third or one half.

Rejuvenation Pruning. Not all trees and shrubs respond to this drastic type of pruning, but, with those that do, it affords a method of correcting specimens that are tall, leggy, deformed, or overgrown, or bare at their bases. This pruning calls for a bold approach.

In many cases the recommended procedure is to cut the plant to within a foot or less of the ground in late winter or early spring before new growth begins, fertilize generously, mulch the soil with rotted manure, compost, peat moss or other suitable material, and keep the cut-back specimens well watered during dry weather in summer and fall. This procedure results in loss of all bloom for one or two years or more. Among the plants that respond to this treatment are Barberries, Dogwoods (Cornus) of the shrubby types, Deutzias, Honeysuckles, Lilacs, Mock Oranges, Privets, Redbud (Cercis), Spiraea, Symphoricarpos, Tamarix, Weigela, as well as nearly all broad-leaved evergreens such as Aucuba, Boxwood, Camellia, Laurel, Mountain Laurel, Rhododendrons and Hollies. Some narrow-leaved evergreens, including Yew and Juniper, also respond to this treatment.

Heading Back or Dehorning. A less drastic type of rejuvenation pruning is the severe "heading back" or "dehorning" that is often practiced on old fruit trees, such as Apples, Peaches and Oranges, and on some shade trees, such as Maples and Sycamores (Platanus), that are overgrown or lack vigor. In these instances the main limbs of the trees are cut back severely but the lower parts of the main branches are retained, as is also the trunk. The cuts are made with a saw in late winter or very early spring, each cut being immediately above (beyond) a side branch so that the cut-back branch is not terminated by a long stub.

It is sometimes advisable to spread the "dehorning" or "heading back" process over 2-3 years rather than to cut back all the main branches of a large tree at one time. Following this "heading back" type of pruning, fertilizing and mulching to conserve moisture and reduce the need for watering during dry weather and to supply nutrients are needed to encourage the development of healthy, vigorous replacement growth.

If the trees or shrubs to be cut back severely are grafted or budded specimens, be sure not to cut below the graft or bud union, but remove, as soon as they appear, any shoots that develop from below that point; these shoots will be of the inferior kind of plant used as the understock rather than the superior kind grafted upon it.

Thinning of the shoots that grow as an immediate result of heading back is necessary. This should be a gradual process, spread, perhaps, over two or three years, but eventually eliminating all shoots not needed to provide a sturdy framework of well-placed branches.

Maintenance Pruning. It is a mistake to think that all trees and shrubs require pruning regularly. Unless they are being trained to some specific form or restricted to a quite definite space, the vast majority grown in gardens need no annual pruning. They make more satisfactory specimens when allowed to develop their natural habits and graces.

But even kinds that do not need regular attention may occasionally need some pruning. A branch may die or be broken, or one may be so badly placed that its removal is desirable. Do not hesitate to cut if it seems necessary.

Flowering Trees and Shrubs. Before attempting to prune these it is necessary to know (and this can be learned by observation as well as by reading or by asking an informed source) whether the flowers are borne on wood of the current season's growth or on older shoots. If the former is true, the new shoots that start into growth in spring bear flowers later in the summer or in fall. It is quite correct to prune woody plants in this category, if they need it, in spring, just before new growth begins. No blooms are lost by doing so and the new shoots that develop following pruning produce flowers later in the same year. Examples of plants that bloom on

An old Apple tree, the pruning of which has been neglected.

An Apple tree which has received adequate maintenance pruning. Note the ample space between the branches.

current-season's shoots are Hydrangea paniculata, Hybrid Tea Roses, Buddleia Davidii, Crape Myrtle, Spiraea Bumalda, Tamarix parviflora, Vitex and Hibiscus syriacus. Pruning may consist of cutting back, as severely as seems desirable, all old shoots.

Spring pruning of trees and shrubs that bear their flowers on second-year or older shoots reduces the show of bloom, because with the shoots are removed buds which would have flowered in spring or early summer if they were given opportunity to do so. The best time to attend to any needed pruning of these kinds of shrubs is immediately after they are through blooming. Pruning in such cases usually consists of thinning out the oldest and most crowded branches and retaining the strong new branches that are developing.

Among trees and shrubs that produce their flowers on old wood are Hydrangea macrophylla (including the varieties called French Hydrangeas), Climbing Roses, Buddleia alternifolia, Spiraea Vanhouttei, Tamarix pentandra, Forsythia, Weigela, Philadelphus, and Kerria. There are many more, all of the spring-flowering and some of the summer-blooming kinds, in fact.

Often it is not possible to generalize about specific groups of plants. As will be noted from listings above, some Hydrangeas, Roses, Buddleias and Spiraeas bloom on old wood, whereas other species of the same genera bear their flowers on shoots of the current season. This variation occurs in some other genera.

When pruning flowering trees and shrubs, every effort should be made to preserve the natural grace and beauty peculiar to the particular kind. Obvious exceptions to this rule are when a specimen is closely trained to clothe a pillar wall or is used in some other formal way. Very often, pruning consists of no more than a judicious thinning out of the oldest and the most obviously ill-placed branches.

When pruning flowering shrubs, in most cases it is necessary, first, to cut out completely dead, diseased and badly overcrowded branches.

After unwanted branches are cut out from an overcrowded flowering shrub it is usually desirable to shorten some of the branches that remain.

Berried Trees and Shrubs. Trees and shrubs valued for their ornamental fruits, such as Barberries, Cotoneasters, Firethorns and Viburnums, should not be pruned more than is absolutely necessary. No matter when the cuts are made, serious pruning is likely to destroy part of the display. Some pruning to correct overcrowding and bad placement of branches and to remove weak shoots may be needed from time to time. Late winter or early spring is the best time to attend to this.

Evergreens. The pruning of evergreens requires special understanding. Most need no regular systematic pruning, merely the occasional removal of an unwanted branch. Many broad-leaved kinds, such as Laurus, Aucuba, Boxwood,

When Pines are to be restricted in size and encouraged to develop into bushy specimens the "candles" of new growth should be cut back before the leaves on them expand.

Yews are among the few evergreens that may be pruned hard back if necessary, but an annual clipping back of the new growth is sufficient to produce dense, bushy specimens.

As a result of cutting back the new growth "candles," this Pine has developed a short shoot terminated by several buds from which will grow the following season's shoots.

Pruning a Red Cedar, Juniperus virginiana, by shortening the new shoots.

The following year, the buds that terminate the cut-back shoot grow freely to produce new branches.

evergreen Privet and Citrus, may be sheared or cut back regularly if desired, and this pruning is usually best done in spring or just before new growth begins. Such annual pruning ordinarily involves only shortening of the shoots formed the previous year, not cutting into older wood. This type of pruning may be performed also with certain narrow-leaved evergreens such as Yews, Hemlocks, Arborvitae, Cypress and Podocarpus.

Most broad-leaved evergreens and a few narrow-leaved ones, such as Yew and Juniper, may, if necessary, be cut back hard and new shoots will grow from the old branches (see Rejuvenation

Pruning, above), but this is not true of Pines, Spruces, Firs and most other conifers (cone-bearing trees).

Any regular pruning of these that is done should receive attention when the new growth is half to three quarters grown and is still soft. The new shoots may then be cut to half or one third their length.

If it is desired to keep evergreens of such kinds restricted, pruning should begin early in the life of the plant and be given annual attention. The severe cutting back of large specimens may be disastrous.

If necessary, whole branches or major portions of branches of conifers may be cut off, but new growth, in most cases, should not be expected from the cut ends. Unless expertly done, the pruning of trees of these kinds is apt to leave ugly, stubbed-back branches that mar the beauty of the specimen and are not hidden by new growth.

Roses. As indicated above, the best time to prune Roses will greatly depend upon whether the flowers are borne on current season's wood or on older shoots. If the former is the case, the cutting out is done in spring; otherwise immediately after blooming is the recommended time.

Shrub or species Roses are treated much as most garden shrubs and are merely pruned, after flowering, in such a way that a fairly open framework of branches is maintained, allowing adequate light and air. From time to time some of the oldest and less vigorous branches are removed and new, vigorous shoots to take their places are encouraged.

Climbing Roses of the Rambler and Pillar types are pruned after blooming by removing as many of the old canes as can be spared with assurance that they are being replaced by strong new canes which spring from the base of the plant about that time. Other types of Climbing Roses, that do not renew themselves entirely or mainly from their bases each season, are pruned after flowering or in winter or spring.

In these cases the gardener seeks to retain a framework of well-placed, permanent branches tied into appropriate positions. The side shoots and old flowering shoots are cut back almost to

By pruning the new growths annually this hedge of Blue Spruce has been well maintained.

their bases each year. Occasionally a new, stout shoot that appears low down on the plant and well located is selected, an old, unwanted one is cut out, and the new one trained into its place.

Hybrid Perpetuals, Hybrid Teas, Floribundas and Dwarf Polyanthas are all pruned in spring, just before new growth begins. The amount of pruning depends upon the amount of winter-killing (if any), the type of Rose and, to some extent, the purpose for which it is being grown. Hybrid Teas may be pruned more severely than the others mentioned but many cultivators now believe that it is a mistake to prune these really severely.

Fruit Trees and Bushes. Most fruit trees and bushes, but not all, require at least some regular pruning for the best results. Details will be found under the names of the various fruits in this Encyclopedia. See also Lorette Pruning.

Vines. Evergreen vines often need pruning or shearing to prevent them from becoming too dense and heavy. The best time to attend to this is before new growth begins, either in late winter or early spring.

Flowering vines are pruned according to the principles followed for flowering shrubs. Those that bloom in spring are pruned immediately after they bloom. In some cases, for example, Wisterias, summer pruning (the shortening back of the young shoots to a length of 12-18 in. in summer) may be practiced with advantage also. Vines that flower on current season's wood are pruned in early spring.

Root Pruning and Lorette Pruning. For discussions of these types of pruning, see Root Pruning and Lorette Pruning.

PRUNUS: THE FLOWERING CHERRIES
And Ornamental Almonds, Peaches, Plums, Apricots, As Well As Cherry Laurels, Portugal Laurel and Other Evergreen Kinds

The Genus Prunus includes the Plum, Almond, Peach, Apricot, Cherry, Bird Cherry and Cherry Laurel. They are leaf-losing and evergreen trees and shrubs belonging to the Rose family, Rosaceae. Nearly two hundred wild kinds or species are known. These grow mostly in the Temperate Zone, but a few are natives of the Andes of South America. Prunus is the ancient Latin name for the Plum.

Many are highly ornamental trees and shrubs on account of the showy flowers which appear before or with the leaves. Cultivated varieties of many kinds of Prunus are largely grown and valued for their fruits, as, for example, the Plum, Peach, Nectarine, Apricot, Almond, Nanking Cherry and Cherry, which see. Botanically, the genus is distinct by reason of its fruit, which is a one-celled, one-seeded drupe.

Trees and Shrubs That Do Well on Lime Soil. Though the different kinds of Prunus vary so much in growth, and include both leaf-losing

and evergreen trees and shrubs, the details of cultivation are very similar. Most thrive best in a deeply cultivated and well-manured calcareous (limy) loam; many are not satisfactory in peat or lime-free soils, though by the liberal use of lime and suitable manures the stone fruits can be grown in districts where lime is naturally absent from the ground.

With the possible exceptions of the evergreen kinds, which will grow in sun or shade, these trees and shrubs thrive best in an open, sunny position. Most, except the evergreen kinds, are hardy in the North.

Methods of Propagation. Propagation is by seeds, layering, budding, grafting and, in a few cases, by cuttings. The species or wild types are grown from seeds sown, when ripe, in very sandy soil. Small quantities can be sown in pots or shallow flats in a frame or greenhouse. If large numbers of plants are required, sow thinly in drills in a bed of prepared sandy soil on a

Prunus serrulata and its varieties are among the most beautiful of the Japanese Cherries. This picture shows Prunus serrulata in full bloom.

The flowers of typical Prunus serrulata are white.

Budding is best done during the second half of July and the first half of August. Grafting should be done in spring when growth is about to recommence, the shoots to be used as scions being removed from the trees in January, and half-buried in soil in a sheltered position to keep them dormant. This is done because it is desirable that the scions shall not be so far advanced in growth as the stocks when the actual operation of grafting is done. Full details will be found under the respective headings of Budding and Grafting.

When to Plant. The planting of the leaf-losing kinds of Prunus is best done during early fall or early spring. The best time to plant the evergreen kinds is in spring.

Pruning. As a general rule, hard and frequent pruning is not desirable. But close attention must be given to the annual pruning of young shoots when the trees and bushes are small, for the purpose of keeping the branches well apart from each other. Both winter and late summer pruning can be practiced. Harm may be done to the trees by the removal of large branches because, however carefully it may be done,

border located in a sheltered area out of doors.

In nurseries large numbers of the common kinds of Prunus are raised from seeds to provide stocks on which to bud and graft the named flowering and fruiting varieties of Cherries, Plums, Peaches, and so on.

Generally, budding is a more satisfactory method of propagating than grafting; beautiful trees are, however, grown by both methods of propagation.

Prunus yedoensis is an early-blooming Japanese Cherry which has delicate pink single flowers which later become white or almost white.

wounds do not heal readily. The Cherry Laurel, Portugal Laurel and the other evergreen kinds may be freely pruned and sheared.

Sweet Cherry Varieties. The Sweet Cherry of Europe and Asia occurs as an escape from cultivation in North America and is known as the Mazzard Cherry. Botanically it is Prunus avium, one of the most attractive spring-flowering trees. There is nothing more beautiful on the lawn than a specimen tree or group of trees of the Double Sweet Cherry, Prunus avium variety plena. Its branches become laden with a profusion of white blossom annually. When grafted on a tall stem, the weeping variety pendula is distinct and showy. Variety salicifolia has very narrow leaves.

Sour Cherry Varieties. The Sour Cherry, Prunus Cerasus, is a native of Asia and southeastern Europe and is cultivated in pomological varieties for its fruits. It also sometimes escapes from cultivation. In addition to the varieties that are grown for their fruits, there are others that are primarily cultivated as decorative subjects, chief among these are P. Cerasus variety Rhexii,

A specimen of the narrow-leaved Sour Cherry, Prunus Cerasus salicifolia, every branch wreathed with clusters of white flowers in early spring.

[10—2]
Golden Larch
(Pseudolarix amabilis)

[10—2a]
Turkey Oak
(Quercus Cerris)

[10—2b]
Upright English Oak
(Quercus Robur fastigiata)

[10—2c]
Red Oak
(Quercus borealis maxima)

[10—3b]
Raft with Orchid growing on it

[10—3a]
Cones of Douglas Fir
(Pseudotsuga Douglasii)

[10—3c]
Buttonwood
(Platanus occidentalis)

[10—3]
Douglas Fir
(Pseudotsuga Douglasii)

Flower clusters of one of the double-flowered Japanese Cherries, which rank among the most valuable of all spring-flowering trees for garden planting.

a small tree with double white flowers; P. Cerasus variety persiciflora, a small tree with double pink flowers; P. Cerasus variety salicifolia, a small tree with leaves much longer than in the typical kind and P. Cerasus variety semperflorens, the All Saints Cherry, a small tree or large shrub which produces a succession of white flowers at a constant rate more or less throughout the summer.

The Japanese Cherries. These are most attractive flowering trees of moderate size, bearing a profusion of blossoms in spring; they are useful alike for large and small gardens. As they have mostly semidouble or double flowers, few of the Japanese flowering Cherries produce fruits. The only pruning required is to thin out the branches lightly, in winter, to prevent overcrowding. These flowering Cherries have been grown in Japan, and, no doubt, China also, for centuries, and the named varieties in Japan are numerous.

The Japanese Flowering Cherries can, in general, be grown wherever Peaches can be grown, and even somewhat further north. Most botanists place the majority of the named varieties of Japanese Cherries under P. serrulata, which, with spreading, almost horizontal branches, is one of the most distinct of all Japanese Cherries.

It bears clusters of double white flowers in spring.

Taking the varieties of Prunus serrulata first, as they are most popular of all, one of the best is Sekiyama or Kanzan (Kwanzan), the most vigorous of the Japanese Cherries; it produces clusters of large, double, rose-red flowers which change to rose-pink when fully developed. A few days later in flowering is Fugenzo or James H. Veitch, a tree of more spreading habit, with double deep rose-pink flowers. Kofugen is similar to Fugenzo but has deeper-colored flowers.

Kirin has double, rather short-stalked rose-pink flowers opening a week earlier than Kanzan and not quite so deep in color. The variety Kiku Shidare is an attractive pendulous tree of distinctive beauty; the long, pendent branches are wreathed in clusters of double rose-pink blossoms.

One of the most remarkable and most distinct kinds, because of its very upright growth, is erecta or Amanogawa, sometimes called the Lombardy Poplar Cherry. Its habit of growth makes it an ideal flowering tree for a sunny position in a small garden. It has large, semidouble, apple-blossom-colored flowers.

The pale yellow-flowered variety, grandiflora

or Ukon of Japanese nurseries, is distinct; the large, greenish-yellow, semidouble flowers contrast with the unfolding, bronze-tinted leaves.

Shimidsu Sakura (Oku Miyako) or longipes is distinct and valuable because of its late flowering. The large double flowers with fringed petals are on long stalks and, opening pale pink, soon change to white.

Shirotae, known as the Mount Fuji Cherry, has snow-white, semidouble or single flowers. It is an early flowering kind and one of the most distinct, with long-stalked, drooping corymbs of white blossoms. The variety albida is the most fragrant of the Japanese Cherries; it bears masses of single white blossoms.

Varieties of Japanese Cherries that have been introduced to the American trade without Japanese names include Paul Wohlert, a low tree (20-25 ft. tall) with deep pink flowers; Jeanne Wohlert, the most dwarf of Japanese Cherries, semidouble, light pink flowers; Ruth Wohlert, a double, blush-pink; and Mrs. A. E. Wohlert, a sport of Kanzan, of somewhat more brilliant coloring.

Ideal Tree for Small Gardens. Because of its moderate size and slow growth, Prunus Sieboldii (Watereri) is an ideal Japanese Cherry for gardens of moderate size. This is the kind named Naden. It has rose-pink, semidouble blossoms closely set along the short branches. A tree may take twenty to twenty-five years to reach 5 or 6 ft. high and, if pruned a little each year, may be kept to a height of 3-4 ft.

Prunus Sargentii is a most beautiful single-flowered Cherry. It is said to grow 80 ft. high in Japan. It is easily raised from seeds and is used largely in Japan as a stock on which to bud and graft the named Japanese varieties. The flowers of the seedling trees vary from pale pink to rich rose-pink, and the young leaves are bronze-green. In autumn the leaves change to rich yellow and red before falling.

An Early-flowering Cherry. Prunus yedoensis, Yoshino of the Japanese, is an early-flowering

In early spring the branches of Prunus subhirtella pendula are wreathed along their lengths with small, pale pink flowers.

Cherry of great beauty. It is said to be a hybrid and is planted more than any other Cherry in the famous tea gardens in and around Tokyo. It is the variety that predominates in the famous planting around the Tidal Basin at Washington, D. C. It is a vigorous tree with blush-white, single flowers opening to pure white, and freely produced. Because of its early flowering, this tree needs a sheltered position with, if possible, a background of evergreens.

Prunus subhirtella, the Rosebud Cherry of Japan and Korea, produces an abundance of small, pale pink flowers early in spring. This and its varieties are among the few Cherries it is possible to propagate from cuttings inserted in a close frame during July or early August.

A Cherry Which Blooms in Autumn. The variety autumnalis of P. subhirtella is most distinct and useful, as the flowers are produced intermittently from October to March or April where winters are mild, and profusely in fall and again profusely in spring where severer winters occur. It should be planted in a sheltered position to give protection to the semidouble, blush-colored blossoms. The variety pendula is of weeping habit and bears a profusion of rose-pink flowers on threadlike branches in early spring.

Prunus serrula has most distinct mahogany-colored bark. When not in flower, this Prunus, with its dark peeling bark, may be taken for a Birch tree.

The Bird Cherry. Prunus Padus, the European Bird Cherry, which bears spikes of small white flowers, is one of the most distinctive and attractive of flowering trees. For garden planting, choose the large-flowered variety Watereri or grandiflora and the double-flowered variety, flore pleno. They are leaf-losing trees 20-45 or 50 ft. tall.

The Mahaleb or St. Lucie Cherry, Prunus Mahaleb, is a native of central and southern Europe. It is a free-growing, leaf-losing tree 25-40 ft. high. Towards the end of April and early in May it is laden with small, fragrant, white blossoms. The variety pendula, budded to form a tall standard, is a graceful tree in leaf and flower. Seedling Mahalebs are used in nurseries as stocks for the fruiting Cherries.

The Flowering Almonds. The Almond is one of our most popular early-flowering trees. Prunus Amygdalus, the Common Almond, is a native of southern Europe or western Asia. During early spring it bears a wealth of delightful pink blossoms on leafless branches. There are several varieties: praecox flowers ten to fourteen days earlier than the type; macrocarpa has larger blossoms and fruits; Pollardii has large, fragrant, rose-red blooms; alba has large white blossoms; and flore roseo-plena has semidouble pink blossoms. (See also Almonds.)

One of the most popular of the plants called Flowering Almonds is Prunus triloba multiplex, or P. triloba flore-pleno, as it is often called. This Chinese kind is usually a low bush but sometimes attains a height of 10 ft. or even more. It bears a profusion of double, pink, rosette-formed flowers in early spring; it is an attractive shrub and, because it flowers early, is especially valued. It is well adapted for espaliering against a wall. There, if pruned each year after flowering, it is a most beautiful object.

The Dwarf Russian Almond, Prunus tenella (nana), is an attractive dwarf bush, 3-4 ft. tall, which bears small, pink blooms in early spring. There is a white-flowered variety, alba, but the best variety of this species is Gessleriana, which has rose-red flowers.

Yet there is another attractive species which is

The weeping variety, Prunus subhirtella pendula, of the Rosebud Cherry forms a shapely specimen with drooping branches.

The white, fragrant flowers of the European Bird Cherry, Prunus Padus, are borne in drooping racemes in spring.

greenhouse; they provide a pretty late winter and early spring display.

Closely related to P. glandulosa, and also really a Cherry although commonly called a Flowering Almond, is P. japonica. This kind forms a shrub up to 5 ft. high. Its flowers vary from almost white to pink and in the forms usually cultivated are double. P. japonica blooms freely in early spring. A hybrid between P. tenella, the Dwarf Russian Almond, and P. japonica is named P. Skinneri.

Belonging with the Almonds and blooming even earlier than the Common Almond, is P. Davidiana, a native of China that is peachlike in appearance and attains a height of 20-30 ft. The flowers vary in color from white to red. In the variety alba, they are white, in variety rubra, red. Because these kinds bloom so very early, there is always danger that their flowers will be damaged by late frosts unless the trees are in a sheltered location. A situation facing west or southwest, which affords the blooms some protection from early morning sunshine, should be selected for them.

commonly called a Flowering Almond, although it more properly belongs in the Cherry group of the genus Prunus, is P. glandulosa. A native of China and Japan, this kind attains a height of 3-5 ft. and bears flowers varying from white to pink. The double-flowered varieties of this Prunus are of considerable decorative value. Of these the one named alboplena, with white blooms, and the one named sinensis, with pink flowers, are especially lovely. These plants are useful for forcing in bloom early in pots in the

The Flowering Peaches are some of the loveliest of small, leaf-losing trees. They are varieties of Prunus Persica, which is generally believed to be a native of China, but it is one of the numerous treasures of China and Japan which were cultivated hundreds and perhaps thousands of

Prunus japonica is a bushy kind that has pink flowers.

The white blooms of weeping Flowering Peach.

The Flowering Peaches are desirable quick-growing small trees. They bear a profusion of beautiful flowers in early spring.

years before their introduction to Western gardens more than three hundred years ago. The trees average from 12-25 ft. in height, and flower in early spring.

Of the numerous varieties in cultivation the best are Clara Meyer, double rose-pink; Cali-

The purple-leaved Plum, Prunus cerasifera atropurpurea, is one of the most handsome of small flowering trees. Its white flowers are produced freely in spring.

fornia Double Red or camelliaeflora, double dark red; Burbank, double rose-pink; and albo-pleno, double white. The variety folis rubris, with red foliage, rose-red flowers and red fruits, is distinctive and attractive. There are also fine weeping varieties with single and double flowers in white, pink and red.

This is an admirable ornamental tree for the garden, for it is attractive through the spring, summer and autumn months.

A severe pruning immediately following flowering is beneficial. It encourages the production of young shoots on which the next year's flowers are borne.

The Japanese Apricot. Prunus Mume, the Japanese Apricot, is a beautiful early-flowering small tree in full beauty about the same time as the Almond. The Japanese have raised numerous named varieties, but unless it is possible to give the trees a sheltered position, the flowers, in some sections, are badly damaged by spring frosts. Most tree nurseries are content to list the double rose-pink and white varieties, roseo-plena and albo-plena.

The Purple Apricot. This small tree, P. dasycarpa, is an attractive kind that attains a maximum height of about 25 ft. Its flowers, which are borne in profusion, are white and are in evidence before the leaves appear. The fruit is

Prunus Laurocerasus schipkaensis is the hardiest of the evergreen Prunus. This specimen is in a garden in Long Island, New York.

dark purple or nearly black but has little value for eating.

Prunus dasycarpa is not known in the wild; it is thought that it may be of hybrid origin.

The Flowering Plums. The best-known tree in this group is the Purple-leaved Plum, Prunus cerasifera atropurpurea (Pissardii), one of the most commonly planted trees with colored leaves. It does particularly well in town and suburban gardens. It withstands frequent pruning better than most kinds of Prunus. The pink buds and white flowers are freely produced on leafless branches in early spring but are soon followed by the rich purplish-crimson leaves. Sometimes the trees bear crimson fruits.

There are several varieties of the Purple-leaved Plum. Blireana has bronze-purple leaves and double, rose-pink blossoms; Moseri has purplish-crimson leaves and pale pink flowers; in the variety nigra the leaves are blackish-purple.

The Myrobalan or Cherry Plum. Except in its purple-leaved varieties, the Cherry Plum, Prunus cerasifera, is not much cultivated as a flowering tree because there are other showier kinds, but it is a useful and free-growing hedge shrub. It is fast in growth and stands clipping well. Grown as a specimen tree, Prunus cerasifera bears plum-colored or yellow fruits on long stalks, like large Cherries, hence the name Cherry Plum.

The Sloe or Blackthorn. The Sloe, Prunus spinosa, is a native of Europe and western Asia. The double white-flowered variety, Prunus spinosa plena, and the purple-leaved variety, P. spinosa purpurea, are compact bushes or small trees for the shrub border and other decorative plantings.

Native American Plums and Cherries. Prunus is well represented in the native flora of North America. Among leaf-losing kinds are both Plums and Cherries, some of which are sufficiently attractive to be included in ornamental plantings; others are less desirable.

The Wild Black Cherry, Prunus serotina, oc-

The creamy white, fragrant flowers of Prunus Laurocerasus schipkaensis are produced in erect spikes in spring.

curs from Nova Scotia to North Dakota and southwards to Florida and Texas. It forms a forest tree, 80-100 ft. tall, and is valued for its timber. It belongs to the Bird Cherry section of the Prunus group.

Over much of its range it is a common weed tree, arising spontaneously from seeds dropped by birds. It is a favorite host of the tent caterpillar. It should be remembered that the wilted foliage of this tree is poisonous if eaten.

The Chokecherry, P. virginiana, is another member of the Bird Cherry group. It occurs from Newfoundland to Saskatchewan and southward to North Carolina and Kansas.

This kind is usually shrubby but sometimes becomes a tree as much as 20 ft. tall. It has no decorative merit and, as it provides a favorite home for tent caterpillars, is not to be encouraged. Its wilted leaves, if eaten, are poisonous.

The Sand Cherries grow in bush form and are very hardy. P. Besseyi is the plant that has given rise to the Hansen Bush Cherries. It is also used as a rootstock for grafting.

P. Besseyi is a native of the plains from Kansas to Manitoba and westward to Wyoming and Colorado. It is a prostrate or nearly prostrate grower.

The other Sand Cherry of importance is P. pumila, which forms a low bush sometimes 6 ft. tall. Its fruits are much smaller than those of P. Besseyi but it is a very attractive shrub in bloom. Its flowers are white.

P. pumila and its varieties occur on sandy shores of the Great Lakes and on other rocky and sandy shores from Quebec and Manitoba southward to Maryland.

The Plums that are natives of North America include P. americana, a small, twiggy tree that is widely spread and that is the ancestor of many varieties that are cultivated for their fruits, particularly in cold, northern regions.

P. angustifolia is the Chickasaw Plum that occurs from Delaware southward and westward to Florida and Texas. It grows 8-10 ft. tall and has given rise to a number of varieties which are prized for the fruits they produce.

P. hortulana, the Hortulan Plum, is the original parent stock from which a number of orchard Plums have been developed. It grows about 30 ft. tall and occurs naturally from Iowa and Oklahoma to Kentucky and Tennessee.

P. gracilis, the Oklahoma Plum, is a bush that grows to a height of about 15 ft. It is found from Arkansas to Texas.

P. mexicana, the Big Tree Plum, is a southern representative of P. americana. It occurs from Kentucky and Tennessee to Oklahoma and Mexico. It does not form suckering thickets as does P. americana, but occurs only as a tree with a distinct trunk. It is hardy in the North.

P. Munsoniana, the Wild-Goose Plum, is related to P. Hortulana. It is native from Kentucky to Tennessee, Kansas and Texas. It is the parent stock of a number of cultivated varieties of Plums.

The Beach Plum, Prunus maritima, is a rather spreading bush, or sometimes a small tree, that occurs along and near the coast from New Brunswick to Virginia. It is very attractive in bloom and produces edible fruits which are usually dull purple but on some plants are yellow. Efforts are being made to develop improved fruiting varieties of this Prunus. Prunus maritima ranges from 4-10 ft. in height.

The Evergreen Kinds of Prunus

In addition to the leaf-losing members of the genus Prunus, which include those mentioned above as well as the Plums, Cherries, Peaches, Apricots and Almonds, cultivated chiefly for their edible fruits, there are a number of evergreen kinds. These latter are highly valuable garden plants but are generally adapted for planting in the South and in the mild climate of the West Coast only. They are not hardy in the North. They include both native and exotic (foreign) kinds.

The native American kinds include P. caroliniana, a Cherry Laurel that occurs as a native from North Carolina to Texas and is most abundant in coastal areas. Known locally as Wild Orange and Mock Orange, it attains a maximum height of about 40 ft. This handsome evergreen is a most useful kind for mild-climate gardens. Its flowers are borne in late winter or early spring. They are cream-colored and are in short, close racemes.

P. myrtifolia, the Myrtle-leaved Cherry Laurel, grows natively from southern Florida and the West Indies to Brazil. It attains a height of 30-40 ft. and is adapted for planting in frost-free, warm climates.

The Islay, Evergreen Cherry or Mountain Holly of southern California is an attractive bush or small tree that occasionally becomes 30 ft. tall. Its botanical name is Prunus ilicifolia. The leaves resemble those of Holly. Its flowers are white. It is adapted for cultivation in the lower South and the warmer sections of the Pacific coast.

The Islands Cherry, P. Lyonii, is by some authorities considered to be a variety of P. ilicifolia; by others it is regarded as a distinct species. The leaves are not spiny-toothed at their edges as are those of P. ilicifolia.

The Islands Cherry is a fine garden subject and is also very useful for growing as a tub plant. At maturity it attains a height of 30 ft. and is of bushy habit. Its flowers are white.

This kind is native to the islands (Santa Cruz and Santa Catalina) off the coast of southern California.

The European Cherry Laurel, Prunus Laurocerasus, if left unpruned, will form a large evergreen bush 15-25 ft. in height, but it is as a hedge shrub, screen plant and evergreen for shade that it is most valued. It withstands frequent and hard pruning; stems 9-12 in. thick, if cut down to the ground in early April, soon start into fresh growth.

Several named varieties are listed; they vary in habit of growth and in the size of the leaves. Angustifolia has narrow, rich green leaves; Bruantii is a bush of upright growth useful for hedges; camelliifolia has large, glossy green leaves; magnoliaefolia has very large leaves, and parvifolia, a bush of low growth, has small leaves. P. Laurocerasus schipkaensis is a hardy Cherry Laurel of slow growth which winters outdoors in sheltered locations as far north as New York City. It grows 3-5 ft. high and flowers freely. Zabeliana, a spreading shrub of free growth, 2-3 ft. high, is a most useful evergreen for underplanting.

The Portugal Laurel, Prunus lusitanica, is usually seen as a large bush or bushy tree, 15-20 ft. high, but it sometimes attains 30-50 ft. in height, forming a wide-spreading evergreen tree. It may be planted as a hedge and also in the form of standards or closely pruned bushes for the formal garden. The variety azorica has larger leaves than the typical kind, and the variety myrtifolia has smaller leaves.

Both the Portugal Laurel and European Cherry Laurel are easily propagated by cuttings 12-24 in. long, inserted, in mild climates, in a border out of doors in late October; or smaller cuttings may be inserted in a frame, under a bell jar or in a greenhouse in September.

Culture of Evergreen Kinds. The evergreen kinds of Prunus known as Laurel, Cherry Laurel, Portugal Laurel and the other kinds listed above are all of easy culture in any reasonably good soil that is fairly well drained. They thrive in sun or shade and stand pruning well.

Planting is best done in spring just before new growth begins, or in late summer or early fall after the new season's growth is completed but while the soil is yet warm enough to encourage new roots to develop and ensure rapid re-establishment of the plants.

The plants should be freely supplied with water until well established after planting. Hard pruning is best done in spring and trimming may be done during the summer.

PSEUDERANTHEMUM (Pseuderan'themum). A genus of shrubs and subshrubs, closely related to Eranthemum and often included in that genus. They are attractive flowering and foliage subjects for warm greenhouse cultivation and for planting outdoors in frost-free localities. They respond to treatment similar to that for Eranthemum, which see. These plants belong to the family Acanthaceae. Their name is derived from *pseudo,* false, and Eranthemum.

Noteworthy kinds include: Pseuderanthemum albiflorum, 3 ft., flowers white; P. albo-marginatum, leaves broadly margined with white, a handsome foliage plant; P. atropurpureum, 4 ft., flowers white and purple; P. indicum, 2 ft., flowers white, veined purple; P. lilacina, 4 ft., flowers bluish-lilac; P. reticulatum, 3 ft., flowers white, spotted purple; P. roseum, rose-pink; P. tuberculatum, small shrub, flowers white; and P. velutinum, rose-pink.

PSEUDO. A word meaning false, used in botany to indicate a close resemblance.

PSEUDOBULB. A term meaning false bulb, used to describe a thickened, bulblike stem. It is

On this Cattleya Orchid, the pseudobulbs, the thick stemlike portions below the flat leaf blade, can be clearly seen.

commonly employed in descriptions of Orchids.

PSEUDOLARIX AMABILIS—*Golden Larch* (Pseudolar'ix). A very interesting and decorative leaf-losing (deciduous) tree from eastern China, whence it was introduced to Western gardens in 1854. In China it grows 100-130 ft. high, with a trunk 5-8 ft. in girth. The name Pseudolarix is taken from the Greek *pseudo,* false, and *larix,* Larch. It has been known as P. Kaempferi. It belongs to the Pine family, Pinaceae.

This tree differs from the ordinary Larch in its longer and broader bright green leaves which turn golden before they fall, and in its erect cones with rather spreading scales, which fall apart and liberate the seeds as soon as they are ripe.

Propagation is by seeds sown in sandy soil in a frame in autumn or spring, and the tree thrives in warm loamy soil that is free from lime. It should have a position sheltered from cold winds and forms a very good lawn specimen where a neat, not very fast-growing tree, is required. The only pruning necessary is the occasional removal of lower branches.

The Golden Larch is not a very common tree even under natural conditions and is rather rare in gardens. It might, with advantage, be planted more frequently, for it is beautiful and does not take up as much room as the ordinary Larches. It is very attractive when the leaves take on their golden autumn tints.

PSEUDOPANAX (Pseudo'panax; Pseudopan'-ax). Tender, evergreen plants with ornamental foliage. They are natives of New Zealand and South America and belong to the Aralia family, Araliaceae. These plants, which grow up to 50 ft. high in their native habitats, are grown outdoors in mild climates, such as that of California, and in greenhouses. They have large digitate (hand-shaped), glossy green leaves. The flowers are in umbels (flattish clusters). The name Pseudopanax is derived from *pseudo,* false, and Panax, the plant which it somewhat resembles.

For a Cool Greenhouse. These plants require a minimum winter temperature of 45 degrees and a soil compost of equal parts of loam and leaf mold, with sand and crushed charcoal added. Repotting is done in April when the plants are set in slightly larger pots. They are well drained with crocks over which a layer of the rough siftings from the compost is placed to keep the drainage free. The plant is taken out of its pot, the crocks and loose soil are removed from its roots, and it is set in the new pot and the soil made firm.

The compost is not watered, as it should contain sufficient moisture for the immediate needs of the plant, but when it becomes moderately dry it is thoroughly saturated. If you follow this system of watering, the roots will develop quickly. When they have entered the new compost freely, the soil is kept moist throughout the summer.

Details of Management. After repotting, the plants are shaded from bright sunlight, but for the remainder of the year they are exposed to full light. They are also syringed frequently and the atmosphere kept moist until they are established; afterwards very little syringing or damping is required, sufficient only being done to keep the atmosphere fresh and the foliage clean.

Outdoor Cultivation. In climates suitable to its growth, Pseudopanax thrives without difficulty in any fairly good soil, in sun or shade.

Propagation by Cuttings. Propagation is by stem or root cuttings or by air layering. Small side shoots are taken off, the lower leaves removed and a cut is made below the lowest joint. The shoots are then inserted in a propagating case with a bottom heat of 70-75 degrees. Each morning the sash is raised and the moisture is wiped from the underside of the glass. This treatment is continued until roots are formed, when the plants are potted separately in small pots and subsequently in larger ones.

Taking Root Cuttings and Air Layering. Pieces of the larger roots may be cut into short lengths and inserted as cuttings. When rooted, they are potted as described. Air layering consists of cutting from the stem a ring of bark $\frac{1}{4}$ in. wide just below the lowest leaves. The cut surface is bound around with moss, which is kept moist and wrapped in polyethylene plastic film until roots are formed. The stem is then severed below the roots and the rooted top is potted in a separate pot. For a more detailed discussion of this procedure, see Air Layering.

The chief kinds are P. crassifolius, P. ferox, and P. Lessonii. The first-named attains a maximum height of 50 ft. The last two do not exceed 20 ft. in height.

PSEUDOPHOENIX—*Cherry Palm* (Pseudophoen'ix). A small group of tropical, unarmed, feather-leaved Palms belonging to the Palm family, Palmaceae. The name is derived from *pseudo,* false, and Phoenix, another genus of Palms, to which the Date Palm belongs, and refers to the general resemblance of Pseudophcenix to the Date Palm.

The only member of the group likely to be cultivated in North America is P. Sargentii, a native of the Florida Keys, the Bahamas and southward. This kind is sometimes planted in southern Florida. It attains an ultimate height of about 25 ft. and grows slowly. The common name of Cherry Palm stems from the appearance of the bright red or orange-scarlet fruits, each ½-¾ in. in diameter.

When grown indoors in pots or tubs, this Palm requires the same treatment as Phoenix, which see.

PSEUDORHIPSALIS (Pseudorhipsa'lis). A small genus of epiphytic Cacti (family Cactaceae), the freely branched plants being of prostrate or drooping habit and free flowering. For details of cultivation, see Cacti.

The principal kind is P. alata, from Jamaica, with flattened stems up to 12 ft. or more long and yellowish white flowers.

PSEUDOSASA (Pseudosa'sa). A small group of Bamboos that are natives of eastern Asia and belong to the Grass family, Gramineae. The name is derived from *pseudo,* false, and Sasa, another genus of Bamboos with which the plants now called Pseudosasa at one time were grouped.

The only kind in cultivation is P. japonica, which has also been known as Sasa japonica, Arundinaria japonica, Bambusa japonica, Arundinaria Metake and Bambusa Metake, and is sometimes cultivated in gardens under these names.

Pseudosasa japonica grows to a height of 10-15 ft. and its leaves are glossy green above and somewhat glaucous blue-green on the underside. This is probably the hardiest of all Bamboos, at

Pseudosasa japonica, the hardiest of Bamboos, thriving in a New Jersey garden.

least of all those that produce imposing stems; it will thrive outdoors in sheltered locations as far north as southern New York and southern New England.

Pseudosasa thrives in moist, fertile soils but they should not be swampy and stagnant. Ideal for it is a position close to a brook or pond where the roots can find moisture some little distance beneath the surface while the crowns of the plants are well above water. Shelter from winds is important, especially in the North. The plants grow in light shade or in sun.

Propagation is effected by division in spring. These plants benefit greatly from mulching with organic material such as rough compost, partly rotted manure, and leaf mold.

PSEUDOTSUGA—*Douglas Fir* (Pseudotsu'ga). Evergreen trees, some of which rank with the finest cone-bearing trees in the world in height, girth of trunk and general magnificence. Some are natives of North America, where they are a definite feature of the flora of the western side of the continent. Others occur wild in China, Japan and Formosa, but the kinds found in those countries do not attain such fine proportions as those that are native to western North America.

The various kinds form pyramidal trees in a

A group of Douglas Fir, Pseudotsuga taxifolia. This native of western North America is one of the most handsome of conifers.

young state, and old trees with trunks clear of branches are very attractive by reason of their reddish bark. On young trees the bark bears many resin blisters, but they disappear as the trees advance in age. The leaves are soft to the touch, green or bluish in color, with two green lines beneath, and most closely resemble the leaves of some of the Firs or Abies.

The winter buds at the ends of the shoots are different from those of other Conifers, for they are brown, and resemble those of a Beech tree in shape. Male and female flowers are borne on the same tree in spring. The male flowers are in spiral clusters from the leaf axils, the female flowers are in cones from near the ends of the shoots, or from the axils of leaves near the ends of the shoots.

Trident-like bracts extend beyond the scales and form a distinguishing character of the cones. The seeds are winged, like those of the Larch, and they ripen in the autumn of the same year the flowers are borne.

Pseudotsuga belongs to the Pine family, Pinaceae, and the name is taken from the Greek word *pseudo,* false, and Tsuga; it refers to the plant's relationship to Tsuga.

The common name of Douglas Fir commemorates David Douglas, an explorer and collector of plants and seeds who did a very great deal between the years 1825-1834 in exploring western North America, and in collecting plants for

Pseudotsuga taxifolia variety pyramidata is a small, compact, pyramidal form of the Douglas Fir.

the Horticultural Society of England, now the Royal Horticultural Society. He originally discovered and sent home seeds of many Conifers of the American West that are now such familiar objects both in European and eastern American gardens. Among the trees he sent home are Picea sitchensis, Pinus ponderosa, P. Lambertiana, P. Sabiniana, P. radiata, Abies nobilis, A. amabilis, A. grandis and many others. Douglas also was the man who introduced the fine tree that bears his name, the Douglas Fir (Pseudotsuga taxifolia).

Unfortunately, the name of P. taxifolia had been used for the tree that was later commonly called Pseudotsuga Douglasii, before the name P. Douglasii was given; therefore, the law of priority demands its use. The common name of Douglas Fir, however, is unlikely to be superseded by any other, and will remain a monument to the memory of a great collector.

Raising the Pseudotsuga from Seed. All the distinct species should be raised from seeds, those of the commoner ones being sown out of doors in beds, in the way recommended for seeds of Pinus. The young plants grow more rapidly in the early years than the Pines, and many may be ready for transplanting from the seedbed to a nursery bed at the end of the first season. Uncommon kinds, more especially those of Asiatic origin, should be raised by sowing seeds in well-drained pots or flats in a frame, using a compost of two parts loam, one part peat moss or leaf mold, and one part sand.

Management of the Seedlings. The young plants of rare kinds should be placed singly in small pots or be planted out in prepared soil in a cold frame for a year or two before being planted in a nursery or in a permanent place. It is a mistake to allow these trees to remain in pots until they are pot-bound, for the roots never spread freely in the open ground when eventually they are planted out. Young plants of the common kinds may be transplanted direct from seed beds to nursery rows.

Varieties that do not come true from seed are grafted on stocks of their respective types previously established in pots, the work being carried out in spring or late summer. It is also possible to root cuttings of some of the dwarf varieties if they are inserted in a greenhouse propagating bench.

Trees for Moist Soil and Sheltered Places. The best results are obtained by planting in moist, but not waterlogged, soil in rather sheltered places; valleys and the lower slopes of hills suit these trees well, although good results are obtained in less-favored places. They do not give good results in thin dry soils, or in lime soils, although P. taxifolia succeeds in places where a deep layer of soil overlies limestone. In such places and where the water table is high—that is, where the soil is flooded to near the surface—the roots do not penetrate very deeply but spread very wide.

The hardiness of P. taxifolia and its varieties differs considerably according to the region from which the seed was obtained. The hardiest is the Rocky Mountain type, which is hardy in New England and southern Ontario.

When planted to form decorative trees, the larger-growing kinds, such as P. taxifolia, must be given plenty of room, for they grow rapidly and branch widely and, when crowded by other trees, their full beauty cannot be seen. P. taxifolia is sometimes used as an avenue tree, but very often is planted too closely. In laying out an avenue with this tree the lines of trees should be spaced 50-60 ft. apart.

Pruning requires very definite consideration in the case of Douglas Firs, and it has to be left entirely to the ideas of the owner as to the form it shall take. Trees may be grown 50-60 ft. high which retain healthy branches to the ground line, or they may be grown as tall, or 30-40 ft. taller, and have their trunks cleared of branches for part of their height. For the first 20-30 years those trees that keep their branches to the ground line are most effective, but in later life, those trees that have a definite length of trunk clear of branches supporting a well-developed head are the best.

At thirty years of age it is too late to begin such drastic pruning as would be required to clear the trunks, unless the branches are dead, a condition that rarely arises in isolated trees: if the lower part of the trunk is to be cleared of branches the work must be carried out gradually, beginning when the trees are a few years old.

This pruning may be done during the summer.

In the case of trees on which the branches are left, pruning is limited to clearing leaders of rival shoots and correcting uneven development.

Economic Uses. The wood of the Douglas Fir, P. taxifolia, is of excellent quality, and of very great value for many purposes. It is used in buildings both in important structural work and in finishing, and it is much used in general carpentry. It is also used for masts and flagpoles, and for many purposes where long and large lengths of timber free from knots are required.

A good deal is used for railway ties, but it is less easily treated with creosote than Pine, the surface of the ties having to be incised before effective impregnation takes place. The wood is greatly used in houses, and whole shiploads of doors and window frames, as well as unfabricated building members, are exported from North America. The wood is variously known as Douglas Fir, Oregon Pine, and British Columbia Pine.

The Commonest Kind. Pseudotsuga taxifolia (P. Douglasii) is the commonest kind. On the Pacific coast it sometimes exceeds 300 ft. in height with a trunk 40 ft. in girth. Trees 200-250 ft. high with a trunk girthing 20 ft. are fairly common. The celebrated flagstaff in the Royal Botanic Gardens, Kew, England, is a single spar of Douglas Fir, 214 ft. long, and, where the top was cut off, it is still 12 in. across.

The common Douglas Fir is a well-known tree by reason of its yellowish-green or dark green, fragrant leaves, vigorous, densely branched habit and cones 3-4 in. long bearing trident-like bracts beyond the scales. The wood is reddish and much like that of Larch in general appearance. This is the best of the Pseudotsugas for general cultivation either as a decorative or forest tree.

Distinctive Varieties. Several varieties have been selected for special names, notably anguina, a monstrosity with long, snakelike branches; brevifolia, with very short leaves; caesia, with grayish foliage; fastigiata, of stiff erect habit; Fretsii, a bush with short leaves; nana, of dwarf habit, suitable for the rock garden; pendula, with weeping branches; revoluta, with curled leaves; and Stairii, with variegated leaves.

P. taxifolia in one form or another covers very extensive areas in the Pacific coast regions of North America from southern British Columbia through Washington, Oregon and the coast region of California to Mexico and Texas. It is at its best in British Columbia, Washington and Oregon.

The Rocky Mountain Douglas Fir. P. taxifolia variety glauca, known as Rocky Mountain Douglas Fir and Blue-leaved Douglas Fir, is a tree of smaller dimensions than the more typical P. taxifolia, although at its best it may be 150 ft. tall. By some botanists it is regarded as a distinct species. The young shoots are olive-green, the leaves glaucous or blue in color with an odor of turpentine when bruised. It is found wild in the central Rocky Mountains, through Montana, Colorado, Utah, Arizona and New Mexico to Mexico. It appears to be hardier in a young state than P. taxifolia, and is less liable to injury from certain insect pests.

The Big-Cone Spruce, despite its common name, is not an Abies (Spruce) but a Pseudotsuga. It is P. macrocarpa, a tree 70-80 ft. high in its native southern California. It is distinguished from other North American kinds by its larger cones, which may be up to 7 in. long and 2½ in. wide. It is seldom cultivated.

The Japanese Pseudotsuga, P. japonica, was introduced to Western gardens in 1910. In Japan it grows 70-100 ft. high. It has dull red-brown bark, light green leaves and rather short and stout chocolate-brown cones. It is a rare tree in North America and is not very hardy.

Other Douglas Firs. P. Wilsoniana is a tree 60-80 ft. high in western China, but very little is known about it outside its native home. From young plants in cultivation it does not appear to be very hardy. P. sinensis is a large tree of western China. It was introduced into cultivation in America early in the present century but is still very rare and is not hardy enough to be grown as far north as Boston.

PSIDIUM—*Guava* (Psid'ium). Tropical evergreen trees and shrubs which have ornamental flowers and bear edible fruits. They belong to the Myrtle family Myrtaceae, and are natives of tropical America. The principal kind, P. Guajava (Guava), forms a branching, shrubby tree up to 30 ft. in height, and has oblong, light green leaves, 3-6 in. in length. The flowers, which are produced in the axils of the leaves in clusters of twos and threes, are white, rotate (wheel-shaped), and five-petaled, and the stamens are numerous.

When the fruits are fully developed, they are round or pear-shaped, 1-4 in. in length, yellowish in color, and of an agreeable flavor. They are chiefly used for making jelly. In large hothouses the shrubs can be made to produce fruits, but principally they are grown under glass as ever-green foliage plants. Their cultivation for their fruits is confined to warm climates. The name Psidium is derived from *psidion,* the Greek name for Pomegranate.

Details of Management in Greenhouses. These plants require a minimum winter temperature of 55 degrees and a soil compost of two parts fibrous loam, one part of leaf mold and half a part of dried cow manure, with sand freely added. The shrubs are grown in large tubs or pots, or are planted in a prepared bed of soil in the greenhouse. Potting or planting is done in March. The pots or tubs are prepared by placing crocks in the bottom to the depth of 3 or 4 in., and these are covered with a layer of rough siftings from the compost. Enough of the prepared soil is then added so that, when it is made firm, the top of the ball of soil is 2 in. below the rim of the pot or tub.

The plant is knocked out of its pot, the crocks and loose soil are removed from the roots, and the plant is set in position; the compost, as it is added, is made firm with the potting stick.

Planting in a Prepared Bed. When planting out in a prepared bed in the greenhouse, a cubic yard of soil is removed and a 9-in. layer of broken bricks placed in the bottom for drainage. These are covered with a layer of coarse leaves. The remainder of the space is filled with the prepared compost. After allowing it a few days to settle, planting is done and the soil made firm.

Watering. After potting or planting, the soil is not watered until it becomes moderately dry; it is then thoroughly saturated, and this method of watering is continued until the plants are established, after which the soil is kept moist until the end of the summer. Plants which are bearing fruits should receive an application of liquid fertilizer twice a week, while the fruits are swelling.

After the plants are potted or planted the atmosphere must be kept moist by frequently damping the floor and benches, and the foliage is syringed twice a day.

Training and Pruning. The shoots are trained to wires or a trellis fixed to the glasshouse wall or roof. Pruning consists of trimming the plants lightly into shape in March.

Outdoor Cultivation. The Common Guava, P. Guajava, is very sensitive to temperature and will not thrive where the mean summer temperature is appreciably below 60 degrees; nor will the plant survive temperatures much below freezing (32 degrees F.).

It is harmed by exceedingly high daytime temperatures such as occur in some of the California valleys. Trees that are killed back by frost will, in warm climates such as that of Florida, renew themselves from the roots and bear good crops of fruit in 2-3 years.

The Common Guava is not particular as to soil; it prospers in a wide variety of earths, from porous, sandy soils to heavy clays, and responds to moderate fertilizing.

The trees should be spaced 15-30 ft. apart. They grow quite rapidly. Pruning, other than the removal of dead or damaged branches, is not necessary; indeed it seems to reduce the yield.

The Strawberry Guava, P. Cattleianum, is hardier than the Common Guava and grows more slowly. It stands cooler summers and more frost. Its soil and cultural requirements are the same as for the Common Guava.

Propagation except by seeds is not easy. Shoots, 3 in. in length, are taken off in spring or summer and are used as cuttings. The leaves are removed from the lower half of the stems and a cut is made below the bottom joint. They are then inserted in a firmly packed bed of sand, or sand and peat moss, in a propagating case with a bottom heat of 75-80 degrees. Each morning the case is ventilated and the moisture is wiped from the underside of the glass.

This treatment is continued until roots are formed, and the plants are then potted separately in 3-in. pots. When well rooted in these, they are repotted in 5-in. pots, and from these they are potted or planted in their permanent quarters.

Budding and grafting are sometimes successful, but not reliably so. Root cuttings are sometimes used with good results.

Air layering, using sphagnum moss and polyethylene plastic film, seems to offer great promise as a means of vegetative propagation that will make the increase of superior varieties easily possible. (See Air Layering.)

Psidiums are easy to raise from seed, and this is the most common method of propagation. Unfortunately, there is considerable variation in the quality of the fruit produced by individual trees.

When selecting seeds for planting, it is important to take them from trees that are known to bear high-quality fruit.

The chief kinds are P. Guajava, the Common Guava, white flowers, yellow fruits; P. Cattleianum, the Strawberry Guava, white flowers, reddish fruits.

PSORALEA—*Scurfy Pea* (Psora'lea). A large genus of plants, few of which have any horticultural value. They are chiefly to be found in botanical collections. The plants belong to the Pea family, Leguminosae, and are found wild in the Mediterranean region, tropical and temperate America and Africa. The name Psoralea is derived from *psoraleos,* scurvy, and refers to the appearance of the stems, which are warted and covered with scurfy scales.

For a Frostproof Greenhouse. The shrubby, tender kinds may be grown in greenhouses. Under such conditions they require a minimum winter temperature of 45 degrees and a soil compost of equal parts of peat and loam with sand freely added.

Repotting is done in March. The plants are lightly pruned into shape and syringed daily. When new shoots form, the plants are taken from their pots and set in slightly larger ones. The new pots are well drained with crocks which are covered with the rough siftings from the compost. Sufficient soil is put in so that when it is made firm and the plant placed in position the top of the root ball is an inch below the rim.

The compost is not watered at once, as it should contain sufficient water for the immediate needs of the plants. When it becomes moderately dry, however, it should be well moistened. This system of watering is continued until the plants are well rooted, after which the soil is kept moist for the remainder of the summer. As autumn approaches, less water is given, and during winter the compost is only moistened when it becomes moderately dry.

No shading is required. Immediately after the plants are repotted they are lightly syringed and the atmosphere is kept moist, but when they

The Pomme Blanche or Indian Breadroot, Psoralea esculenta, is native from Saskatchewan to Montana.

are established no syringing or damping is required and the greenhouse is freely ventilated.

Propagation by Cuttings. Shoots of the shrubby kinds, 2 in. in length, are taken off in early summer. The leaves are removed from the lower halves of the stems and cuts are made just below the bottom nodes. The shoots are inserted in sand in a propagating case or under a bell jar.

For Outdoor Cultivation. Hardy, herbaceous perennial kinds can be grown without difficulty outdoors in any reasonably good soil. One, P. esculenta, the Indian Breadroot or Pomme Blanche, is native from Saskatchewan to Montana. Its edible roots were an important source of food to the Indians. Others occur in other parts of North America.

These hardy herbaceous kinds are easily increased by seeds and by division of the roots in spring.

The tender, shrubby kinds can be cultivated outdoors in mild climates that are frost-free or nearly so.

The Chief Kinds. P. aphylla, a tall, usually leafless shrub from South Africa, flowers pale blue; P. esculenta, Pomme Blanche, Indian Breadroot, a hardy perennial 1½ ft. tall, flowers bluish, in dense heads; P. glandulosa, shrubby, to 5 ft. tall, native to Peru, flowers blue and white; P. hypogaea, low, hardy perennial, native from Nebraska to New Mexico, flowers blue, in dense spikes; P. Onobrychis, 4-5 ft. tall, hardy perennial, flowers pale purple, native from Ohio to Iowa and southward to Tennessee and Missouri; P. pinnata, shrub to 12 ft. tall, native to South Africa, flowers blue and white.

PSYCHOTRIA—*Wild Coffee* (Psychot'ria). Tropical flowering shrubs with ornamental berries. They are not widely cultivated and are chiefly to be found in greenhouses, botanical collections and, occasionally, planted outdoors in the far South. These plants are natives of tropical America, Malaya and Africa, and belong to the family Rubiaceae. They have oval, pointed, smooth, hairy or coriaceous (leathery) leaves, 3-5 in. in length, and bear small clusters of insignificant white or greenish flowers in early summer. The flowers give rise to small, roundish, blue, yellow or red berries, which are ornamental but not edible. The name Psychotria is derived from *psyche,* soul, and alludes to the medicinal properties of some of the kinds.

Cultivation. Outdoors, in warm, frost-free regions, these shrubs grow without difficulty in any average soil. When grown in greenhouses, they require a minimum winter temperature of 55 degrees, and a soil compost of equal parts of loam and peat with sand and crushed charcoal freely added.

Repotting is done in March. The plants are taken out of their pots, the crocks and loose soil are removed from their roots, and the plants are set in slightly larger pots. These are well drained with crocks which are covered with the rough siftings from the compost. The plants are potted firmly and placed in the warmest part of the greenhouse.

No water is applied to the soil until it becomes moderately dry. It is then thoroughly moistened,

and the same treatment is continued until the plants are well established; for the remainder of the summer the soil is kept moist. During the winter the compost is moistened only when it becomes moderately dry.

The atmosphere is kept moist throughout the year, except when the fruits are setting, by damping the floor and benches, and the foliage is regularly syringed. Less syringing and damping are required in winter, when the temperature is lower and the evaporation not so rapid. From April until September the foliage is shaded from bright sunlight, but for the remainder of the year shading is not required.

Taking Cuttings. Propagation is by cuttings or seeds. Cuttings are taken at any time from April to August and rooted in a propagating case with a bottom heat of 70-75 degrees. Each morning the sash is raised and the glass wiped on the underside until the cuttings are rooted. They are then potted separately in 3-in. pots and subsequently in larger ones.

Raising Seedlings. Seeds are sown in spring or summer. The seed pots or pans are well drained and filled with finely sifted soil, which is well moistened by immersing the vessels in water. After allowing a few minutes to drain, the seeds are sown thinly on the surface and lightly covered with soil. A pane of glass is laid over the pot, which is plunged in a propagating case with a bottom heat of 65-70 degrees.

The glass is wiped on the underside or reversed each day until the seedlings appear, after which it is removed and they are exposed to full light, but shaded from the sun. When the seedlings are 2 in. in height they are potted separately in 2-in. pots and subsequently in larger ones.

The chief kinds are P. capensis, yellow, fragrant flowers, black fruits; P. cyanocarpa, white flowers, blue berries; and P. jasminiflora, white flowers.

PSYLLA. See Pests and Diseases.

PTELEA TRIFOLIATA—*Hop Tree, Wafer Ash* (Ptel'ea). A leaf-losing shrub or small, round-headed tree, up to 25 ft. high, with, usually, three-parted leaves, fragrant, greenish flowers in large clusters in May or June and bitter, elmlike fruits, containing a central seed

Foliage and flowers of the Hop Tree or Wafer Ash, Ptelea trifoliata.

surrounded by a thin wing. The wing suggested the second common name of Wafer Ash.

Ptelea belongs to the Rue family, Rutaceae, and the name is the Greek name for the Elm tree, given to Ptelea by reason of the similarity of the fruits.

Ptelea trifoliata is a native of North America and occurs wild from New York to Florida, and westward to Ontario, Michigan, Iowa and Mexico.

The Hop Tree is easily raised from seeds. It thrives in any good garden soil, but should be given a sheltered place, for the branches are liable to be broken by wind. A little pruning in summer suffices to train the tree to form a well-

The round flat fruits of Ptelea trifoliata hang in clusters.

balanced head, but it cannot be induced to form more than a short trunk.

The fruits and, in fact, all parts of the tree have a bitter, hoplike taste and tonic properties. There are several well-marked varieties—aurea, with golden leaves; heterophylla, with much-divided leaflets; fastigiata, of stiff, erect habit; and mollis and pubescens, with downy leaves.

There are a few other little-known and very closely related kinds of Ptelea, all of North American origin.

PTERETIS—*Ostrich Fern* (Pteret′is). A small group of robust Ferns that are natives of North America, Europe and Asia. They belong to the Polypody family, Polypodiaceae. The name is

The Ostrich Fern enjoys wet, semishaded locations and humus-rich soil.

derived from the Greek *pteris,* a Fern. By some botanists this group of Ferns is named Matteuccia.

The Ostrich Ferns are plants of swamps and moist, wooded slopes. The North American kind grows naturally from Newfoundland to Alaska, southward to Virginia, Ohio, Missouri and British Columbia.

These Ferns are handsome, bold-foliaged subjects for growing in wild gardens and bog gardens. They are propagated by spores and by division in early spring. (See Ferns.)

Kinds. P. pennsylvanica (nodulosa), the largest native Fern of temperate North America, has fronds 6-10 ft. long; P. Struthiopteris is a closely allied European kind.

PTERIDIUM—*Bracken, Brake* (Pterid'ium). A genus of the Ferns belonging to the Polypody family, Polypodiaceae, and containing only one species, P. aquilinum. The name is a diminutive of Pteris, another kind of Fern.

The Bracken is not ordinarily cultivated in gardens, as it is too rampant in growth. The rhizomes spread rapidly underground and, once well established, are difficult to eradicate; the smallest portion left in the ground is capable of forming a new plant.

The Bracken has an almost world-wide natural distribution and is found in many parts of North America.

PTERIDOPHYLLUM—*Fern Poppy* (Pteridophyl'lum; Pteridoph'yllum). Pteridophyllum racemosum is a most charming little rock plant from Japan. It belongs to the Poppy family, Papaveraceae, but looks much more like a dainty Fern bearing small white flowers. The name Pteridophyllum means fern-leaved and refers to the resemblance of the foliage to a Fern frond.

The leaves are 3-4 in. long, dark and glossy green. The pure white flowers, in loose, graceful spikes, 6-9 in. high, open in June–July.

Pteridophyllum is rare in gardens, but is a great treasure for a cool corner of the rock garden, in light loam and leaf mold. It may be increased by careful division of the rather thick fleshy roots in spring, or by seeds sown in spring in a pan of loam, sand and leaf mold in a cold frame; the seedlings must be protected from slugs, which have a great liking for the plant.

PTERIS (Pter'is). A large genus of Ferns, some of which are popular pot plants. There are hothouse, greenhouse and hardy kinds, including evergreen and deciduous (leaf-losing) types. They grow wild in many parts of the world, including the West Indies, tropical America, tropical Asia, India, China, Japan, South Africa, Australia, New Zealand and Europe. The name Pteris is derived from *pteron,* a wing, and refers to the shape of the fronds of some of the species. They belong to the Fern family, Polypodiaceae.

Popular House and Greenhouse Ferns. The various kinds of Pteris differ greatly in size and appearance. Some are a few inches, others several feet, in height. The fronds of most kinds are

Pteris cretica Wimsettii, a splendid Fern for house decoration and for cultivation in a shady cool greenhouse.

deeply divided into a number of long, ribbon-like segments. P. cretica is the most popular kind; the crested forms of this kind are sold in large numbers as pot plants. Another favorite kind is P. tremula, which is a native of Australia and New Zealand and has fronds 2-3 ft. in length. There is a variety with crested fronds named Smithii.

Management of Hothouse and Cool Greenhouse Kinds. The hothouse kinds require a minimum winter temperature of 55 degrees and the cool greenhouse kinds one of 45 degrees. The best soil compost for most of these consists of equal parts of loam, peat, leaf mold and sand. The quick-growing, popular kinds such as P. cretica and P. tremula do best in equal parts of loam and leaf mold made porous with sand. Repotting of hothouse kinds is done in February, and of the cool greenhouse kinds in March, or as soon as the young fronds commence to develop.

At these times, the plants are taken out of their pots and the roots examined. Those which are well rooted are repotted in slightly larger pots. Those with comparatively few roots are slipped back into the pots and repotted at a later date, or they may remain in the same pots for another season. Those which have decayed roots (caused by poor drainage and the resulting sour soil) must be repotted in smaller pots after all the old compost has been removed.

Repotting. Well-established plants are taken out of their pots, the crocks and any loose soil are removed from the roots, and the plants are repotted in slightly larger pots. The new pots are prepared by draining them with crocks over which is placed a layer of the rough siftings from the compost. Potting is done by pressing the soil firmly with the fingers.

After potting, no water is given until the soil becomes moderately dry, and then it is thoroughly moistened. This system of watering must be continued until the plants are well rooted. Overwatering the soil will cause it to become sour and the roots will decay.

The atmosphere is kept moist by damping the floor and benches throughout the year, but less moisture is needed during the winter, when the temperature is lower and evaporation very slow. No syringing or wetting of the foliage is required.

After potting, the plants are shaded from the direct rays of the sun until the autumn, but for the remainder of the year they rarely need shading.

Treatment of These Ferns in Houses. Plants growing in houses must be protected from damage due to being close to radiators or other sources of dry heat. They require an abundance of water but the soil must not become stagnant. Repotting is done in the same way as for those which are grown in the greenhouse.

As the atmosphere cannot be kept moist by damping, the plants must be placed in cool, shady corners away from draughts. On warm, showery days they should be placed out of doors, to cleanse and freshen the foliage.

Propagation is by spores and division. The spores may be sown as soon as they are ripe, or kept in seed packets and sown at a later date. To ascertain if the spores are sufficiently ripe for sowing, a frond is gathered having spores of a dark-brown color. This is dropped into a paper

Pteris longifolia withstands drier atmospheric conditions than most Ferns. Along the path in this greenhouse the Pteris flourishes along with desert Cacti.

bag which is placed in a well-ventilated room for a few hours. The spores which are then found at the bottom of the bag are fit for sowing. (See Ferns.)

Propagation by division is done at potting time. The plants are taken out of their pots and the soil is washed or shaken from the roots. They are then pulled apart or divided by cutting through the rhizomes with a sharp knife. Each portion should consist of a piece of rhizome or crown with roots and a few fronds or buds attached. Each piece is potted in a small pot and treated as advised for repotting.

Favorite kinds for greenhouse and house cultivation are: P. cretica, 12 in., and its varieties, albo-lineata, green and silver fronds, Mayii, crested fronds, and Wimsettii, crested fronds; P. tremula, 3 ft., soft, green fronds, and its variety Smithii, with fronds that are marked with a checkered pattern; P. multifida (serrulata), 18 in.; P. ensiformis, 12 in.; and P. longifolia, 18 in. The last mentioned kind withstands dry atmosphere better than most Ferns.

PTEROCACTUS (Pterocac'tus). A small genus of the family Cactaceae, natives of Argentina. The name is derived from pteron, wing, and Cactus, and refers to the winged seeds. They produce, from a tuberous root, short-jointed stems furnished with bristly spines and terminated by yellow flowers. For details of cultivation, see Cactus.

The chief kinds are P. Fischeri; P. pumilus, of prostrate habit; and P. tuberosus.

PTEROCARYA – *Wing Nut* (Pterocar'ya). Leaf-losing trees of considerable size, natives of the Caucasus, China and Japan. They have long and ornamental pinnate leaves made up of an indefinite number of oblong leaflets. The flowers are small, and male and female are produced in separate catkins on the same tree. The female catkins are in some instances of considerable length; the flowers are succeeded by numerous winged, nutlike fruits.

These trees are hardy in the North but may need some protection from winter cold while young. They have little general economic use, but form handsome, decorative trees which are specially interesting by reason of the distinctive fruits. Pterocarya belongs to the Walnut family,

Juglandaceae, and the name is derived from the Greek *pteron,* a wing, and *karyon,* a nut, and refers to the winged nuts.

The most satisfactory means of propagation is by seeds, although the rarer kinds are sometimes grafted on stocks of P. fraxinifolia, and cuttings can be rooted. Seeds should be sown in a frame as soon as possible after they are ripe. When the seedlings appear, they should be set in separate pots and finally planted in a nursery bed; they must be transplanted every second year until they can be permanently placed.

Pruning will be necessary in order to keep the young trees to a definite central trunk, for there is a decided tendency for forked trunks to develop. This pruning may be carried out during summer.

The Best-known Kind. Pterocarya fraxinifolia, often called P. caucasica or the Caucasian Wing Nut, was introduced to France from the Caucasus in 1782. It attains a height of 100 ft. and has a large trunk and widely spreading head of branches. The leaves are 9-18 in. long, and those of the largest size may be composed of as many as twenty-seven leaflets. The male catkins are 3-5 in. long, and the female catkins may be 12-20 in. in length, bearing numerous winged nuts.

This tree thrives in loamy soil that is moist but well drained; also in wet ground such as the margin of a lake or stream. In moist places it is very apt to produce suckers from the roots, and a thicket is formed around the parent plant.

Other Noteworthy Kinds. P. hupehensis, the Hupeh Wing Nut, was introduced from Hupeh, China, in 1901. The leaves may be up to 12 in. or more long, and the female catkins 12-18 in. long. The numerous nuts, each with a pair of wings, form rounded fruits about 1 in. across. This tree grows 60-70 ft. high in China.

P. Paliurus, from central China, was introduced in 1901. In its native country it grows 40-50 ft. high. The leaves are about 9-12 in. long, the fruiting catkins are up to 10 in. long. The fruits are very distinct, for the central seed is entirely surrounded by a wing, the whole sometimes exceeding 2 in. in diameter. P. Rehderiana is a vigorous hybrid between P. fraxinifolia and P. stenoptera. It grows freely, and bears fruiting catkins that are upwards of a foot long.

P. stenoptera is a tree 80-100 ft. high, native to China, whence it was introduced about 1860. The leaves are 15 in. long, and sometimes include as many as twenty-one leaflets, the midrib of the leaf being winged on the upper side. The female catkins are 6-8 in. long, and the nuts have each two narrow erect wings. R. rhoifolia grows 90-100 ft. high in Japan. The leaves are sometimes more than 12 in. long, and the female catkins 8-10 in. long, the nuts having conspicuous wings.

The wood of the Wing Nuts is not of very good quality, and has no general commercial value. All these trees should be set in an open position and planted in loamy soil.

PTEROCEPHALUS—*Pincushion Plant* (Pteroceph'alus). Pterocephalus Parnassi is a mat- or cushion-forming rock plant, that is known also as Scabiosa pterocephala. It belongs to the Teasel family, Dipsaceae, and its name is from the Greek *pteron,* wing, and *cephala,* head, and refers to the formation of the seed heads.

For the Rock or Wall Garden. Pterocephalus Parnassi is a hardy plant for the rock garden or the wall garden. It makes a low-spreading cushion a foot or two across, and only 2 or 3 in. high. The leaves are a soft gray-green and feathery, and in July and August the plant covers itself with innumerable heads of scabious-like flowers, 1½ in. in diameter, and carried low down on stems only 1 or 2 in. high. The flowers are a delicate rosy-lilac, and contrast charmingly with the gray-green leaves. The plant should be given a sunny, well-drained position in the rock garden, well raised up among the rocks, so that it may trail down and form a half-hanging cushion. Light loamy soil suits it.

Pterocephalus is a first-rate plant for the wall garden, for which its trailing habit is particularly well adapted, and its flowering comes at a time of year when flowers of this type are all too scarce in the wall and rock garden.

Propagation. Pterocephalus may be propagated by careful division of the roots in spring, by seeds sown in a pan of light loam, leaf mold and sand in a cold frame in spring, or by soft cuttings taken in early summer before the formation of flower buds, and rooted in sand in a cold frame.

PTEROSTYRAX—*Epaulette Tree* (Pterostyrax; Pterosty'rax). Chinese and Japanese leaf-losing trees or large shrubs which are of considerable beauty when in flower in June. They were at one time included with Halesia, but conspicuous differences are seen in the flowers.

In Halesia the flowers are larger than in Pterostyrax; they are produced singly or in small clusters, and the stamens do not protrude beyond the petals. In Pterostyrax the flowers are small and borne many together in large pendent clusters; the stamens protrude beyond the petals. The fruits in Pterostyrax are much smaller than in Halesia.

Whereas Pterostyrax is purely Asiatic, Halesia is a North American genus. Pterostyrax belongs to the Styrax family, Styracaceae, and the name is derived from the Greek *pteron,* a wing, and *Styrax,* and refers to the winged fruit of P. corymbosa, and the relationship of the genus to Styrax.

Propagation is most readily effected by seeds. The branches may be layered. Pterostyrax require a sunny position in well-drained, but reasonably moist, loamy soil. They are hardy as far north as New England.

The most familiar kind is P. hispida, the Epaulette Tree of China and Japan, whence it was introduced in 1875. It may be found from a bush 12 ft. high to a spreading tree of 50 ft. The leaves are more or less oblong, up to 8 in. long and 4 in. wide, and the creamy white, fragrant flowers are in pendent clusters 4-9 in. long. The seeds are small and definitely ribbed.

P. corymbosa, with distinctly winged seeds, has been introduced; it seems to be less hardy than the other kind.

PTILOTRICHUM (Ptilo'trichum). A genus of dwarf subshrubby plants previously included in the genus Alyssum and belonging to the family Cruciferae. The name is from *ptilon,* feather, and *thrix,* hair, and refers to the starry down with which the growth is covered.

For the Rock Garden. The principal cultivated kind is P. spinosum, commonly grown as Alyssum spinosum, a spiny bush of dense, dwarf, spreading growth suitable for a sunny, well-drained position in the rock garden. It has tiny, silvery leaves, and in June–July is literally smothered with white flowers. There is also an attractive pink-tinted variety named roseum. Propagation is by seed sown in spring, or cuttings of the little new shoots inserted in sand in a frame in summer.

PTYCHOSPERMA—*Australian Feather Palm* (Ptychosper′ma). A small group of Palms from Australia, New Guinea and other Pacific islands. The characteristic features of these plants are the tall, slender, ringed trunks which are surmounted by large tufts of finely divided, feathery, arching leaves, several feet in length. This group belongs to the Palm family, Palmaceae. The name is from *ptyche*, a fold, and *sperma*, seed, and refers to the formation of the seed.

The only kind in common cultivation is P. elegans, which is the plant that was previously known to botanists as Seaforthia elegans, but is not the plant that is often wrongly named Seaforthia elegans in gardens. This last kind is properly named Archontophoenix Alexandrae.

P. elegans is a native of Queensland, Australia. It is planted in southern Florida and southern California.

Indoor Cultivation. Ptychosperma elegans forms an attractive decorative plant when grown in pots or tubs, and at one time was popular for greenhouse cultivation. It is easily grown and gives the cultivator no particular trouble.

Summer and Winter Treatment. These Palms require a minimum winter temperature of 50 degrees and a compost of equal parts of loam and leaf mold, with sand added freely. Repotting is done in March, or as soon as the new leaves commence to develop in the spring. The plants are taken out of their pots, the crocks and loose soil are removed from the roots with a pointed stick, and the plants are then set in slightly larger pots.

The pots must be well drained with crocks so that the water can pass freely through the compost, a layer of rough siftings from the compost or a layer of coarse leaves being placed over them. When potting these plants, ample space must be left for watering and the compost made firm.

Watering. The soil is not watered until it approaches dryness, and then enough water is given to moisten the whole ball of soil. If this system of watering is adopted, the roots quickly penetrate the compost. When well established, the plants are watered copiously during the remainder of the summer. In autumn the supply is gradually lessened and throughout the winter the compost is moistened only when it becomes moderately dry.

The atmosphere is kept moist by damping the floor and benches, and the foliage is syringed throughout the year, but these operations are performed less frequently in the winter when the temperature is much lower and evaporation consequently less rapid. From April to September the plants should be shaded from sunlight, but for the remainder of the year, shade is only afforded from the fiercest rays of the sun.

Plants in small pots are repotted annually, but when they become large enough to occupy large tubs they should not be disturbed for several years. They should be top-dressed with rich soil each year to keep them growing vigorously, and during the summer regular applications of liquid fertilizer are given.

Propagation Is by Seeds. These are sown in spring or summer, 1 in. deep, in well-drained seed pans. A light, sandy compost is used and this is afterwards thoroughly moistened. The seed pans are plunged into a propagating case with a bottom heat of 75-80 degrees, and the compost is kept uniformly moist until the seedlings appear. When 2 in. high, they are potted separately in 3-in. pots and subsequently in larger ones.

The chief kind is P. elegans, 20 ft., with leaves several feet long. This plant is often misnamed Hydriastele Wendlandiana in cultivation.

PUBESCENS. A botanical term meaning pubescent—that is, covered with soft hairs or down.

PUCCOON. Lithospermum canescens, which see.

PUDDLING. A term used by gardeners to denote the practice of placing the roots of seedling plants, more particularly those of Cabbage and other Brassicas, in a thick mixture of clayey soil and water before planting them. This is of especial benefit when planting is carried out in hot, dry weather, for it helps very considerably to keep the roots moist and so enables them to start into fresh growth as soon as they are planted.

The term "puddling" is also used to describe the practice of setting a plant in the hole in which it is to be planted, partly filling the hole with soil, and then soaking it with water before adding more soil and completing the planting.

PUERARIA THUNBERGIANA — *Kudzu Vine* (Puerar'ia). This is a vigorous subshrub with long, twining shoots, fleshy roots, and large three-parted leaves. The flowers are pea-shaped, violet-purple, and produced in dense, erect clusters. The plant is grown as a decorative plant and a fodder crop. The fleshy, tuberous roots are also used for food and as a source of starch.

The Kudzu Vine is propagated by seeds and cuttings and by root division. It thrives without difficulty in any ordinary soil, and under favorable conditions grows shoots 40-60 ft. long in a single season. In the South the tops are perennial, but north of Washington, D. C., they do not ordinarily persist over winter, although they sometimes do. In the North the soft shoots die to the ground in winter, but the rootstock remains alive and new shoots appear in spring. In cold climates the rootstock should be protected with straw, salt hay, leaves or ashes.

Pueraria belongs to the Pea family, Leguminosae, and the name commemorates M. N. Puerari, a Geneva botanist. The plant is a native of China and Japan.

PUERTO RICAN HAT PALM. See Sabal causiarum.

PULCHELLUS. A botanical term meaning pretty and used frequently in plant nomenclature.

PULCHER. The Latin word for beautiful, sometimes used as the specific name of plants. Senecio pulcher is an example.

PULMONARIA—*Lungwort, Blue Cowslip* (Pulmona'ria). A genus of hardy plants which are found wild in various parts of Europe and belong to the Borage family, Boraginaceae. They grow 9-12 in. high, and chiefly bear blue flowers. The name Pulmonaria is derived from *pulmo,* a lung, because of the supposed value of the leaves in the treatment of lung diseases.

These plants are perfectly easily managed and thrive in ordinary soil that is fairly moist, in sunny or shady places. They may be planted on

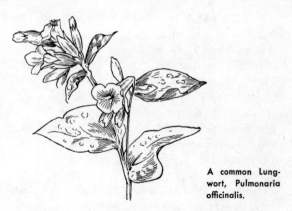

A common Lungwort, Pulmonaria officinalis.

the outskirts of the rock garden, or towards the front of the flower border, but are chiefly valuable in gardens for setting in shady positions where comparatively few plants are happy.

The Lungworts may be planted in autumn or spring. If an increased stock of plants is required, it can be obtained without difficulty by lifting them in October, separating them into rooted pieces and replanting the latter where they are to grow.

The chief kinds are P. angustifolia, 12 in., blue, early spring, and its varieties alba, white,

Pulmonaria saccharata blooms in early spring, the flowers opening rose-colored, then changing to blue.

and azurea, the best blue kind; P. arvernensis, 9 in., blue, spring; P. officinalis, 12 in., early spring; flowers reddish at first and fading to violet-blue; P. saccharata, Bethlehem Sage, 12 in., rose fading to blue, spring.

PULSATILLA. See Anemone.

PULTENAEA (Pultenae'a). Uncommon, tender, flowering shrubs, all of which are natives of Australia. They belong to the Pea family, Leguminosae, and grow up to 3-6 ft. in height. The principal kind, P. rosea, has virgate (round or wandlike) branches with linear (long and narrow), terete (roundish), evergreen leaves. The pink, pea-shaped flowers are borne in terminal heads in April. The name Pultenaea commemorates Dr. R. Pulteney, a botanist of the eighteenth century.

Outdoors in California. In California and similar climates these shrubs may be grown outdoors. They thrive in sun in well-drained soils.

Flowering Shrubs for a Greenhouse. These plants are almost hardy and do not need a higher temperature than 40 degrees minimum in winter. They do best in a compost of sandy peat.

Repotting is done after flowering. The plants are first lightly pruned into shape and are then set in slightly larger pots. The new pots are well drained with crocks, and these are covered with a layer of coarse leaves.

The plants are taken out of their old pots, and the crocks and loose soil removed from the roots. The tips of the main roots are then gently loosened with a pointed stick so that they may more readily enter into the new compost. When potting, the compost is made very firm to encourage short-jointed, prolific flower-bearing growth.

After potting, the plants are shaded from bright sunlight until established, after which they are exposed to full light; during the latter part of the summer they are stood out of doors on a bed of ashes to ripen the shoots. Early in October they are taken into a well-lighted, frost-proof greenhouse for the winter. No damping of the greenhouse is required, and they are only syringed for a few weeks after they have been repotted, or until they have become established.

Summer and Winter Treatment. The soil is not watered immediately after repotting, but is allowed to become moderately dry before it is moistened; then enough water is given to saturate the whole ball of soil. This system of watering is continued until the plants are well rooted, after which the soil is kept moist for the remainder of the year. Much less watering is required during the winter. Extremes of wetness or dryness of the soil must be avoided at all times, as both are injurious to these plants.

Propagation Is by Cuttings. Well-ripened shoots, 2 in. in length, are taken in August. The leaves are carefully trimmed off from the lower part of the stem with a sharp knife to avoid tearing the bark, and a cut is made below the bottom joint.

The cuttings are inserted firmly, 1 in. apart, in a well-firmed mixture of peat moss and sand. They are covered with a bell jar which is wiped dry inside each morning until roots are formed. Then the bell jar is removed, and after a few days the cuttings are potted separately in 3-in. pots and subsequently in larger ones. To ensure bushy plants the tips of the main shoots are pinched out and the resultant side shoots are treated similarly.

The chief kinds are P. daphnoides, 6 ft., red and yellow, summer; P. rosea, 3 ft., pink, April; and P. stricta, 3 ft., yellow, June.

PUMMELO OR SHADDOCK. Citrus maxima. See Shaddock under Citrus.

PUMPKIN. The popular name given to the fruits of certain varieties of Cucurbita Pepo, a tender plant related to the Gourd. The fruits, which may reach an immense size, are borne on long, sprawling, prostrate vines.

The Pumpkin is strictly a warm-weather crop. Seeds are sown outdoors in hills spaced 6 ft. or more apart or, in regions where summers are short, are raised early indoors in pots and are planted in hills outdoors after the weather is warm and settled. These plants are often interplanted with a crop of Corn.

Pumpkins are gross feeders and, for the best results, a generous amount of manure or rich compost fortified with fertilizer should be put in each hill.

Plants grown in very rich soil should have their vines pinched back occasionally to limit leaf growth and encourage fruiting.

The term Pumpkin is not applied with exactitude. Sometimes varieties of Cucurbita moschata and C. maxima are called Pumpkins as well as varieties of C. Pepo; and other varieties of C. Pepo are known as Squash. The term

Squash is sometimes restricted to varieties of C. maxima.

PUNCH AND JUDY ORCHID. An Orchid suitable for cultivation in a warm greenhouse. The botanical name is Gongora, which see.

PUNICA GRANATUM—_Pomegranate_ (Pu'-nica). A tender, leaf-losing shrub or small tree, native to western Asia and southern Europe but widely grown in tropical and subtropical countries, in several of which it has become naturalized. It is often grown as a large bush, but may form a tree 25 ft. high. The small, deep green leaves are willow-like, up to 3 in. long, and usually less than ¾ in. wide. The flowers are vivid scarlet and 1½-2 in. across. The fruit, when ripe, is the size of a large Orange, golden, flushed with red, with hard rind covering numerous seeds embedded in pulp.

Punica is the only member of the family Punicaceae, and the name is taken from Pliny's name for the plant, Malum Punicum, probably an allusion to the apple-shaped fruits and red flowers.

The Pomegranate is hardy as far north as southern Maryland and, if planted against a wall in a sheltered location, may be grown further north. As a flowering shrub it is worth a position on a wall. It should be given well-drained soil.

The Pomegranate, Punica Granatum, in fruit.

The most favored regions for the cultivation of the Pomegranate are Florida and other parts of the deep South, and California. The trees succeed on a variety of soils and should be planted 15-20 ft. apart when grown for their fruit.

When planted for a hedge, Pomegranates should be set about 6 ft. apart. They are very attractive plants for this purpose, as they flower freely over a long period in spring and bear attractive fruits in summer.

When Pomegranates are to be grown as individual specimens, they should be encouraged to develop a treelike habit by removing the numerous shoots that develop around their bases and retaining only one trunk. In the case of hedges, however, all basal shoots that do not trespass beyond the limits set for the hedge are allowed to remain.

Propagation is easily effected by means of seeds, and the plant can also be increased by cuttings of short, half-ripened side shoots inserted in a bed of sand or sand and peat moss in a close cold frame or propagating case in June or July. The easiest method of securing new plants is by digging up and replanting the sucker growths that appear around the bases of the old plants. This should be done in early spring before new growth begins. As a flowering shrub, the Pomegranate is worth a position on a wall. It should be given well-drained soil.

In addition to the type, there are several named varieties; albescens has white or cream-colored flowers; flore-pleno has large, double, scarlet flowers; and nana is of dwarf habit, with small leaves and small scarlet flowers which are produced with great freedom. There are also named varieties that bear superior fruits such as Wonderful.

The variety nana may be grown in pots or tubs placed in a cool greenhouse for winter and spring, and set out of doors in a sunny position for summer and autumn.

The fruits of the Pomegranate are eaten; the bark is used for tanning; the roots have medicinal properties as a vermifuge, and the dried rind of the fruits has been used in cases of diarrhea and dysentery.

PUNK TREE. Melaleuca Leucadendra.

PUPA. The intermediate or resting stage of

many insects. It is most familiar in the moths and butterflies; in the latter group the alternative name of chrysalis is more often used. When the caterpillar or grub casts its skin for the final time, it enters the pupal stage. In this stage it undergoes a complete metamorphosis, and later the perfect insect emerges, very different in appearance from the grub stage.

PURPLE BEECH. See Fagus.

PURPLE BELL VINE. Rhodochiton volubile, which see.

PURPLE CONEFLOWER. See Echinacea.

PURPLE-LEAVED NUT. See Corylus.

PURPLE-LEAVED PLUM. Prunus cerasifera atropurpurea (Pissardii), which see.

PURPLE LOOSESTRIFE. See Lythrum.

PURPLE OSIER. Salix purpurea, which see.

PURPLE WILLOW. Salix purpurea, which see.

PURPLE WREATH. Petrea, which see.

PURSHIA TRIDENTATA—*Antelope Brush* (Pursh'ia). A western American, leaf-losing (deciduous) shrub that belongs to the Rose family, Rosaceae. It is a plant of arid soils and dry climates that has little horticultural value although it is sometimes transferred to grounds. The name honors the German botanist, Frederick T. Pursh, who traveled in North America and wrote of its plants.

Propagation may be effected by seeds and by layers. P. tridentata grows to a height of 4-6 ft. Its foliage is silvery, its flowers yellow but of little decorative value.

PURSLANE. Portulaca oleracea is best-known as a pestiferous and persistent weed of cultivated ground; it is often called "Pussley" colloquially. This plant was probably originally a native of western Asia but is now widespread and occurs in many parts of the world.

A variety of the common Purslane identified as Portulaca oleracea sativa is sometimes grown in gardens as a summer salad for the sake of its edible leaves. Like kinds of Portulaca valued for their flowers, it thrives best in light or well-drained soil and must be sown on a sunny border. The usual time to sow seeds is in spring, as soon as soil and weather conditions are suitable; it is useless to sow when the ground is sodden or when the weather is cold.

The seeds are sown in rows 10 in. apart, and need but a slight covering of soil. The only attention required during the summer months is to hoe between the rows to keep down weeds, and to water the plants in prolonged dry weather. The leaves are cut for use when about 3 in. high. Further sowings may be made during June and July if a succession of produce is required.

PUSCHKINIA SCILLOIDES—*Striped Squill* (Puschkin'ia). An attractive spring-flowering bulb belonging to the Lily family, Liliaceae. It was named in honor of Count M. Puschkin.

A Hardy, Spring-flowering Bulb. Puschkinia scilloides (libanotica), the Striped Squill, is a hardy bulbous flower closely resembling a Scilla, growing 4-6 in. high, and flowering in spring. It is an extremely attractive flower of the easiest possible cultivation, thriving in ordinary soil,

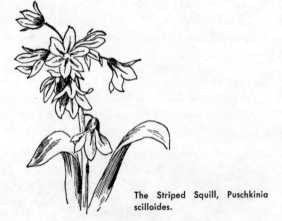

The Striped Squill, Puschkinia scilloides.

and enjoying an open sunny position. The bulbs may be planted any time in autumn. The flowers, about ½-¾ in. across, are carried in an erect spike, and their color is palest blue-white, with three darker porcelain-blue lines down the sides and center of each petal.

Propagation is most readily effected by lifting and dividing the bulbs every two or three years, or seeds may be sown as soon as gathered, but this is a slower method of increase.

Puschkinia scilloides is a native of Asia, the Caucasus and Afghanistan. It is a first-rate bulb for the rock garden and the alpine lawn, and for flower borders generally. A pot or two, moreover, will add greatly to the attractiveness of the cool greenhouse and windows of a living room; the plant is a welcome change from the other spring bulbs more commonly grown in this way.

PUSSYTOES. Antennaria, which see.

PUSSY WILLOW. Salix discolor, which see.

PUTORIA CALABRICA (Putor'ia). A charming dwarf evergreen shrub, suitable for planting in well-drained gritty soil in a sheltered position in the rock garden. It bears clusters of deep pink, daphne-like flowers in summer. Cuttings of young shoots, inserted in sandy soil under a bell jar in summer, provide the best means of increase. The leaves have a disagreeable odor; hence the name, derived from *putor,* a foul smell. The plant belongs to the family Rubiaceae and is a native of the Mediterranean region.

PUTTYROOT. Aplectrum, which see.

PUYA (Puy'a). A group of tender, perennial plants remarkable for the striking colors of their flowers. The Puyas are found wild in South America and they belong to the family Bromeliaceae. Puya is the Chilean name of this plant.

Puyas are mostly plants for warm, sunny greenhouses and for cultivating outdoors in frost-free or nearly frost-free climates. One kind, P. alpestris (also known as P. Whytei), successfully withstands several degrees of frost and is cultivated in the open air in favored places in the south of England.

For their satisfactory cultivation these plants require a well-drained soil; one containing an appreciable amount of peat seems to suit them best, although they are not very particular as to the composition of the rooting medium, provided it is not stagnant or waterlogged.

Puyas may be grown in large pots or tubs in a well-drained compost of loam and peat, with sand added freely. During the summer months they may be placed out of doors. In winter, water must be applied sparingly; it should be given only when the soil is dry. Propagation is effected by detaching and potting the offsets or suckers.

Kinds. P. alpestris, stem short, leaves to 2 ft. long and 1 in. wide, inflorescence much branched and many-flowered, 4-5 ft. tall, flowers metallic blue-green with orange-colored anthers; P. Berteroniana, 10-12 ft. tall, flowers blue-green, leaves white on their undersides and strongly

Flowering spike of Puya alpestris, the hardiest kind of Puya.

Puya spathacea has stiff gray leaves and large, branched flower stems. The flowers are blue, the bracts pink.

recurved; P. caerulea, to 4 ft. tall, leaves 2 ft. long, narrow, inflorescence somewhat branched, flowers blue; P. chilensis, to 5 ft. tall, leaves to 4 ft. long, narrow, glaucous, inflorescence branched, flowers greenish yellow; P. spathacea, 2 ft. tall, leaves 12-15 in. long, less than an inch wide, inflorescence much branched, flowers blue, bracts pink.

PYCNANTHEMUM—*Mountain Mint* (Pyc-nanth'emum). Hardy, perennial, herbaceous plants that are natives of North America and belong to the Mint family, Labiatae. The name derives from *pyknos,* dense, and *anthos,* a flower, and refers to the dense, clustered arrangement of the flowers.

These plants are of no great horticultural importance. Their chief value is as subjects for planting in the wild garden; they may also be used occasionally in perennial borders and in herb gardens. Their leaves release a minty, aromatic odor when bruised.

Pycnanthemums are easily grown in any ordinary soil and adapt themselves to a variety of conditions. In nature some inhabit dry, upland soils, others moist woods and meadows.

Mountain Mints are easily propagated by means of seeds sown when ripe or in spring, and by division in early fall or spring.

Kinds that may sometimes be cultivated include P. flexuosum, 2-2½ ft., a dry-soil kind; P. incanum, 3 ft. a native of upland woods; P. muticum, 3½ ft., a plant of moist woods and meadows; P. virginianum, 3 ft., a native of upland woods and moist prairies. All have white or purplish flowers in late summer or fall.

PYCNOSTACHYS (Pycno'stachys; Pycno-stach'ys). Tender, evergreen, perennial flowering plants of great beauty. They are found growing wild in tropical Africa, and belong to the Mint family, Labiatae. The principal kind, P. Dawei, grows 5 ft. in height, has stout erect, square, semiwoody stems clothed with lanceolate, bright green leaves, 6 in. in length and 1 in. in width. The leaves have serrate (sawlike) edges, and the tips taper to a fine point.

At the end of each shoot there is a large densely packed spike of cobalt-blue, labiate (two-lipped) flowers. The name Pycnostachys is derived from *pyknos,* dense, and *stachys,* a spike,

The rich blue flower spikes of Pycnostachys Dawei open in midwinter. A warm greenhouse is required to grow them successfully.

and refers to the flower spikes of the plants.

Winter-flowering Plants for a Warm Greenhouse. These plants, which flower in December and January, are very useful for decorating the greenhouse in midwinter. They require a minimum winter temperature of 55 degrees and a soil compost of two parts of loam, one part leaf mold, and a little well-decayed manure, with sand added freely.

Although the plants can be kept for several years to form large specimens, it is usual to raise young plants annually. If cuttings are inserted early in the spring, bushy plants 5 ft. in height are obtained in 9 months, and, by taking cuttings in successive batches up to the end of June, plants varying in height from 18 in. to 5 ft. are obtained.

Taking Cuttings. Side shoots 2 in. in length are taken off, the leaves from the lower halves of the stems are trimmed off, and a cut is made just below the bottom joint. The cuttings are placed in a propagating case.

To prevent the cuttings from damping off, the case is opened each morning, and the moisture is wiped from the underside of the glass. When roots are formed, the cuttings are potted separately in 3-in. pots and subsequently in larger ones. Those which are rooted in March will eventually occupy 9- to 10-in. pots, and those rooted in June will finally be put in 6- to 7-in. pots. To obtain bushy plants, the tips of the main shoots are pinched when the plants have recovered from their first potting, and the subsequent side shoots are stopped after the second repotting. Extra-bushy plants are obtained by planting three rooted cuttings in a 3-in. pot and repotting without separating them.

Raising the Plants from Seeds. Seeds of these plants are sown in well-drained pots of sandy soil in spring. The soil is moistened by immersing the pot in water, and a pane of glass is laid over the pot. The pots are placed in a greenhouse with a minimum temperature of 55 degrees, and the underside of the glass is wiped dry each morning until the seedlings appear above the surface. When 2 in. in height, they are potted separately in 3-in. pots, and treated as advised for the cuttings.

After each repotting no water is applied until the plants are well rooted, after which the soil is kept moist. When established in their final pots, a biweekly application of dilute liquid fertilizer is applied. The soil is kept moist until the plants have finished flowering. They are then rested by keeping the soil moderately dry until March, when they are restarted into growth to finish young shoots for cuttings.

The atmosphere must be kept moist and the foliage syringed with water daily until the plants are established in their final pots. They need shade from strong sunlight. Afterwards they are freely ventilated and fully exposed to the light to ripen the shoots. When in flower, they are placed in a cool greenhouse or conservatory to prolong the period of blooming.

The chief kind is P. Dawei, 5 ft., blue, winter. P. urticifolia, 7 ft., has paler blue flowers than P. Dawei and is less handsome.

PYRACANTHA — Firethorn (Pyracanth'a). Tender and hardy evergreen trees or, more frequently, spreading shrubs of large size with dark green leaves covering spiny branches. The white flowers are produced in flattened heads in June and they are followed by attractive, usually coral-red fruits which ripen in early September and remain in good condition for several months if protected from birds.

These plants are natives of southern Europe,

Orange-red fruits of the Firethorn, Pyracantha coccinea Lalandii.

Asia Minor and China, and, with one exception, are among the newer shrubs in our gardens. Pyracantha belongs to the Rose family, Rosaceae, and is related to both the Crataegus and Cotoneaster; the name is from the Greek pyr, fire, and akanthar, a thorn, and alludes to the red berries and spiny shoots.

The hardiest, P. coccinea and its varieties, lives outdoors as far north as southern New England but often has its foliage severely damaged in winter. Other kinds are adaptable for outdoor cultivation only in mild climates.

Propagation by Seeds and Cuttings. Propagation is effected by seeds, which may lie dormant in the soil for twelve months before they germinate, or by cuttings of short side shoots taken with a slight heel of old wood in July and inserted in a close frame or under a bell jar. It is usual to cultivate young plants in pots until they are set out permanently.

Planting and Pruning. Firethorns may be grown in the open ground or against a wall. In colder parts the protection of a wall is very helpful. Well-drained, loamy soil and a sunny position are required. Bushes growing in the

Pyrethrums, Painted Daisies, come in a variety of colors and are excellent for cutting.

Flowering at the same time as May-flowering Tulips, Pyrethrums combine well with them in perennial borders.

open ground do not require regular pruning; those against a wall may be cut back in early spring when they are becoming too large for their places.

The Common Firethorn. Pyracantha coccinea, the Buisson Ardent of southern Europe and Asia Minor, is the best-known kind. In the open ground it will grow 12-15 or more feet high and spread over a wide area. Planted against a wall it may be expected to grow at least 20 ft. high if required.

This is a good evergreen at all times. It is beautiful in June when covered with white flowers, and doubly so in autumn, when bearing its crop of brightly colored, coral-red fruit.

The variety Lalandii, with orange-red fruits, is usually preferred to the type. If this shrub is planted against the wall of a house, it is necessary to train the shoots in the direction required and secure the main branches firmly to the support. The frontal shoots must be cut back far enough to keep the plant compact. The variety Lalandii

is considered to be somewhat hardier than P. coccinea itself.

Other Attractive Kinds. P. angustifolia, a native of western China, is more tender than P. coccinea, and is only of use for planting where winters are mild. It will attain a height of 12 ft. and is easily distinguished by its narrower leaves, which are green above and with gray felt-like covering beneath; the flowers are white, the fruits orange-yellow. It has been grown since 1899.

P. crenulata is a native of the Himalayas, and is rather like P. coccinea in general character, except that the fruits are orange-yellow.

P. atalantioides (Gibbsii) grows 12-14 ft. high, forming a dense bush with dark, glossy green leaves. White flowers are produced freely and are followed by a good crop of small, coral-red fruits which remain in good condition for several months. It is useful alike as a bush in the open and for planting against a wall. P. crenato-serrata is an evergreen shrub from

A young Pyracantha being trained as an espalier against a wall. Pyracanthas are well adapted to this mode of training.

central and western China, with glossy leaves and clusters of coral-red fruits.

P. crenulata variety Rogersiana is possibly the most attractive of all, both as a bush and as a wall shrub. It is of good habit and bears orange-red fruits freely. This small-leaved species is very charming in flower as well as fruit, and there are several grand forms of it, notably flava, with bright yellow fruits, and aurantiaca, with rich orange-yellow fruits.

P. Duvallii is a kind of horticultural origin that has fine, bright red berries and attractive foliage.

The Pyracanthas are shrubs that form good hedges in the warmer parts of North America; this is because they grow and stand clipping very well, are evergreen, and pract cally impenetrable.

PYRAMID. A term used by gardeners to denote a fruit tree or other tree or plant which has a central stem on which the branches develop, from ground level to the top, and which gradually narrows above.

PYRAMIDALIS. A botanical term used to denote a conical habit of growth.

PYRETHRUM (Pyre'thrum). Although the various Pyrethrums are now included by botanists in the genus Chrysanthemum, the familiar hardy herbaceous kinds, which bear large, daisy-like, single or double flowers in many attractive colors, are still grown in gardens as Pyrethrum. They belong to the Daisy family, Compositae. The name Pyrethrum is from an old Greek name, *Pyrethron*. These plants are sometimes called Painted Daisies.

The species or wild type from which the present-day race of garden varieties of Pyrethrum is chiefly descended is Chrysanthemum coccineum (roseum), which is found wild in the Near East. These varieties are in full beauty in May and June, and are valuable because they provide masses of color in the garden at a time when the last of the spring flowers have faded and before most of the summer kinds are in bloom. The flowers are long-stemmed and invaluable for cutting for decorative purposes indoors.

The Pyrethrum thrives best on well-drained soil; on heavy, clayey soil it is not happy and may perish during excessively wet weather in the winter months. It should be planted in a sunny position. Light land can be made suitable for Pyrethrum by digging in well-decayed manure or compost to prevent the plants suffering from the effect of drought during hot summer weather; clayey ground is improved by adding leaf mold, manure or compost and sand.

The best time to plant Pyrethrum is late August or September; the soil is still warm and

A Pyrethrum or Painted Daisy, one of the many attractive varieties of Chrysanthemum coccineum.

the plants have a chance of becoming well rooted before cold weather sets in. If planting cannot be done then, it is preferably deferred until spring, when soil and weather conditions are likely to be more suitable than in winter.

It is the practice in some gardens to cut down the plants after the first crop of flowers is over, as is also done with Lupine and Delphinium, for the purpose of obtaining a second crop of blooms later in the summer. The second display, however, is a comparatively poor one, and it is very doubtful if this practice is worth following, because it must have a weakening effect on the plants, which are forced into fresh activity when they ought to be going to rest. If the plants are cut down in June, the soil must be enriched by a top-dressing of decayed manure or a dressing of fertilizer and kept moist in dry weather.

Propagation by Division. If an increased stock of Pyrethrum is wanted, it is supplied either by raising seedlings or by division of the old plants. Growers have different opinions as to which is the best time to lift and separate Pyrethrum for the purpose of providing an increased number of plants. The work can be done in September on light or really well-drained land, but if it is carried out at that time on heavier ground, the plants are liable to perish during the winter months.

Probably the most suitable time to lift and divide Pyrethrum is late in spring, just when fresh growth is about to begin. The roots are then active and soon take possession of the soil. Still another plan is to wait until the flowers have faded, and then to lift and divide the old plants. If the work is carried out then, it is most important that the roots be kept moist in dry weather and that the plants be shaded for a week or two after the operation.

The plants must be separated very carefully to avoid unnecessary damage to the roots.

Varieties. There are many beautiful single and double named varieties of Pyrethrum. These will be found described in the catalogues of specialists in hardy perennial plants. Mixed varieties can be raised from seed.

PYRETHRUM POWDER. This powder, once known as Dalmatian or Persian Insect powder, is made from the dried flowers of Chrysanthemum (Pyrethrum) cinerariaefolium and other species, and is used against insect pests in the garden as well as flies and other pests that may infest the house. It does not lose its efficiency when exposed to the atmosphere and is harmless to plants. It enters into the composition of many insecticides.

PYROLA—*Shinleaf* (Py'rola). A small genus of hardy perennial herbs, natives of Europe, northern and central Asia, and North America, belonging to the Heath family, Ericaceae. The name Pyrola is a derivation of Pyrus, a Pear tree, from a supposed resemblance of the leaves to those of the Pear, though the resemblance is not easy to see. The plant is sometimes called Wintergreen.

The Shinleafs are very beautiful plants, well worthy of a place in the rock garden and wild garden, though some of them are by no means easy to grow successfully. They are mostly woodland and bog plants, growing in moist, sandy, peaty, or sometimes damp, mossy places. Their roots are rambling, threadlike, white thongs.

The best means of propagation is by very careful division of the roots in spring, and the greatest care must be taken not to let them become dry during transplanting. Seeds are produced, but they are as fine as snuff, and are rather difficult to manage. They should be sown in woodsy, moist soil, in a cold frame, when ripe.

Pyrola elliptica, a native of North America, has white, cup-shaped flowers in few-flowered racemes, about 6 in. high; the flowers are fragrant and appear in June and July. P. minor grows natively in North America, Europe and Asia. It has white or pinkish flowers.

The Best of All. Pyrola rotundifolia is a native of Europe, and its variety americana of eastern North America. These are decidedly the most easily grown and satisfactory, as well as the most beautiful of the Shinleafs. The leaves, 3-4 in. high, are glossy, evergreen, and spoonshaped, while the flower stems are erect and wiry, 6-12 in. high, carrying from ten to twenty large, waxy, white bells of a delicious fragrance in May and June. This lovely and uncommon plant is easy to grow in spite of its reputation of

[10–4]
Red Raspberries

[10–4a]
Red Raspberry variety Amber

[10—5]
Raspberries in staked rows

[10—5a]
Turban Ranunculus

[10—5b]
Raphiolepis indica

[10—5c]
Rhubarb

being difficult. The first essential to success is to procure sound healthy plants established in pots.

The Secrets of Success. Having secured good plants, the rest is simple. Choose a shady or half-shady position, dig out the soil 18 in. deep, and fill in with fine, well-decayed leaf mold. Then turn the Pyrolas out of the pots and plant them 9-12 in. apart. The shade afforded by shrubs such as Azalea or Rhododendrons is most suitable for sheltering Pyrolas from too much sunshine; or they may be planted in light woodland. During periods of severe drought an occasional watering may be necessary, but, apart from this, Pyrola will need no attention. It will soon root through the leaf mold and produce great quantities of its lovely flowers which look and smell like Lilies of the Valley and are equally good for picking for the house. In certain rich, soft vegetable soils the provision for a leaf-mold bed may be unnecessary, but when the natural soil of the garden is unsuitable, it provides a sure and easy way to success.

Pyrola asarifolia is another North American kind similar to the last-named. It has pale pink or lavender flowers. Its variety incarnata has beautiful rose-pink flowers. It is rare in gardens, a choice and lovely plant which responds well to the same treatment as P. rotundifolia.

Pyrola secunda, a native of northern Asia, northern Europe and North America, is smaller than P. rotundifolia, 4-5 in. high, with spikes of greenish-white flowers in June and July. It is pretty, but less valuable and attractive than P. rotundifolia, though worthy of a place in a garden where rare and interesting plants are appreciated.

Other North American kinds that may be cultivated include P. picta, which occurs from British Columbia to Montana and southward to California and Arizona. This kind has greenish or purplish flowers, and leaves that are purple beneath and blotched with white on their upper surfaces. P. uliginosa occurs from Nova Scotia to Minnesota, and from British Columbia to Colorado and California. Its flowers are pink to purplish.

PYROSTEGIA IGNEA (Pyroste′gia). Pyrostegia ignea (venusta) is a showy, tender, climbing

Pyrostegia ignea clothing a wall in the deep South. It bears beautiful crimson-orange, tubular flowers.

shrub from Brazil, which produces its rich crimson-orange, tubular flowers in large drooping panicles. The name Pyrostegia is derived from *pyr,* fire, and *stega,* roof, and refers to the upper lip of the flower. The plant was previously included in the genus Bignonia, and belongs to the family Bignoniaceae.

This high climber is a grand subject for clothing the rafters of a large greenhouse and for growing outdoors on arbors and similar locations in the far South.

Cultivation. Pyrostegia ignea thrives in any ordinary soil and grows rapidly. It has three-forked tendrils that cling to wood, masonry and similar surfaces.

In the far South it blooms over a long period in winter and often again in summer, but summer flowering is usually less profuse than that in winter.

When grown in greenhouses, this fine flowering vine should be planted in a bed or border or in large boxes and the shoots trained under the roof glass, up a pillar, or against a wall.

A rich, well-drained soil is needed and planting should be done in early spring. At all times the atmosphere should be kept moist. To assure this, frequent damping of the paths, benches and other interior surfaces should receive attention, particularly from spring to fall; in winter less damping and syringing are usually required.

The temperature of the greenhouse should be maintained at a minimum of 45-50 degrees in winter. From spring (after new growth begins) until fall the minimum temperature should be 65 degrees.

Plants grown in northern greenhouses flower in summer; winter is their season of rest. During winter, water should be applied sparingly, but freely from spring to fall. Weekly applications of dilute liquid fertilizer during the season of active growth are highly beneficial.

Pruning is carried out after the plants flower, the side shoots being cut back to within 1-3 ft. of the old wood. This strengthens the lateral buds, which in turn produce flowering branches.

All superfluous and weak branches should be removed in late winter, and those that remain should be tied neatly to their supports.

Propagation is readily effected by means of cuttings, each consisting of about three joints, taken in spring or early summer from side shoots and planted in a moist propagating case in a warm greenhouse.

PYRRHOCACTUS (Pyrrhocac'tus). A small group of South American Cacti that are closely related to Malacocarpus and by some botanists are included in that genus. They belong to the Cactus family, Cactaceae. The name is derived from *pyrrhos,* reddish. For their cultivation, see Cacti.

Kinds that are likely to be grown by fanciers of Cacti include P. curvispinus, flowers yellow-red; P. Strausianus, flowers salmon-pink; P. tuberisulcatus, flowers brownish-yellow striped red; P. umadeave, flowers pale yellow.

PYRUS—*Pear* (Py'rus). At one time this was a large genus, embracing many ornamental and economically important trees, but these have now been reclassified and separated into different genera, the name Pyrus being reserved for the Pear group. The Crab Apples and cultivated Apples are placed under Malus; the Rowans, White Beams, and Service Trees are called Sorbus; the Chokeberry is Aronia, under which generic names they are dealt with in this work.

Pyrus belongs to the Rose family, Rosaceae, and the name is the old Latin name for the Pear tree. (See also Pear.)

Ornamental Flowering Pear Trees. Pyrus communis, the tree from which the garden Pears were raised, is a native of Europe and western Asia. It is a long-lived tree that may grow 30-40 ft. high with a trunk of large dimensions. The flowers are white, and the fruits of the wild kinds are hard and gritty.

The Birch-leaved Pear. P. betulaefolia is a hardy tree from North China growing 20-30 ft. high. The white flowers appear in spring. The fruits are not attractive.

The Almond Pear, P. amygdaliformis, usually grows less than 20 ft. high. It is a native of western Asia, and has thick-textured leaves, white flowers, and small hard fruits. There are several varieties, such as lobata, cuneifolia and oblongifolia, but they have no decorative significance.

The Willow-leaved Pear, P. salicifolia, has narrow green leaves with a white felt-like covering which wears off as the leaves age. It is found wild in southeastern Europe and western Asia. The flowers are white, the fruits green and hard. The variety pendula has weeping branches.

The Sand Pear, P. pyrifolia (serotina), sometimes called P. sinensis, is a Chinese tree, and the parent of the Chinese and Japanese cultivated Pears. Varieties such as Kieffer and Leconte are hybrids between P. pyrifolia and P. communis. The white flowers of P. pyrifolia are attractive, as are the yellowish, sweet, but rather insipid fruits, in which the part near the stalk is wider than the apex.

P. Pashia is a tree from the Himalayas and western China, with spiny branches, white, rose-tinged flowers and small rounded fruits.

Other kinds occasionally cultivated in collections are P. elaeagrifolia, P. nivalis, the Snow Pear, and P. Calleryana.

PYXIDANTHERA BARBULATA (Pyxidanthe'ra; Pyxidanth'era). A prostrate evergreen shrub with slender branches spreading into a matlike mass, bearing small, dark green, leathery leaves, and white or pinkish flowers in spring. It is native from New Jersey to North Carolina, where it grows on sandy Pine-barrens and is known as the Pyxie Plant, Pine-barren Beauty and Flowering Moss. Although rarely seen in cultivation, it is sometimes grown in rock gardens, where it requires acid, sandy soil and a sunny position. It can be grown from seeds or from cuttings of short shoots inserted under a bell jar or hand light in summer. Pyxidanthera belongs to the Diapensia family, Diapensiaceae, and the name is taken from *pyxis*, a box, and *anthera*, an anther, owing to the lidlike opening of the anther.

PYXIE. Pyxidanthera, which see.

PYXIE MOSS. Pyxidanthera, which see.

QUADRANGULARIS. A botanical term, used chiefly in reference to stems and meaning four-angled. It occurs in species names.

QUAKER-LADIES. Houstonia, which see.

QUAMASH. See Camassia.

QUAMASIA. See Camassia.

QUAMOCLIT—*Star Glory* (Qua'moclit). A genus of climbing herbaceous plants, chiefly from Mexico, which are annuals or are best treated as annuals. They belong to the family Convolvulaceae, and were previously included in the genus Ipomoea. The origin of the name Quamoclit is unknown.

The Quamoclits are of easy cultivation. One of the best-known kinds is Q. lobata (also called Ipomoea versicolor and Mina lobata), which bears crimson flowers which later turn to orange and yellow. Seeds can be sown in pots in a warm greenhouse in March and the seedlings planted out of doors in a sunny position in late May, or, as soon as the weather is warm and settled, seeds can be sown outdoors in the place where the plants are to grow. Q. lobata is actually a perennial.

The Cypress Vine, Quamoclit pennata, an annual, is another popular kind for summer display. Under favorable conditions it attains a height of 20 ft. Both its foliage, which is fine and feathery and green, and its funnel-shaped scarlet flowers are attractive. There is a white-flowered variety of this plant named alba.

Q. pennata is a native of tropical America and the southern United States. It requires the same culture as Q. lobata.

The Star Ipomoea, Quamoclit coccinea, has flowers that are scarlet with a yellow throat (in variety luteola the flowers are yellow or orange). It is a 10-ft.-tall annual that is a native of tropical America and is naturalized in the warmer

Quamoclit lobata is a fast-growing vine that is grown as an annual.

The Cypress Vine, Quamoclit pennata, is a popular summer - flowering annual.

other rooting media that may contain such pests and diseases. The laws and regulations by which these controls are effected are called plant quarantines.

Quarantine regulations are changed from time to time to keep abreast of current needs. Some regulations are relaxed or eliminated, others are strengthened or new ones are imposed as occasion demands.

Any person who contemplates moving plants from state to state or country to country should secure the latest information on the regulations in force at the time from the Bureau of Entomology and Plant Quarantine, United States Department of Agriculture, Washington, D. C., and from the State Agricultural Experiment Stations of the states involved. In Canada such information can be obtained from the Plant Protection Division, Canada Department of Agriculture, Ottawa, Canada.

QUEEN ANNE'S LACE. The wild Carrot, Daucus Carota, which see.

QUEENCUP. Clintonia uniflora, which see.

QUEEN LILY. See Phaedranassa.

QUEEN OF THE MEADOW. Filipendula Ulmaria, which see.

QUEEN OF THE PRAIRIE. Filipendula rubra, which see.

QUEEN PALM. Arecastrum Romanzoffianum, which see.

QUEEN VICTORIA'S WATER LILY. Victoria regia, which see.

QUEENSLAND NUT. Macadamia ternifolia, which see.

parts of the United States. Its culture is the same as for Q. lobata.

The Cardinal Climber, Quamoclit Sloteri, is a hybrid between Q. coccinea and Q. pennata. Its attractive flowers are crimson with white throats. It requires the same culture as the others here mentioned.

QUARANTINES, PLANT. The Governments of the United States and Canada and those of many other countries, as well as State and Provincial Governments, exercise controls over the transportation of living plants and parts of living plants that may transmit diseases or pests deemed to be harmful to horticulture and agriculture. These controls extend also to soil and

QUERCUS: THE OAK

Valuable Evergreen and Leaf-losing Trees and Shrubs, Both Native and Exotic

Quercus (Quer'cus). A large group of evergreen and deciduous trees and shrubs widely distributed in Europe, northern Africa, Asia, and North and South America. Some are definitely tropical in their requirements, others require subtropical conditions, but the majority are hardy in the North. The Oaks belong to the Beech family, Fagaceae, and the name Quercus is the ancient Latin name of the Oak.

Of Varied Appearance. In outward appearance the various kinds of Oak exhibit a good deal of difference, and it is hard to believe that some kinds can be associated with the more familiar species. The evergreen Oaks such as the Live Oak, Q. virginiana, the Coast Live Oak, Q. agrifolia, the Holm Oak, Q. Ilex, and the Kermes Oak, Q. coccifera, with their thick, leathery, dark green leaves, are very different from leaf-losing kinds; the Willow Oak, Q. Phellos, and the Chestnut Oak, Q. montana, differ much in appearance from kinds with more typical oak-shaped leaves.

The Oaks, however, have one very definite character in common. The seed, usually called an acorn, is carried in a definite cup, different in appearance from the seed receptacle of other members of the family.

Remarkable Differences Between Acorns of Various Kinds. In different kinds the acorns and their cups show a remarkable degree of variation. Some have stalked, others stalkless, cups; in some, the cup only encloses the base of the acorn; in others, the tip of the acorn only is exposed. In some, the cups are roughened by large irregular scales; in others, they are smooth by reason of the uniform and symmetrical arrangement of the scales. Some kinds mature their acorns six months after the flowers appear; in others eighteen months elapse between flowering and the ripening of the acorns.

Male and female flowers appear on the same tree, the male flowers in slender, conspicuous catkins of varying length, the female flowers as small inconspicuous bodies, sometimes singly, sometimes two or more on a short stalk.

Acorns lose their vitality quickly if allowed to become dry, but may be kept for several months if kept moist, either by spreading them on a damp floor or mixing them with slightly moist peat moss, leaf mold or sand. When being shipped long distances, they must not be sent in a dry state, but packed in slightly damp moss, sawdust, peat moss or powdered charcoal.

Some of the Oaks have two growing periods, one in May and June, the other in July and August. Very often the young leaves are brightly colored, and some take on brilliant shades of red and gold before they fall in autumn. Three of the best for autumn color are the North American Scarlet Oak, Q. coccinea, the Northern Red Oak, Q. borealis, which is also North American, and the Pin Oak, Q. palustris, another native kind.

When several kinds of closely related Oaks are growing together, a good deal of natural hybridization may take place, particularly among young trees. They intermingle both in their native state and in cultivation and many hybrids occur which have part of the characters of one kind and part of another's.

Even widely separated kinds may hybridize, as was the case when pollen of Q. Suber, the Cork Oak, was inadvertently carried to a female flower of the Turkey Oak, Q. Cerris, and a hybrid appeared in the form of the subevergreen Q. hispanica.

Some Oaks show a good deal of variation in the same kind or species, in habit of growth, color and shape of foliage, and many of these have been selected for variety names. It will thus be understood that although Quercus is an important genus for decorative gardening, it is also a very puzzling one for the beginner.

Raising Oak Trees from Seeds. Propagation should be effected by seeds whenever possible. As previously stated, acorns lose their vitality quickly if allowed to become very dry. Those that lie on the moist ground beneath trees germinate quite freely in spring if not injured by animals or birds, but as they are the natural food of squirrels, mice, and some large birds, and are eaten by pigs and cattle, it is not wise to rely on being able to find acorns in spring. They should be collected as they fall, stored, and sown in spring after being rolled in red lead. This latter treatment discourages mice and other animals and birds from disturbing them.

Acorns may be sown in autumn, but if that is done many are likely to be disturbed during winter unless they are in a cold frame and are protected by fine wire mesh from invaders. Even after spring sowing a certain number may be pulled up by mice, birds, or other animals.

Acorns can be protected from damage by birds by covering the bed with a double thickness of wire mesh. If only a few trees are wanted, the acorns may be placed singly in 4- or 5-in. pots filled with soil and set in a frame or greenhouse; they will germinate in the window of a cool room if care is taken to keep the soil moist.

When larger numbers are needed, the seeds are best sown an inch or two apart in nursery rows, or they may be sown in the locations where the trees are to grow. Direct sowing has one great advantage. Oaks form long taproots with few fibrous roots during the first year or two and transplanting usually results in the taproot being cut or broken and a check to growth follows.

Small quantities of seeds, and seeds of rare kinds should be sown in a frame; when a few acorns only are involved it is wise to sow them singly in small pots. Seedlings raised in pots or flats should be planted in a nursery border or in permanent places as soon as possible.

The only other practical means of propagation is by grafting. This must be practiced in dealing with varieties that do not come true from seeds. Understocks of closely related kinds are necessary, and shoots at least two years old must be used as scions. Neither layers nor cuttings are of use in the propagation of Oaks.

When acorns are wanted of rare kinds that are growing near other Oaks it is wise to isolate the female flowers in muslin bags and convey pollen to them by hand as soon as the stigma is in a receptive state, otherwise cross-fertilization is almost sure to take place.

Most Oak Trees Should Be Planted While Small. Oaks should be planted in their permanent places as early as possible. This is especially necessary with the evergreen kinds. While they are grown in the nursery garden they must be transplanted every two to four years to ensure a compact mass of fibrous roots; all injured roots should be cut back. The leaf-losing kinds may be planted at any time between autumn and the beginning of new growth in spring, provided the weather is mild and the ground moist. Early fall or spring is the best transplanting time. The Pin Oak is one kind that transplants well even when of considerable size.

When to Plant Evergreen Oaks. The evergreen kinds, such as Q. virginiana and Q. Suber, succeed best when transplanted in early fall or rather late spring (but before new growth begins), provided care is taken to reduce the branch system at the same time in order to lessen the demand for moisture on the disturbed roots. A good watering should be given when the work is completed.

Should the leaves fall from newly planted evergreens there is no cause for alarm—it is just Nature's way of assisting recovery. However, if the leaves die and remain on the branches, root action is unsatisfactory. In such a case, cut the branches back and keep the tree stems moist.

Oaks thrive in various kinds of soil, but most kinds give the best results in deep, loamy soil that is fairly moist without being waterlogged. The Scrub Oaks succeed in poor, dry soils.

When Oaks are to be planted in places where the soil is poor, extra-large holes should be dug; the bottom soil should be spaded deeply and enriched with liberal amounts of manure, compost or other decayed organic material, and good, rich, loamy soil should be used to fill in the hole at planting time. This is especially important when Oaks are used as street trees.

Pruning should receive regular attention from the time the trees are a year old. Aim at keeping a clear central leading shoot, check the development of side shoots, and remove them as may be necessary. After setting out the trees in permanent places, continue the pruning every second year until they are able to maintain their symmetry without further aid. The object in pruning the larger-growing kinds is to obtain a good length of clear trunk with a uniform head of branches.

How to Preserve Old Trees. Fine old specimens that show signs of deteriorating can often be improved in appearance and their lives prolonged by cutting out dead wood, cleaning out and disinfecting cavities, and fertilizing. Trees that have become stag-headed (a condition in which the ends of the branches are dead) may be greatly improved and induced to produce new branchlets by cutting off the dead parts to a point 9-12 in. below where they are dead and protecting the wounds with tree-wound paint.

While the work is in progress, care should be taken to preserve the contour of the original head as far as possible. If the ground is very hard beneath such trees, fork it over to admit air and water, and provide a surface dressing of rich compost or manure.

Evergreen Oaks

Evergreen Oaks include a number of fine trees of both American and exotic origin. Among those native to America are Q. virginiana, the Live Oak, of the southeastern United States and Mexico; Q. chrysolepis, the Maul Oak or Canyon

Oak, of the Pacific coast; Q. agrifolia, the Coast Live Oak, of California; Q. durata, the Leather Oak, of California, a spreading shrub that attains a height of about 5 ft.; Q. dumosa, California Scrub Oak, a shrub to 8 ft. tall; Q. Engelmannii, a 60-ft.-tall native of southern California; and Q. Wislizenii, a native of California that grows to a height of 75 ft.

Among exotic (foreign) evergreen Oaks that are worthy of note are Q. acuta, the Japanese Evergreen Oak, a small tree that is rarely cultivated; Q. coccifera, the Kermes Oak, a shrubby kind from southern Europe, northern Africa and western Asia; Q. glauca, a Japanese kind that grows about 70 ft. tall and is planted in California; Q. Ilex, the Holm Oak or Holly Oak, of southern Europe; Q. myrsinaefolia, a tree of eastern China that grows 60 ft. tall; Q. phillyraeoides, a native of China and Japan that attains a height of about 30 ft.; and Q. Suber, the Cork Oak of southern Europe and northern Africa.

None of the evergreen Oaks is hardy in the North. Washington, D. C., seems to be about the northern limit for the cultivation of the hardiest, and some kinds need even milder winters than occur there.

The Live Oak, Q. virginiana, is one of the most beautiful of American Oaks. It sometimes attains a maximum height of about 70 ft., but more often does not exceed 50 ft. It is a noble, wide-spreading tree, its branches horizontal or nearly so, its leaves dark, glossy green above and whitish beneath.

The Live Oak occurs as a native from Virginia to Florida and Mexico. Because of its fine appearance, as well as the comparative rapidity of growth and the ease with which it can be transplanted, this species is a great favorite in the South for planting as a shade and avenue tree. It produces valuable timber.

The Canyon or Maul Oak, Q. chrysolepis, is native from Oregon to California and reaches a height of 50 ft. or more. Sometimes it grows to 90 or even 100 ft. tall. This tree, which is one of the most handsome of West Coast Oaks, forms a wide-spreading specimen of imposing appearance.

The Live Oak, Quercus virginiana, is one of the most handsome of native American shade trees. It has wide-spreading branches and evergreen foliage. This kind is easy to transplant.

A magnificent Holm Oak, Quercus Ilex. This kind is a native of the Mediterranean region.

The Coast Live Oak or, as it is sometimes called, the California Live Oak, Q. agrifolia, is similar in appearance to the Canyon Oak. It grows to be 100 ft. tall and is native to California.

The Holly or Holm Oak. Q. Ilex, the Holm Oak, is a native of the Mediterranean region. It forms a large tree with a wide-spreading head, and when grown among other trees it develops with a long clean trunk. The wood is very hard, heavy and well marked. It grows well near the sea as well as inland, and can be used with

effect as an avenue tree. It is very variable in size and shape of leaf even on the same tree.

Good varieties are macrophylla and latifolia, with very large leaves; rotundifolia, with rounded leaves; and crispa and Fordii, with deeply lobed or dissected leaves.

The Holm Oak can be grown as a high and strong hedge. When it is used in that way, an annual pruning is necessary. This, with all other pruning required by Oaks, may be done between June and early fall, though there is not the same objection to spring pruning as there is

Quercus glauca is a fine evergreen kind, well adapted for planting in the South and in California.

The foliage of Quercus glauca, a beautiful Japanese Oak.

in the case of Birch, Maple and Walnut trees.

The Cork Oak, Q. Suber, is a rather similar tree in foliage, but it has corky bark. A native of southwestern Europe and northern Africa, it is not so hardy as Q. Ilex. It is planted fairly commonly in California. This is the tree from which commercial cork is obtained. Q. Coccifera, the Kermes Oak, is a tree or bush of the Mediterranean region with small, spiny leaves and spiny acorn cups.

Three Japanese Kinds. Q. phillyraeoides is a small Japanese tree with broadly elliptic or obovate, rather small, dark green leaves. It forms a handsome bush when allowed to branch low down, or a small tree when suitably pruned. Q. acuta is another Japanese evergreen tree with

A Japanese evergreen Oak, Quercus acuta, thriving in a Virginia nursery.

handsome, glossy leaves. It is of small dimensions. Q. glauca is a handsome kind that has leaves about 5 in. long that are toothed above the middle and, when young, are silky and glaucous on the underside.

American Leaf-losing Oaks

North America has many splendid Oaks, both leaf-losing and evergreen. The evergreen species are discussed above; here the leaf-losing kinds only are considered. Most of the leaf-losing Oaks are hardy in the North and most are trees of noble dimensions; a few are shrubs or small trees and are generally known as Scrub Oaks.

Among native leaf-losing Oaks are magnificent kinds for planting as shade trees, park trees and roadside specimens. They are deep-rooting and it usually is possible to grow a lawn beneath them without undue difficulty.

The American Oaks fall into two distinct groups, the White Oak tribe, in which the leaves and lobes of the leaves do not end in bristles and on which the acorns ripen during the first year, and the Black Oak tribe, which bears acorns that do not ripen until their second year and in which the lobes of the leaves are usually bristle-tipped.

The White Oak tribe contains White Oak, Swamp White Oak, Oregon Oak, Valley Oak, Overcup Oak, Burr or Mossy-Cup Oak, Chestnut Oak, Chinquapin Oak, Yellow Chestnut Oak, Basket Oak and Post Oak.

The Black Oak tribe includes Scarlet Oak, Jack Oak, Spanish Red Oak (a native American despite its name), Scrub Oak, Shingle Oak, California Black Oak, Laurel Oak, Blackjack Oak, Water Oak, Pin Oak, Willow Oak, Northern Red Oak, and Black Oak.

The White Oak, Q. alba, grows natively from Maine to Florida and Texas. It is a wide-spreading kind that attains a height of 100 ft. It is one of the largest, if not the largest, of native Oaks and forms a fine rounded head.

The White Oak, Quercus alba, develops a large, rounded head and stout, spreading branches. It is a magnificent tree for planting in parks and other places where there is room for it to develop.

In fall the leaves of this tree assume attractive, deep purplish red hues. The White Oak forms a magnificent specimen tree where it has space to develop.

The Swamp White Oak, Q. bicolor, is valued for its timber but is less esteemed as an ornamental than many other kinds. It grows from Quebec to Georgia and Arkansas and is a tree of moist soils. It attains a height of 70-80 ft.

The Oregon Oak, Q. Garryana, grows from British Columbia to California and attains a height of 80-100 ft. It is an important timber tree.

The Valley Oak of California is Q. lobata. It has wide-spreading main limbs, drooping branches (for which reason it is sometimes called the Weeping Oak), and grows to 100 ft. tall. It has not proved adaptable to cultivation except in climates similar to that of California.

The Overcup Oak, Q. lyrata, grows in wet woods and swamps from New Jersey to Florida and Texas and to southern Indiana, southern Illinois and Missouri. Its name refers to the fact that the cup of the acorn covers from half to all of the seed or nut.

This Oak is not much cultivated. Hardy as far north as Massachusetts, it prefers a moist soil. It attains a maximum height of about 100 ft.

The Burr Oak or Mossy-Cup Oak, Q. macrocarpa, forms a rough-barked tree that at its finest attains a height of 150 ft. or even more, but is often of smaller dimensions. It has a wide-spreading head and is of picturesque appearance. It grows from Nova Scotia to Pennsylvania and Texas, generally favoring moist soils, but occurring also in dry upland regions.

The Chestnut Oak is Q. Prinus, a kind that grows natively from Maine to South Carolina and Alabama. It has leaves that closely resemble those of the Chestnut (not Horse Chestnut).

This really handsome Oak grows well on either fairly moist or comparatively dry soils. It grows 70-100 ft. tall and has leaves that turn a dull orange-yellow in autumn.

The Chinquapin Oak, Q. prinoides, is native from Maine to Alabama and Texas. It is one of the Scrub Oaks, growing not more than 8 ft. tall and usually lower. It spreads by sucker growths and in nature prefers rather dry, calcareous (limestone) soils and is most often found near the coast.

This Oak is a good-looking kind for planting on dry banks and in similar difficult locations.

The Yellow Chestnut Oak, Q. prinoides variety acuminata, grows naturally on limestone soils from New England to Michigan and Nebraska and southwards to Virginia, Alabama and Texas. It forms an erect specimen to 100 or even 150 ft. tall. This is an especially handsome species. It has beautiful leaves, in shape somewhat like those of Q. montana; they are glossy on their upper surfaces and silver-white beneath.

The Basket Oak is Q. Michauxii. This species forms a tree that attains heights up to 100 ft. It inhabits low, moist soil from New Jersey to Florida and Texas. It is, without doubt, one of the most lovely of Oaks and is excellent for planting where the soil is not excessively dry.

The Basket Oak is sometimes known as the Cow Oak and the Swamp Chestnut Oak. It has leaves resembling those of the Chestnut Oak.

The Post Oak grows from Massachusetts to Ohio, Indiana and Iowa, and southward to Florida and Texas. This tree, Q. stellata, is a native of dry and often rather barren soils.

In the northern part of its range this kind is often shrubby, but to the south it becomes a sizable tree and may attain a height of 100 ft., although it is usually lower. It is a handsome kind, hardy and well suited for planting near the sea. It is round-headed.

The Scarlet Oak, Q. coccinea, is one of the most handsome of American Oaks. In fall its foliage turns a brilliant scarlet. It thrives well on dryish soils. In nature it occupies such soils from Maine to Florida and Missouri.

The Scarlet Oak grows to a height of 80 ft. and forms an upright, more or less cylindrical specimen. Because it has a good mass of fibrous roots, this Oak can be transplanted, even when large, with much less chance of harm than many other Oaks.

The Jack Oak, Q. ellipsoidalis, attains a height of about 70 ft. and occurs as a native from Michigan to Minnesota and Missouri. It favors dry, upland soils.

The Spanish Red Oak, Q. falcata, grows to 80

This specimen of the Spanish Red Oak, Quercus falcata, is located at Williamsburg, Virginia.

ft. or more tall and is native from New Jersey to Florida and Texas, and to Ohio, Indiana and Missouri. This is one of the trees that were once known as Q. rubra, a name that is now rejected.

In the eastern part of its range Q. falcata is usually found on dry soils, but more to the west it occupies moist soils. This is a very handsome, round-headed tree but it is not hardy far north.

The Scrub Oak, Q. ilicifolia, is a shrub or small tree to about 10 ft. tall. It grows in poor, sandy and rocky soils from Maine to Ohio, West Virginia and North Carolina. It is of value for covering barren hillsides and rocky places.

The Shingle Oak, Q. imbricaria, is a very beautiful kind that attains a height of 80-100 ft. In fall its handsome foliage turns a fine red color. The tree is of conical habit when young but with age becomes round-topped. Its branches are slender and slightly pendulous.

This species inhabits dry, upland soils from Pennsylvania to Michigan, Iowa, Arkansas, Georgia and North Carolina. It is especially plentiful in the Middle West.

The California Black Oak, Q. Kelloggii, grows to 80 ft. or more tall and develops erect main limbs and an open, round-topped head. It is found as a native from Oregon to California at elevations ranging from 200 ft. to 8,000 ft. above sea level. It is the only native California Oak that belongs in the Black Oak group. It is a graceful tree.

The Laurel Oak of the southeastern United States is Q. laurifolia. It is a handsome kind that finds frequent use in the South as a shade tree and avenue tree.

The Laurel Oak grows to a height of about 60 ft., and occasionally considerably more, and has rather slender branches that form a dense, round-topped head. Its foliage is glossy, dark green and almost semievergreen. It prefers moist soils and is found as a native from southern Virginia to Florida and Louisiana. This Oak is not hardy in the North.

The Blackjack Oak is Q. marilandica. This species inhabits dry and poor soils, especially sandy soils from New York to Michigan and Iowa and southward to Florida and Texas. It is of good appearance and forms a small or medium-sized (30-50 ft. tall) tree with a narrow, rounded,

The Water Oak, Quercus nigra, is a native of the southeastern United States and is there valued for planting as a shade tree.

or often irregularly shaped head. The leaves are large, dark green and glossy.

The **Water Oak,** Q. nigra, usually occurs naturally in damp or wet soils from Delaware to Florida and Texas and to southeastern Missouri. It is favored in the South for planting as a specimen tree and for avenue planting; it may be grown as far north as New Jersey, but is not reliably hardy farther north.

The Water Oak grows rapidly and may be transplanted without difficulty. It attains a maximum height of about 80 ft. and has comparatively slender branches that form a more or less round-topped head.

A favorite native American Oak, Quercus palustris, the Pin Oak. The drooping lower branches are characteristic of this kind.

The **Pin Oak,** Q. palustris, is one of the most important Oaks from the gardener's point of view. It is much valued as a shade tree, avenue tree, and street tree. It forms a rather narrow, pyramidal specimen, with its lower branches somewhat drooping. In fall its foliage turns bright red.

This species grows naturally in moist, somewhat acid soils, and in cultivation prefers similar soils; it will not thrive on alkaline soils. Its natural range extends from Massachusetts to Michigan, Iowa and Kansas and southward to

The Willow Oak, Quercus Phellos, thrives best in moderately moist soil. It is an excellent shade tree and is particularly well adapted for seaside planting. This is a young specimen.

North Carolina, Tennessee and Oklahoma.

A maximum height of 100 ft. may be attained by the Pin Oak but most specimens are less tall even at maturity. The Pin Oak grows rapidly and transplants easily.

The **Willow Oak,** Q. Phellos, occurs as a native in swamps and moist soils from New York to Florida and Texas and to southern Illinois. It forms a tall shrub or a tree to 50 ft. in height When it is mature it forms a round-topped head Its slender branches form a round-topped head and its narrow willow-like leaves turn light yellow in fall. This kind is well suited for planting near the sea.

The **Red Oak and the Northern Red Oak or Gray Oak.** The Northern Red Oak or Gray Oak, Q. borealis, attains a maximum height of about 80 ft. and inhabits the region extending from Nova Scotia to Minnesota and southward to

The Red Oak, Quercus borealis maxima, may attain an ultimate height of 150 ft. It grows fairly rapidly.

Pennsylvania. It forms a broad, round-headed specimen of good appearance and has foliage which turns dark red in fall.

The variety of this Oak named Q. borealis

The Black Oak, Quercus velutina, grows quite rapidly and thrives in dryish soils. It is a native of eastern North America.

maxima is the Red Oak. It is a tree of more imposing proportions than the Northern Red Oak, attaining a height of 150 ft., and has stout, spreading branches that furnish a large, round-topped head. The foliage of the Red Oak turns dark red in fall. Q. borealis maxima occurs as a native from Nova Scotia to Florida and Texas.

Both of these Oaks prefer soil that is moderately moist, but the Northern Red Oak succeeds better in dryish soils than does the Red Oak. Both kinds make comparatively fast growth. Both kinds have been known as Q. rubra.

The Black Oak, Q. velutina, usually grows naturally in dry, poor soils and on dunes from Maine to Michigan and southward to Florida and Texas. It attains a maximum height of about 125 ft. and has rather slender branches that spread to form a narrow, open head. The foliage turns orange-brown or dull red in fall. The Black Oak grows quite rapidly.

Exotic Leaf-losing Oaks

Of the many foreign leaf-losing (deciduous) Oaks, those now to be described are among the most interesting.

The English Oak, Q. Robur (pedunculata), has stalkless, or almost stalkless, leaves, and long-stalked acorns quite distinct from the stalked leaves and stalkless acorns of its near relative Q. petraea (sessiliflora), the Durmast Oak. Q. Robur forms a tree 60-100 ft. high, with a large trunk and a heavy, spreading head of branches. It is a native of Europe, northern Africa and western Asia and is hardy in the North.

Many named varieties of Q. Robur exist, of which the following are distinct. Most are rare in cultivation.

A Golden-leaved Oak. Q. Robur variety Concordia has leaves that are distinctly golden in spring and more yellow than those of other kinds in summer. In Q. Robur filicifolia (asplenifolia) the margins of the leaves are divided into many narrow segments. Q. Robur heterophylla has leaves of various shapes on the same tree, some of the leaves are distinctly lobed, others almost without lobes. Q. Robur pendula has weeping (drooping) branches. Q. Robur purpurascens

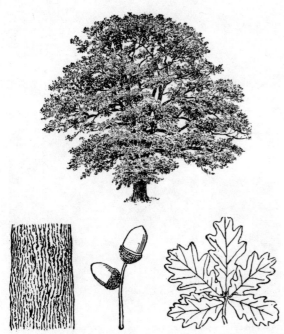

Quercus Robur, the English Oak. Bark, acorns and leaf cluster are shown in the detail drawings.

A fine specimen of the English Oak, Quercus Robur, at Greenbrier Farms Nursery, near Norfolk, Virginia.

has leaves that are purplish when young but become green as they mature. The leaves of Q. Robur atropurpurea are dark purple. Q. Robur fastigiata is distinguished by its narrowly upright (columnar) habit of growth, the branches being erect and close to the trunk rather than spreading, and Q. Robur variegata has its leaves margined or otherwise variegated with white.

The Durmast Oak, Q. petraea (sessiliflora), occurs as a native of Europe and western Asia. It forms a fine tree, as big as Q. Robur and equally as hardy. It thrives on poorer soil. It, also, has many varieties. Of these, Q. petraea mespilifolia is curious by reason of its long,

The century-old golden-leaved English Oak, Quercus Robur Concordia, that shades this pleasant lawn is located at Irvington, New York. A few feet above ground level there can be seen on the trunk a line marking the graft union between the understock and the golden-leaved variety grafted upon it.

A fine specimen of the columnar Quercus Robur fastigiata, at Yonkers, New York.

few-lobed leaves. The branches of Q. petraea pendula are weeping (drooping). The leaves of Q. petraea purpurea are purple.

The Turkey Oak. Q. Cerris, the Turkey Oak, grows into a very large tree and.is very handsome. It retains its rich green leaves until late in the fall. It is easily recognized by the hairlike scales that surround the winter buds, and by its mossy acorn cups. It is a native of southeastern Asia and Asia Minor. After transplanting, young trees become established better than young trees of some other kinds of Oaks.

A Caucasian Chestnut-leaved Oak. Q. castaneifolia, a Chestnut-leaved Oak, has leaves rather similar in appearance to the leaves of the Spanish Chestnut, Castanea sativa. It grows into a tree of moderate size and is a native of the Caucasus. The variety algeriensis, which is semievergreen, is found wild in Algeria. Q. castaneifolia is probably not hardy north of New York City; its variety is less hardy.

Q. Frainetto, the Italian Oak, is a shapely tree

The Turkey Oak, Quercus Cerris, retains its foliage late in the year, long after most native eastern American trees have dropped their foliage. This is one of the most beautiful of Oaks.

A handsome specimen of Quercus castaneifolia.

[10—6]
Rhododendron catawbiense

[10—6a]
Rhododendron Fortunei

[10—7]
Dexter Hybrid Rhododendron

[10—7a]
Catawbiense Hybrid Rhododendron

from Italy, Hungary and adjacent countries. It is allied to Q. petraea by its large, evenly lobed leaves, which are often 6-8 in. long and half as wide, and by its stalkless acorn cups. It forms a very decorative tree, and grows to a large size.

A Striking Tree. Q. canariensis (Mirbeckii) is an even more striking tree than Q. Frainetto. It grows over 100 ft. in its native countries, Algeria and Portugal. The leaves on young trees are often 5-7 in. long and half as wide. They often remain on the tree until very late in the season. This kind is suitable for mild climates only.

The Lebanon Oak. Q. libani, the Lebanon Oak, from the Syrian Mountains and Asia Minor, is one of the lesser-known trees. Of graceful habit when young, it forms slender branchlets clothed with rather narrow, deep green leaves with many-toothed margins; the acorns are large and about three parts embedded in the cup.

Q. hispanica has already been mentioned as a chance hybrid between Q. Cerris and Q. Suber. It is semievergreen, or in some instances the leaves may fall before new ones appear. Mature trees may be 70-80 ft. high, with a large trunk and heavy head of branches. The leaves are rather like those of Q. Cerris, and the bark is corky. The trees seen in cultivation are very variable in character, owing to many of them having been raised from seed. Several have been given variety names. Of these crispa, Lucombeana and diversifolia have very corky bark.

Q. Aegilops, the Valonia Oak, is a tree of moderate size found wild from Italy to Asia Minor. It succeeds only in mild climates and is not hardy in the North. The acorn cups of this Oak are rich in tannin and are in demand by the tanning industry.

Some Asiatic Kinds. Not many Asiatic Oaks appear to be in cultivation. Among leaf-losing kinds Q. dentata is a remarkable species. It is hardy in the North and has extraordinarily large leaves, sometimes 1 ft. long. It forms a round-topped tree some 80 ft. tall and grows fairly rapidly. This kind is a native of China, Korea and Japan.

Q. aliena is another hardy kind. It is known as the Oriental White Oak and is a native of Japan, Korea and China. It attains a height of

about 70 ft. when it reaches its full maturity.

Q. glandulifera is semievergreen, a native of Japan. In its native country it forms a tree 40-70 ft. tall, but in cultivation is usually much lower, and shrubby. It has attractive foliage and is hardy as far north as Massachusetts.

Q. mongolica, from Siberia, China, Korea and Japan, attains a height of 100 ft. Its variety grosseserrata has smaller leaves. This handsome tree is hardy in the North.

Economic Uses

Timber Values. The wood of Oaks has for many generations been pre-eminent for many kinds of work. It was at one period extensively used for the roof timbers of important public buildings, churches, cathedrals, and the like. It was also used for paneling, doors, and furniture, and there is still a considerable demand for Oak for this kind of work. At one period it was widely used for shipbuilding.

A great deal of Oak timber is used in cooperage, particularly American Oak, and farm implements use a proportion. Timber cut radially is very beautifully marked and in demand for furniture and paneling, while the wood of some old trees is of a beautiful warm brown color, owing to the presence of a fungus. This wood has a good market in the cabinet trade.

Oak bark is very rich in tannin, and at one time was extensively used. Comparatively little is used for this purpose at the present time owing to the exploitation of cheaper extracts and tanning substances.

Cork. The bark of the Cork Oak is the cork of commerce. Quercus Suber is a native of Spain, Portugal, Algeria and other parts of northern Africa. Cork stripping is an important industry in each of these countries. The first bark taken from a tree is known as virgin cork and it is of inferior quality. This cork is used for horticultural purposes, and, when ground, it is in demand for the manufacture of cork mats, linoleum, etc. After removal from the tree, the cork is submitted to pressure and is marketed as flat sheets. Waste cork from the manufacture of bottle corks is ground and used as virgin cork.

QUICK. A name given in Great Britain to the

Hawthorn when it is used for hedge planting. Thus a Hawthorn hedge is commonly referred to as a Quick or Thorn Hedge. This shrub makes a splendid hedge, close, thick and impenetrable when well grown and correctly treated. The plants should be hard pruned in spring after planting, to ensure a well-furnished base to the hedge.

QUICKLIME. See Lime.

QUILLED. This term is used to describe certain varieties of flowers, more particularly those of Aster, Marigold, Dahlia and Chrysanthemum, in which the petals are rolled inwards from the margins, giving them a quill-like appearance.

QUINCE. The Quince, Cydonia oblonga, a native of the region from Iran to Turkestan, has been cultivated since ancient times, but it has never become of much commercial importance. It is cultivated mostly in dooryards and gardens, but it is grown to a limited extent commercially in New York, Ontario and California. The fruit is highly prized for jelly, jam and preserves, but it is too harsh for use uncooked.

The trees are not much hardier than the Peach, the wood being seriously injured by temperatures of 15-20 degrees below zero F. Quinces should be grown only in regions where Peaches are hardy. The plants bloom late, after the Apple, and consequently the flowers are not apt to be damaged by frost.

Quinces have the same site and soil requirements as most other deciduous fruit trees. Good air circulation, such as is provided on a slope, is desirable. Good drainage is essential, and rather heavy soil types are preferred, although good tree performance may be had on fertile sandy loams.

Either one- or two-year-old trees may be set out, and planting is done in the same way as for the Apple. The tree is shaped at planting time in the same manner as recommended for Apples, except that more scaffold branches may be retained. Quinces are sometimes grown as bushes with several stems. They are planted about 12-15 ft. apart each way; they normally develop into small trees not over 15 feet in height.

The soil should be managed as for the Pear. Growth should be moderate rather than vigorous, as succulent, vigorous-growing twigs are

Foliage and young fruits of the Quince.

The Quince is a small tree that produces fruits much valued for making jams and jellies.

very susceptible to fire blight, the most serious disease of Quinces. Clean cultivation with a cover crop, or mulching, if only a plant or two are grown in the garden, is satisfactory. Nitrogen fertilizers and manure should be used with great caution.

Pruning. The Quince tree grows slowly and makes rather crooked branches. Very little pruning is needed; in fact, heavy pruning stimulates vigorous growth that is susceptible to blight. Dead wood and blight-killed twigs should be removed. Branches that interfere with one another should be removed, and the tree should be thinned lightly to stimulate a moderate amount of new growth. Large cuts should be avoided.

When to Gather the Fruits. The fruits must be allowed to hang on the tree until fully matured and ripened, and are usually ready for gathering from the middle of October to early November, according to the season. On no account should the fruits be gathered until they will part readily from the tree with but the slightest leverage, or they will quickly shrivel and spoil. Well-ripened fruits give off a powerful aroma, and at that time should practically drop off into the hand when lifted to a horizontal position.

Storing the Fruits. When gathered, the fruits may be stored in any cool, frostproof room or shed for a month or two, providing they are picked when quite dry and are wiped with a clean cloth before being laid out in single layers on a shelf, or in shallow trays. It is unwise to store the Quinces in the general fruit store, however, for neighboring Apples and Pears will be quickly tainted with their peculiar odor and flavor.

Propagation. Quinces are propagated by budding on the Angus Quince (East Malling A) rootstock, or on Quince seedlings. Some varieties may be raised from hardwood cuttings. Layering is also practiced, especially for increasing the rootstocks.

Two Methods of Layering Are Followed. The mound or stool method of layering is perhaps the most common method adopted. A young tree is cut down to near the ground in winter, and the young shoots springing from the base during the next season are layered by pegging them down to the ground, or, more usually, by mounding soil over the base of the whole stool. The buried portions of the shoots produce roots readily, the stool is uncovered in autumn and the rooted growths are pulled off for planting in rows, ready for grafting or budding later.

Another method is to plant one- or two-year-old Quince trees at an angle of 45 degrees, in long rows. These are bent down to the ground along the row and pegged in position during winter. New growths springing up in the next season are then gradually "earthed up" with soil, finally to a depth of 6 in. or so, during summer. By autumn they will have formed roots, and are then stripped off and planted in rows. One strong young growth is left near the end of each old layer, this in turn being bent down, and subsequent new growth is "earthed up" as in the previous year. In this way the stock beds remain productive over many years.

Varieties. The Orange Quince is the best and most widely grown variety. Others are Champion, Pineapple and Van Deman. The varieties have not changed for many years and are not likely to change, as new varieties are not being produced. Quinces are self-fertile, so provision for cross-pollination is not necessary.

QUINCE, JAPANESE. See Chaenomeles.

QUINCUNX. A method of planting whereby the plants are spaced alternately; those of the second row come midway between those of the first and third rows.

QUININE. This valuable drug is one of several alkaloids present in the bark of various kinds of Cinchona, those most frequently grown for the bark being C. officinalis, producing Crown Bark; C. Calisaya, from which Yellow or Calisaya Bark is obtained, and C. Calisaya Ledgeriana, which produces Ledger's Bark.

These quinine-producing trees are natives of South America, chiefly of Ecuador and Peru, where the medicinal value of the bark has been appreciated for centuries.

QUINOA. A name given to the seeds of Chenopodium Quinoa, which are used for food in parts of South America.

QUISQUALIS—*Rangoon Creeper* (Quisqual'-is). Tropical climbing shrubs, with ornamental flowers, which are found wild in tropical Asia and belong to the family Combretaceae. The principal kind, Q. indica, has opposite, entire (undivided) oblong, sharp-pointed leaves, and bears spikes of slender, tubular, reddish flowers in summer. The name Quisqualis is derived from *quis,* who, and *qualis,* what kind; when the plant was first named it was uncertain to which family it belonged.

Q. indica may be grown outdoors in southern Florida. It is also a good plant for a large greenhouse.

For a Warm Greenhouse. These shrubs are grown in a greenhouse with a minimum winter temperature of 55 degrees, and a compost of two parts loam, one part of peat, and a scattering of sand is required. Repotting of small plants is done in March; when eventually they are established in 7-in. pots, they are planted out in a bed or set in large tubs.

When repotting, the plants are removed from their pots and the crocks and loose soil extracted from the roots with a pointed stick. The new pots are prepared by draining them with crocks which are covered with the rough siftings from the compost. The plants are then set in position and the compost is made firm.

The bed in the greenhouse is prepared by taking out a hole to a depth of 30 in.; a layer of broken bricks, 9 in. in depth, is placed in the bottom and covered with turfs from which the finest particles have been shaken.

Wires or a trellis is fixed to the greenhouse wall or roof, to which the shoots are secured. Pot plants are tied to stakes inserted in the centers of the pots. During the summer the compost is kept moist, but as autumn approaches drier conditions are maintained, and throughout the winter the soil is only moistened when it becomes quite dry.

Summer and Winter Management. After potting or planting and until the plants are established they must be shaded from sunlight, but for the remainder of the year they are only shaded from the strongest sun. To assist the roots to enter the new compost quickly, the floor and benches are damped and the foliage is syringed daily, but afterwards very little damping and syringing are required, sufficient only being done to prevent the atmosphere from becoming excessively dry.

Pruning is done as soon as the flowers have faded, when the shoots are cut back to within three or four buds of the base.

Propagation Is by Cuttings. Side shoots are detached with a "heel" (portion of the main stem), the leaves from the lower half of the stem are removed and the "heel" is pared smooth. The cuttings are inserted firmly, 1 in. apart, in a propagating case having a bottom heat of 70-75 degrees. Each morning the case is ventilated for a few minutes and the moisture wiped from the underside of the glass. When roots have formed, the rooted cuttings are potted separately in 3-in. pots and subsequently in larger ones.

The chief kind is Q. indica, which grows 12 ft. high and bears orange-red flowers when it blooms in summer.

R

RABBIT. See Pests and Diseases.

RACEME. A botanical term used to describe an inflorescence of flowers which are on separate stalks on an undivided branch or axis. The difference between a raceme and a spike is that the flowers of the latter are sessile, that is, they are without stalks. The name is from the Latin *racemus*.

RACEMOSE. An inflorescence is said to be racemose when it is in the form of a raceme, which see.

RADISH. This familiar salad vegetable, of which the botanical name is Raphanus sativus, is a hardy annual which is found wild in various parts of Europe. There are numerous varieties in cultivation; they vary in shape and in color. There are round, ellipsoid, and long-rooted Radishes, and of each type there are white, crimson, scarlet and rose-colored varieties. By making sowings at different times it is possible to maintain a supply of Radishes throughout the cooler months when the temperature is high enough for growth.

The secret of success in the cultivation of this vegetable is to provide rich, well-cultivated soil, so that the plants will grow quickly and the roots be crisp and of good flavor. If Radishes are given indifferent cultivation the roots will be soft and flavorless, while on light soils lacking humus they quickly become woody and hot-flavored. Radishes will not thrive in hot weather.

It is a mistake to sow large quantities of Radish seeds at one time; the aim should be to maintain a succession of produce by sowing small quantities at frequent intervals. Radishes are palatable only when the roots are young, and the way to ensure a supply of young roots is to raise crops in quick succession.

The First Sowing. Most amateur gardeners are content to rely on supplies which result from seeds sown out of doors in the open garden. The first sowing should be made in spring, as soon as soil and weather conditions are suitable to the germination of the seeds.

In preparation for sowing the seeds, the soil should be dug over and broken down to a fine condition with the garden fork. It is a great advantage to mix some compost and fertilizer with the soil. Crumbly, fairly rich soil is necessary to ensure quick growth. After the ground has been dug and fertilized it should be raked to ensure a fine surface.

Sowing in drills is preferable to broadcasting, for it allows the soil between the rows to be cultivated. The rows should be 9-12 in. apart, and the seeds sown thinly to prevent the need for excessive thinning of the seedlings. The seeds only need a slight covering of soil therefore the drills should not be more than $\frac{1}{2}$ in. deep.

Protection from Birds. In some gardens it is necessary to protect the seeds from damage by birds, either by placing netting or cheesecloth, supported by short sticks, over the bed, or by black thread stretched between short sticks.

In the absence of some protection the birds may take a heavy toll of the seeds and the small seedlings.

The plants must be thinned out before they become crowded; to ensure quick growth it is most important that the seedlings have sufficient room for development. Several thinnings will be necessary; finally, the plants ought to be about 1 in. apart.

Further sowings of the seeds ought to be made when the plants from the previous sowing are half-grown; if this practice is followed there will be a prolonged supply of young and succulent roots.

The later sowings should be made in a slightly shady part of the garden where the soil dries out less quickly than in a position fully exposed to the sun. In times of drought it is necessary to water the plants freely.

Sowings for autumn supplies may be made in late summer.

Winter supplies of Radish are assured by sowing seeds of the large Black Spanish and the Chinese rose-colored Radishes in late summer. In cold districts it is usual to lift and store these

Radish French Breakfast, a favorite variety.

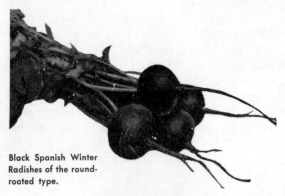

Black Spanish Winter Radishes of the round-rooted type.

Radishes are a quick - maturing crop. They are ready for pulling just a few weeks from the time the seeds are sown.

Raffia is easier to handle for plant tying if soaked in water before use.

RAFT. A term used by gardeners for a piece of wood on which certain epiphytal Orchids are grown when it proves more convenient than flowerpots, flower pans or baskets. The wood is covered with osmunda fiber and sphagnum moss, or other compost suitable for the kind to be grown. The term is also used for a platform con-

An Orchid raft made from the limb of a tree. The Orchid growing on it is one of the epiphytic Angraecums.

roots in autumn, but in mild districts they may be left in the ground to be dug as they are required. Incidentally, they are an excellent substitute for Horse-radish.

The Rat-tailed Radish, Raphanus caudatus, is an annual, grown for the sake of the seed pods, which are used as a pickle. It is raised from seeds sown out of doors in spring and is grown in the way already described, except that, as the plants are larger, they must be given more room; the seedlings should be thinned to 5 or 6 in. apart.

RAFFIA. Material used for tying plants, and for plaiting into mats, hats, baskets and other articles. It is actually the split and dried young leaves of a Palm from Madagascar, Raphia Ruffia. The young leaves are collected, shredded and carefully dried, the sections then being made up into thick plaits and baled for export.

structed of strips of hardwood, preferably teak, cypress or redwood, with spaces between the strips and with wires or chains attached at the corners so that the raft can be suspended in a horizontal position. Suitable rooting compost is placed on the raft and Orchids, Ferns, Bromeliads or other epiphytic or semiepiphytic plants are planted in it.

RAGGED ROBIN. See Lychnis Flos-cuculi.

RAGWORT. See Senecio.

RAGWORT, AFRICAN. See Othonna.

RAIN TREE. Samanea Saman, which see.

RAISIN TREE, JAPANESE. Hovenia dulcis, which see.

RAKE. The iron-toothed rake is an indispensable garden tool which is used chiefly in the preparation of seedbeds for the purpose of breaking down the surface soil into fine particles or, as the gardener would say, to obtain a fine tilth (crumbly condition at the surface). Soil which has been thrown up roughly for the winter, and has been forked over in spring, can quickly be reduced to fine tilth by using an iron-toothed rake.

In preparing ground for seed sowing, after it has been dug, all lumps are broken down by treading, or by knocking them with the back of the rake, and the tool is then used in the ordinary way to remove large stones and other foreign matter. As a result the surface is made fine and even, and small seeds can be sown at the correct depth, a proceeding which is impossible in rough, lumpy ground.

A wooden rake is useful for a preliminary clearing of ground which has been dug over, especially if the area is large, before the iron-toothed rake is used for finishing off the work. A wire- or bamboo-toothed rake is commonly used for raking fallen leaves from the lawn, flower beds and shrubberies; wooden rakes are also sometimes used for this purpose.

RAMBLER. A term used to describe certain vigorous types of climbing Roses. The two chief types of Rambler Rose grown in gardens are those which are descended from Rosa Wichuraiana and Rosa multiflora (polyantha). See Roses.

RAMIE. Boehmeria nivea, which see.

RAMONDA—*Rock Mullein, Pyrenean Primrose* (Ramon'da). A small genus of beautiful hardy rock plants belonging to the Gesneria family, Gesneriaceae. There are only three or four kinds known; they are natives of southern Europe,

The beautiful Pyrenean Primrose, Ramonda pyrenaica. It thrives in moist, shady crevices in the rock garden, producing its lovely lavender-blue flowers in May or June.

Siberia and Greece. Ramonda (commonly misspelled Ramondia) was named in honor of L. F. Ramond, a French botanist and traveler, who died in 1827. Ramonda Heldreichii is a synonym of Jankaea Heldreichii, which see.

Beautiful Rock Garden Plants. R. Nathaliae is a rare plant from Serbia and Bulgaria, with flat rosettes of rich, glossy green leaves, crinkled and corrugated, and edged with brown fur. Each rosette is 4-5 in. across, and the plant eventually forms a clump of these rosettes. The flowers, carried several on a 4-5 in. stem, are an inch or more in diameter, are numerous, and of lavender-blue color, with a prominent central beaklike cluster of anthers. All the Ramondas have flowers which bear a strong superficial resemblance to the flowers of the Potato.

Needs a Cool Rock Crevice. R. Nathaliae is best grown in a rock crevice in loam, leaf mold and sand, in a cool northern exposure, and the plants should be well watered in dry, hot weather. It also makes an excellent plant for the alpine house when grown in a pot or pan of loam and leaf mold mixed with lumps of sandstone or limestone, the size of Walnuts, buried among the roots. There is a very rare and extremely beautiful variety with pure white flowers.

The Pyrenean Primrose. Ramonda pyrenaica

Ramonda Nathaliae, a rare alpine plant from the Balkan Peninsula, forms rosettes of glossy, corrugated leaves, above which rise sprays of clear lavender-blue flowers.

is the commonest and best-known kind, coming from shady, moist, limestone cliffs in the Pyrenees and that strange, interesting mountain, Montserrat, behind Barcelona. The dark green, crinkled velvet leaves will form rosettes 12 or even 18 in. across and a strong, well-grown plant will often form a cluster of such rosettes. The large, lavender-blue flowers, with prominent golden centers, are borne, two to four, on 4-5-in. stems, in May and June.

R. pyrenaica is a plant for deep rock crevices, for pots or pans in the alpine greenhouse or for a wall garden with a northern exposure. It grows equally well on limestone or sandstone, but it should be given ample root space in loam and leaf mold, must always have a cool northern exposure, and should be well watered in dry weather. It does not thrive in hot summers.

Must Be Kept Moist in Dry Weather. The plant is very sensitive to drought and the leaves will shrivel badly if not kept moist in dry weather; it has quite remarkable powers of recovery after such neglect, and if thoroughly soaked both at the root and also over the shriveled leaves, the latter will soon recover.

Ramonda pyrenaica varies considerably in the size and depth of color of its flowers, some being poor and narrow petaled, others large, round, well proportioned and handsome, some a pallid lavender, others rich lavender-blue or lilac. There are also white-flowered varieties, the best of which are extremely beautiful, and there are some pale rose-pink forms, which at their best are lovely.

Ramonda serbica is a desirable plant for the rock garden or the alpine house. It is intermediate in habit and general appearance between R. Nathaliae and R. pyrenaica and requires the same conditions for cultivation and propagation as those plants.

Propagation. Ramondas may be increased by division of the roots in early spring. Seeds may be sown in peaty soil in a pot in a shaded cold frame, in September, or leaf cuttings may be set in sand and peat in summer and kept close in a cold frame. The seeds, which are almost as fine as snuff, must be sown on the surface of a pot or pan of sand, leaf mold and loam, and kept covered with a sheet of glass and paper in a shaded cold frame.

The seedlings should be pricked off into pans of similar soil at an early stage, and grown in shade.

In two seasons they should be large enough to pot, or to plant out in their permanent quarters.

RAMPION. The common name of a hardy

herbaceous plant, Campanula Rapunculus, which grows wild in Europe. It is sometimes grown in gardens for the sake of its tuberous roots, though far less commonly now than in former days. It thrives in ordinary soil that is well drained, in a sunny or slightly shady place.

This plant is raised from seeds sown out of doors in spring in soil which has been pulverized by using fork and rake. Shallow drills are drawn at 6 or 8 in. apart and the seeds are sown thinly; the seeds are covered sufficiently by passing the rake lightly over the surface of the ground. When the seedlings are well developed they should be thinned to about 5 in. apart. During the summer months the only attention needed is to hoe between the rows occasionally to keep down weeds. The roots are lifted and stored in early autumn; they must be protected from damage by frost, and a cool root cellar is a good storage place.

The roots may be used raw in salads, or cooked; the leaves, too, may be used in salads.

RAMPION, HORNED. Phyteuma, which see.

RAM'S HORN. Pithecellobium guadelupense, which see.

RANGOON CREEPER. Quisqualis indica, a vigorous climbing shrub from tropical Asia. See Quisqualis.

RANUNCULUS: THE BUTTERCUP

A Varied Group of Easy-to-Grow Plants Adapted for Many Garden Uses

Ranunculus (Ranun'culus). A group of hardy and tender herbaceous plants, widely distributed but especially numerous in temperate and frigid regions. In the tropics they are chiefly found high up in mountain regions. The Latin name is from *rana,* meaning a little frog, and was given by Pliny because of the fact that many of the kinds are found in damp places.

Ranunculus gives its name to the family Ranunculaceae, to which also belong such diverse plants as Monkshood, Clematis, and Columbine. Many lovely rock-garden and border plants are included.

Fair-Maids-of-France. R. aconitifolius (Fair-Maids-of-France) is an extremely beautiful European plant of alpine marshes and streamsides up to an altitude of six and seven thousand feet. It has handsome glossy-green foliage, suggesting that of an Aconite—hence its name—and much-branched stems 2 or 3 ft. tall, carrying loose sprays of small, white flowers in immense numbers. The variety flore-pleno, with double white flowers, is very attractive and a good plant for sunny or semishady borders.

A Double Yellow Buttercup. R. acris flore-pleno is a double-flowered variety of a common European field Buttercup that is naturalized in North America, and is a very ornamental plant for the flower border and for cutting for the house. It is sometimes called Yellow Bachelors' Buttons. It grows 18 in. to 2 ft. tall, is of erect habit, and has numerous, golden-yellow, double, button-like blossoms. It flourishes in ordinary soil, flowers in May and June, and is easily increased by division of the roots in spring or autumn.

A Lovely Alpine Buttercup. R. alpestris is a beautiful high alpine Buttercup, widely distributed in the Alps of Europe. It grows 2-3 in. high, has rich green leaves and bears large white

A double-flowered Buttercup, Ranunculus acris flore-pleno.

flowers with golden centers. It varies a good deal in different localities. In the rock garden it should be given loamy soil in which has been mixed a good proportion of broken stone, and it needs abundant moisture during the growing and flowering period. Seeds may be sown as soon as ripe in a pot of loam, leaf mold and sand in a cold frame, or the plants may be lifted and divided in spring every three or four years.

The Most Beautiful Mountain Buttercup. R. amplexicaulis is perhaps the most beautiful and the most satisfactory of all the white Mountain Buttercups. It is found in the Pyrenees, in the

Ranunculus amplexi-caulis, a beautiful alpine Buttercup with gray-green leaves and snow-white flowers.

high pastures, and in broken soil. It forms fine sturdy clumps of gray-green leaves, and in May or June bears numerous 9-12-in. stems, branched and each carrying a number of snow-white flowers, sometimes an inch in diameter. Each stem has one or two leaves which clasp or encircle it in a curious and characteristic way.

In the rock garden R. amplexicaulis is not only of the utmost beauty, but of simple cultivation. Give it rich loamy soil and an open sunny position, and it will flourish and flower profusely in May and June. In a few years' time a single root will form a strong clump. In spring, this may be lifted, divided, and replanted at once— the forked, fleshy roots come apart quite easily. But such division should only be resorted to as a means of increase, for clumps left undisturbed are naturally more effective than single crowns.

Seed may also be sown, as soon after gathering as possible, in pots of loam, leaf mold and sand

in a cold frame, the seedlings being left alone for a year, and then planted out in their permanent quarters.

R. amplexicaulis varies greatly in the size and splendor of its flowers. Varieties occur with extra-large flowers, and often with many extra petals; now and then one with pale rose-pink flowers is discovered.

The White Water Crowfoot. R. aquatilis is the charming native water plant known as White Water Crowfoot. It is extremely pretty for growing in shallow water, in ponds or slow-moving streams, where in spring it stars the surface of the water with myriads of white blossoms looking like miniature Water Lilies. The foliage of this plant is interesting; there are two distinct types of leaves—the smooth, round, floating leaves, and other finely divided hairlike leaves beneath the surface.

R. circinatus is a closely related kind differing only in minor technical characters.

Another Double-flowered Buttercup. R. bulbosus flore-pleno is a handsome double-flowered variety of the dwarf early-flowering field Buttercup, R. bulbosus, a native of Europe naturalized in eastern North America. This double variety, 9-12 in. high, is a handsome plant for the flower border, thriving in ordinary soil and flowering in May or June. It is increased easily by division of the roots in spring or autumn.

The Lesser Celandine. R. Ficaria, a pretty European plant naturalized in eastern North America, is known as the Lesser Celandine. It is

The Lesser Celandine, Ranunculus Ficaria, is a pretty, bulbous plant that may be grown outdoors in moist places or in pans of soil in a cold frame or cool greenhouse.

The double-flowered Lesser Celandine, Ranunculus Ficaria flore-pleno.

one of the earliest of spring flowers and has shining leaves and golden blooms. In the garden there are many shady places, in shrubberies and unconsidered corners, where the ground is fairly moist, where it might well be introduced as a cheerful ground cover for the early months of the year. Soon after flowering, the whole plant, leaves and all, disappears underground and is no more seen until the following spring.

There is a double-flowered variety in cultivation, one with pale cream-white flowers (albus) and a giant form (grandiflorus) four or five times the size of the type in all its parts; the last-named is a fine plant for woodland and wild gardens. The variety cupreus has copper-yellow flowers. Propagation is by root division after flowering.

The Rue-leaved Buttercup. Ranunculus rutifolius, also known as Callianthemum rutifolium, is a charming high alpine plant with blue-gray fern- or ruelike leaves, and anemone-like greenish-white flowers. It grows only 2-3 in. high, and is suitable for the rock garden in light loam in which is mixed a good proportion of stones.

Although it enjoys abundant moisture during the growing season, this plant should have a well-drained and sunny position. Propagation is by seeds sown as soon as ripe in a pot of loam, sand and leaf mold in a cold frame, or by careful division of the roots in spring.

A Beautiful Plant. R. asiaticus, from the Levant, is the original parent of the brilliant Turban and Persian Buttercups or Florists' Ranunculus. It is a fine plant for rock gardens and sunny flower borders but is not hardy in the North. This plant grows 9-12 in. high and has beautiful, large, single anemone-like flowers, usually intense scarlet with an almost black, occasionally white or yellow, boss or knoblike organ in the center. The curious clawlike tuberous roots should be planted with the claws downward in light, well-drained soil from November to February in mild, nearly frost-free climates.

After flowering, when the leaves begin to turn yellow, the roots should be dug up, placed in a paper bag and hung in a dry cellar or storage room until planting time comes around again.

Turban and Persian Ranunculi. The garden varieties of R. asiaticus known as Persian Ranunculus and Turban Ranunculus are neat

The large double-flowered Turban Ranunculi are unrivaled for their brilliant colors.

and compact in flower and in habit. The Turban varieties are larger, more robust in constitution, if less refined in form, but both sorts are extremely beautiful and are well worth cultivating for garden decoration and as cut flowers. They are suitable for outdoor cultivation only where mild winters prevail. They are excellent for greenhouse cultivation.

How to Plant. These plants prefer a light,

Turban Ranunculi flowering in April from a planting of tubers made in October in a cold frame.

sandy, fertile soil. When grown outdoors, the bed in which they are planted should be prepared, after first making sure that the subsurface drainage is good, by spading it to a depth of 9-12 in. Liberal amounts of well-decayed compost, leaf mold or old, rotted manure, commercial humus, sedge peat or peat moss should be mixed with the soil and, in addition, bone meal, at the rate of half a pound to each 10 sq. ft. of surface.

The Time to Plant. November to February is the best time to plant. Set the tuberous roots about 6-8 in. apart each way and 3 in. deep, with the points of the claws downward. Keep the surface of the bed loose by occasional hoeing or stirring of the surface or, preferably, mulch it with peat moss, leaf mold, or some other suitable material. Make sure that at no time do the plants suffer from dryness; it is important that the soil be reasonably moist throughout the growing season.

When the foliage has died down naturally after the blooming season is over, the tubers may be dug up and stored until the next planting season or may remain in the ground undisturbed until the bed becomes so crowded that the need for lifting, separating and replanting them is clearly indicated. If they are stored over summer they should be kept in peat moss in a cool, dry place.

Both Persian and Turban Ranunculus roots may be bought either in collections of named varieties or in mixture; these flowers are invaluable for cutting and a good mixed strain is perhaps the most suitable. The double flowers, two or three inches in diameter, vary through endless shades of red, pink, scarlet, yellow, primrose, gold and white, with numerous bizarre and picotee variations.

A handsome and vigorous strain, possibly derived from the Turban Ranunculus, and called Tecolote Giants, is very popular. The flowers are large, the plants vigorous and free-flowering and the colors varied and extremely fine. In some mixed strains single flowers sometimes occur, and although from a cultural point of view this may be a defect it should not unduly distress the amateur gardener, for these single flowers are admirable for cutting.

Cultivation in the Greenhouse. The Florists' Ranunculi, the Turban and Persian kinds, are among the finest flowers that can be grown in cool greenhouses to provide a supply of cut flowers in late winter and spring. They come in a splendid range of colors and in general appearance remind one of the Poppy Anemones that are grown in similar fashion for similar purposes. One main difference is that the prevailing colors of the Poppy Anemones are red, blue, and white, while those of the Florists' Ranunculus are yellow, orange and red.

Persian and Turban Ranunculi, when grown in greenhouses, require a light, rich, well-drained soil that contains an abundance of organic matter.

Tubers may be planted, as early as they can be obtained from dealers, in fall, in pots, flats or benches. If planted in benches or flats they should be spaced about 8 in. apart; if in pots, they may be set singly in 4- or 5-in. pots or three together in 6-in. pots.

Watering should be done with considerable restraint at first, but when the plants are in active growth and have rooted through the soil allotted to them, they must never be allowed to suffer from dryness. At this time, too, dilute liquid fertilizer may be applied with advantage at weekly intervals.

It is very important that the greenhouse temperature be not too high. At night it should not exceed 45-50 degrees when outside temperatures are at those levels or lower. Daytime temperatures in bright weather may be ten degrees or so higher. These plants need full sunshine for their successful growth.

As an alternate to purchasing tubers in the fall, it is easy to obtain a good supply of these plants by raising them from seeds. The seeds should be sown in a cool greenhouse or in a cold frame in late April or May in a humus-rich soil that is well-drained but kept evenly moist.

The young plants are transplanted individually to small pots as soon as they are large enough to handle conveniently, and are grown through the summer in a well-ventilated, lightly shaded greenhouse or cold frame. In fall they are planted in benches, pots, or flats at the same distances as tubers. Seedling plants bloom later than early-planted tubers. They produce their flowers in early spring. Greenhouse-grown plants should be discarded after their blooming season has finished.

Culture in Cold Frames. In regions where winters are too severe to permit the outdoor cultivation of Persian and Turban Ranunculus, excellent results can be obtained by growing them in a cold frame. Suitable planting conditions are provided by a bed of fertile soil, well mixed with leaf mold, humus, good compost or other decayed organic matter, made porous by the liberal addition of coarse sand and enriched with a generous dressing of bone meal.

Plant the tubers in fall, 7-8 in. apart, and keep the soil moderately moist but not sodden. At night in winter and on extremely cold days (unless a good thick layer of snow protects the glass), cover the glass with mats, straw, or some other protective covering that will prevent the inside temperature from dropping excessively low.

On all favorable occasions—that is, whenever the outdoor temperature is above 32 degrees—ventilate the frame and, whenever the weather is really mild, remove the glass sash entirely.

Raising Ranunculi from Seeds. In mild climates the Asiatic Ranunculus and the Turban and Persian varieties derived from it may be raised from seeds sown on a prepared bed of rich soil similar to that recommended for roots. Sow thinly in spring, and lift and dry the roots in summer when growth has finished and the leaves begin to turn yellow.

The Double Creeping Buttercup. The double-flowered variety of the Creeping Buttercup, Ranunculus repens pleniflorus, although a handsome plant with its fine golden buttonlike blossoms, should be used with caution as it creeps about, rooting as it goes, and may soon become a nuisance. For clothing rough and unimportant places it is both useful and attractive.

It propagates itself by strawberry-like runners.

Ranunculus bilobus is a rather rare high mountain Buttercup from South Tyrol, allied to R. alpestris, with white, five-petaled flowers and kidney-shaped leaves. It grows two or three inches high and is not difficult in the rock garden if set in gritty loam.

R. Buchanani, from New Zealand, grows about 12 in. high, has kidney-shaped leaves and large white flowers. It is rare in cultivation, and should be given a cool half-shady position in the rock garden in deep loam.

R. crenatus is a rare white-flowered alpine Buttercup, dwarf and attractive, closely related to R. bilobus and R. alpestris, and a plant whose chief appeal is to the specialist in rare plants. It is beautiful and not difficult to grow, and is native to Styria, Bosnia, and Macedonia. It is said to hate lime.

A Lovely High Alpine Buttercup. Ranunculus glacialis is a plant of the highest alpine screes and moraines, found on granite formations. It is widely distributed in the European Alps, Norway, Iceland, and Greenland. It grows naturally in mixtures of stiff claylike loam and broken stone, always where it is kept extremely wet at the root during the growing and flowering period, watered from above by melting snow and ice. It is an extremely beautiful plant, with thick, fleshy rootstocks, long, thonglike roots, gray-green fleshy leaves and large flowers on slightly branched stems. The flowers open white and with age fade to rose-pink, deep rose or wine-red. It often grows in amazing abundance in the European Alps and is then a splendid sight.

How to Grow Ranunculus glacialis. In the rock garden this plant is by no means easy to manage, but success can be achieved, in localities where summers are not excessively hot, by planting it in a deep bed of a mixture of broken granite, loam, leaf mold and sand, and ensuring that the plants receive ample moisture from the time they start into growth in spring until the flowering is finished.

Seeds may be sown, as soon as ripe, in a pan of loam, leaf mold and sand in a cold frame; the seedlings should be left undisturbed the first year and planted out in their permanent quarters the following spring. Large clumps may also be lifted in spring and then carefully divided.

Ranunculus Gouani, from the Pyrenees, is regarded as a form of R. montanus. It grows 6-9 in. tall, and has large, golden-yellow flowers, almost an inch in diameter in the best varieties. It is a fine plant in the rock garden. Loamy soil suits it, and it should be given an open, sunny position. Seeds may be sown, as soon as ripe, in a pot of loam, leaf mold, and sand in a cold frame, or the plants may be lifted and divided in spring.

R. Gouani is seldom seen in cultivation, but, on account of its dwarf growth, easy management, and brilliant flowers, it deserves to be better known. The plant varies considerably in the size and splendor of its flowers, so that it is important to secure a good form.

The Grass-leaved Buttercup, Ranunculus gramineus, is a handsome mountain plant from southwestern Europe and Morocco, forming clumps of erect, narrow, grasslike leaves and branched 9-12-in. stems carrying large golden flowers. It is a fine plant in the rock garden. It flowers in May and June. Loamy soil suits it, and an open, sunny position is necessary. There is a variety with extra-large flowers, known as R. gramineus grandiflorus, which is particularly desirable.

The plant may be raised from seeds sown as soon as ripe in a pan of loam, leaf mold, and sand in the cold frame; or plants may be lifted in spring, the roots divided and replanted where they are to flower.

Ranunculus insignis, from New Zealand, is a big yellow-flowered Buttercup, akin to R.

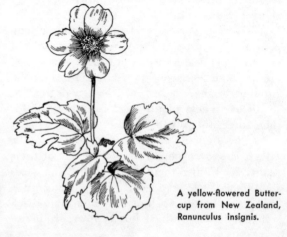

A yellow-flowered Buttercup from New Zealand, Ranunculus insignis.

Ranunculus Lingua grandiflora, a
wet-ground or water plant.

Lyallii, but with hairy leaves. It is handsome,
but rare in cultivation, and difficult to grow.

For Planting in Shallow Water. Ranunculus
Lingua grandiflora is a giant form of a European wild Water Buttercup, which, in Great Britain, is called the Greater Spearwort. It has long,
narrow leaves, grows about three feet tall, and
has golden-yellow flowers. An extremely handsome plant for shallow water, it spreads so rapidly that it should be planted with caution, and restrained, otherwise it will soon overrun its neigh-
bors and become an intolerable nuisance.

Ranunculus Lyallii is an extremely handsome
and beautiful New Zealand alpine Buttercup,
2-3 ft. tall, with curious round fleshy leaves of
glossy green borne singly on the tops of tall
stems, and with loose heads of very large, white
flowers. It requires moist loam, but is not easy to
manage and is seldom seen in gardens. It could
probably be grown with greatest expectation of
success in the Pacific Northwest.

A Golden-yellow Rock-Garden Ranunculus.
Ranunculus montanus is a dwarf, golden
flowered Buttercup, widely distributed in the
Alps of Europe. It is variable in nature, but is
usually extremely attractive, forming compact
clumps of erect stems, 4-5 in. tall, carrying immense numbers of golden-yellow flowers in
spring. Loamy soil in an open sunny position
suits it, and it is best propagated by division of
the roots directly after flowering in early summer. The variety albus has pale lemon-yellow

flowers, and is generally considered very pretty.

For the Moraine. Ranunculus parnassifolius
is a beautiful mountain Buttercup found in the
highest limestone screes from the Pyrenees in the
west to Austria in the east. It has thick, leathery,
rounded leaves of a somber green, and big white
flowers on 4-5-in. stems. Where summers are
fairly cool it is reasonably easy to grow in the
rock garden, and should be given limestone scree
or moraine, with ample moisture in the flowering and growing season.

Propagation is by division of the roots in
spring, or seed may be sown as soon as ripe in a
pot of loam, leaf mold and sand in a cold frame;
the seedlings should be left undisturbed during
their first season of growth and planted in their
permanent quarters the following spring. For
such treatment the seed should be sown thinly.

The Pyrenean Buttercup. Ranunculus pyrenaeus is rather near R. amplexicaulis in general
appearance, but of slighter growth, with narrower, almost grasslike leaves, which do not clasp
the stems as do those of R. amplexicaulis. It is
extremely abundant in high mountain pastures
in many parts of the European Alps, growing in
colonies in the short turf in such profusion as to
give almost the effect of a thin fall of snow. The
erect stems are 6-9 in. tall, carrying lovely white
flowers which are about as big as a quarter.

The plant varies considerably in the size and
splendor of its blossoms, and superior forms with
a double row of petals exist; fully double varieties are sometimes, though rarely, found. R.
pyrenaeus is easy to grow in the rock garden in
light loam in an open position.

Ranunculus Seguieri is near R. glacialis, but
smaller in growth, with pure white flowers
which do not fade to pink as do those of R. glacialis; it is a lime-lover, and is far easier to grow
than the lime-hating R. glacialis. It is distributed
rather widely and irregularly in the Alps of Europe. It is best grown in limestone scree, and
should be kept moist during the flowering and
growing period. It grows only 2-3 in. high, and
the white flowers are large for the size of the
plant.

Beautiful but Poisonous. Ranunculus Thora
is a curious Buttercup found on limestone formations at moderate altitudes in the European

Alps. The golden flowers are carried on stems some 4-5 in. tall, and each erect stem is furnished with one curious broad, fan-shaped leaf of dull-green, leathery texture.

The plant forms a clump and is most readily increased by division of the roots in spring; or seeds may be sown as soon as ripe in a pot of loam, sand and leaf mold in a cold frame, and the seedlings left undisturbed until the following spring, when they may be planted out in their permanent quarters.

It should be noted that Ranunculus Thora is an extremely *poisonous* plant, though there would seem to be no reason why anyone should be tempted to eat it.

RAOULIA (Raou'lia). A group of interesting plants belonging to the Daisy family, Compositae, natives of New Zealand and Tasmania. Although many species are known to botanists, few are cultivated. The name honors Edouard Raoul, a French naval surgeon. The Raoulias are closely allied to the Helichrysums or "Everlastings," and their flowers are, in effect, little "everlasting flowers." These are the principal sorts at present in cultivation:

Raoulia australis forms a spreading mat of silvery leaves, closely hugging the ground; it is one of the most fascinating of all dwarf carpeters for the rock garden. The flower heads are inconspicuous and yellowish. It requires light, well-drained soil and fullest sun; the scree or moraine suits it admirably, and it is ideal for growing as a ground cover over small choice bulb plants in the rock garden. Propagation is by division of the stems in early summer; they root freely as they creep.

Raoulia glabra is of the same dwarf creeping habit as R. australis, but the foliage is green and the plant somewhat hardier and less particular as to perfect drainage. The flowers are yellowish. Being more vigorous than R. australis, it is capable of holding its own in the alpine lawn. It is easily propagated by division of the creeping rooting stems in spring or early summer. R. glabra is a valuable plant for the crevices of paved paths.

Raoulia subsericea is a minute carpeting plant, smaller than either of the other two. It is gray-green and suitable for a sunny spot on the scree. The flowers of this variety are white.

R. eximia is perhaps the most remarkable of all this interesting genus. It forms big, rounded masses of densely congested growth of grayish color. In New Zealand it is called Vegetable Sheep because of the strange, superficial resemblance groups of the plants bear to a flock of sheep, when observed from some distance away. It is doubtful that it will ever be grown successfully in North America, and even in New Zealand it has never been kept healthy under cultivation for any considerable period.

RAPE. A cabbage-like plant (Brassica Napus) grown extensively in India, Japan and various European countries for the sake of its oily seeds, from which colza or rape oil is obtained. Rape is also occasionally sown as a green manure, but is not recommended where Clubroot disease is prevalent.

RAPHANUS (Ra'phanus). The botanical name of the Radish. Details of cultivation will be found under the heading of Radish.

RAPHIA RUFFIA—*Raffia* (Raph'ia). A member of a group of mostly African Palms that is the source of the well-known fiber raffia, which is used for tying plants and for other purposes. It belongs to the Palm family, Palmaceae. The name is derived from *raphis,* a needle, and alludes to the short, sharp beak of the fruit.

This Palm attains a height of 25-30 ft. and dies after its first fruiting. Its leaves are as large as, or larger than, those of any other known plant. They are of the feather type and are often 65 ft. long, with stalks 10-15 ft. long. The leaves stand nearly straight up, are green on their upper surfaces and whitish-powdered beneath.

This plant is practically unknown in cultivation in North America, though it could be expected to thrive in southern Florida. It is a native of Africa and Madagascar. In the latter place most of the raffia fiber that enters commerce originates. See Raffia.

RAPHIOLEPIS (Raphio'lepis; Raphiolep'is). Tender, evergreen flowering shrubs which grow wild in China and Japan. They are closely allied to Photinia and belong to the Rose family, Rosaceae. The name Raphiolepis is derived from *raphis,* a needle, and *lepis,* a scale, and refers to the needle-like scale leaves.

Raphiolepis indica has lanceolate leaves and heads of pale pink flowers.

The hardiest kind is R. umbellata. It forms a sturdy bush 9 ft. in height, and the young leaves are coriaceous (leathery), serrate (saw-edged), obovate, 2½-3 in. long and 2 in. wide. The flowers, which are produced in late spring or early summer, in upright spikes, are pure white and fragrant. They are rotate (roundish) and five-petaled.

Prefer Mild Climates. Raphiolepis is for the deep South and for California. The shrubs succeed in any fairly good soil, in sun or part shade. Planting is done in early spring or fall and the soil is made firm. Afterwards the soil is thoroughly soaked with water to settle it around the roots.

Tenderness. Raphiolepis withstands some frost but temperatures much below freezing are damaging. In parts of the South where such temperatures are likely to occur occasionally, it is wise to select protected or sheltered positions when planting these shrubs.

Pruning. Very little pruning is required, as plants are compact in growth. Straggling shoots, or those which are growing faster than others, are pruned back in spring to preserve the symmetry of the bushes.

For the Greenhouse. R. indica is less hardy than R. umbellata and cannot be grown out of doors except in the very mildest regions. It is, however, an excellent plant for a large greenhouse or conservatory. It is more graceful in habit of growth than R. umbellata, and has lanceolate (lance-shaped) leaves and pinkish-white flowers. It is best grown in a large, well-drained pot or tub in a compost of equal parts of loam, peat moss and sand with a liberal amount of old, rotted manure added.

Potting is done in March, and the soil is made firm with a potting stick. It is watered moderately until the plants are established, and then kept moist throughout the summer. From September to March much less water is required, sufficient only being given to prevent the leaves from falling. During winter it is best to allow the soil to become nearly dry, and then thoroughly saturate it.

The method of pruning is the same as for outdoor-grown specimens.

Propagation is by cuttings, which are inserted in August or September. Firm, well-ripened shoots are removed with a heel or piece of the

Raphiolepis umbellata, an evergreen shrub, bears white, fragrant flowers in June. It is hardy only in mild climates.

main stem attached. Enough of the lower leaves are removed to enable the shoot to be inserted in a well-packed bed of sand or of sand and peat moss in a cold frame or greenhouse. When roots are formed, the shoots are set in separate pots.

The chief kinds are R. umbellata (japonica), 10 ft., white, and R. indica, 8 ft., pinkish-white. R. Delacouri, pink, is a hybrid obtained by crossing R. umbellata and R. indica. It was raised at Cannes, France, at the end of last century.

RASPBERRIES: RED, BLACK AND PURPLE

Easy-to-Grow Fruits for the Home Garden

The cultivated Raspberries are derived from three species, the European Red Raspberry, Rubus idaeus, the wild Red Raspberry of North America, R. idaeus variety strigosus, and the Blackcap Raspberry, R. occidentalis. Hybrids between Blackcap and Red Raspberries are known as Purple Raspberries and are grown extensively commercially in New York, and occasionally in other states and in Canada. Several species of Oriental Raspberries are now being crossed with American varieties to produce varieties suitable for cultivation south of the latitude of Washington, D. C., where the American varieties do not thrive.

Red Raspberries were introduced into America before 1800, and selections of the American Red Raspberry were grown later. Red Raspberries became important about 1870. Black Raspberry cultivation began about 1850.

The Raspberry requires a cool, moist climate, such as is found north of the Potomac and Ohio River valleys. The commercial industry is mostly in New York, Michigan, Oregon, Washington, and Ontario, but Raspberries may be grown successfully in the other northern states, except in the Great Plains region, which is too cold and dry for them.

The soil may range from a deep sandy loam to a clay loam, the former being preferable. Good drainage is important, as Raspberries die out readily where the water table is near the surface for more than a few hours after a heavy rain during the growing season. The water table should be down at depth of about 3 ft. The soil should be well-supplied with organic matter.

Good air drainage is desirable because minimum winter temperatures are lower in frost pockets from which cold air cannot easily drain, and fungus diseases, especially anthracnose, and spur blight are more serious where air circulation is poor.

Wild Red Raspberries and run-out cultivated Raspberries should be eliminated before starting a new planting because these may harbor virus diseases and insect pests. Land that has grown Tomatoes, Potatoes, Peppers or Eggplants should be avoided as a site for a Raspberry planting for at least three years because these crops may infect the soil with verticillium wilt, a troublesome soil-borne disease of Black and Purple Raspberries.

Soil preparation should be as thorough as for vegetables. Organic matter may be supplied by the addition of stable manure or by plowing under green manure crops. Perennial weeds

Raspberries, a favorite summer fruit, are easy to grow in the amateur's garden.

should be eliminated before the Raspberries are set.

Propagation. The Red Raspberry increases by producing many sucker plants from the roots. When increase is desired, these are dug when dormant and are used for planting. Nurseries often grow them in nursery rows for a year and sell them as transplants or two-year plants. The new shoots which come up in the spring are sometimes used as planting stock and, if transplanted carefully during cool cloudy weather, are entirely satisfactory. They should be dug before they are over 6 in. high.

Black and Purple varieties are propagated by tip layering. This is done by inserting the tip of the new cane vertically in the soil to a depth of about 4 in. in late August or early September, before autumn winds have injured them. Roots develop rapidly on the tips, and the "tip plants," as they are called, are dug in the spring and used as planting stock, or grown for a year in the nursery to become transplants, or two-year plants.

Planting. Red Raspberries may be planted in the fall or early spring. They are usually grown in hedge rows, the plants being set 2 ft. apart in the row and the suckers filling in a solid row which should be restricted to a foot in width. Rows in the garden should be 6-7 ft. apart, or, in commercial plantings, 9-10 ft. apart, according to tillage machinery that is to be used. They are also grown in hills 5-6 ft. apart and tied to stakes.

Trellises are often used to support the fruiting canes of Red Raspberries, especially in the West, where they grow very tall. Trellises are of doubtful value in the East, although home gardeners often use them. A simple trellis consists of two wires about 5 ft. high and about a foot apart. The fruiting canes are tied to these wires in the spring before growth starts. Often a single wire is used rather than a pair of wires.

When the red varieties are grown in hills, a stake extending 6 ft. above the ground is used. Seven or 8 canes may be left in each hill and tied to the stakes.

The Black and Purple varieties are set 3 ft. apart in the row and, as they do not produce suckers, the plants remain in hills. The tip

plants by which they are propagated are best set out in the spring, but the two-year plants may be planted out in the fall.

Care after planting consists mostly of weed control. Cultivation should be shallow and frequent enough to keep down the weeds. After the first year the suckers of the Red varieties will spread out into the row, and these must be removed periodically to prevent the hedge rows from becoming over a foot in width. After the planting is in full bearing, which will be the third year, cultivation should be stopped soon after harvest and a cover crop sown between the rows to check late fall growth of the canes, which may predispose them to winter injury.

Mulching with straw, hay, or a similar material is a very effective method of managing the soil, especially for light soils, or where the summers are hot and dry. The mulch may be put on in early summer and allowed to remain until it decays.

Nitrogen is the material most likely to be profitable for fertilizing Raspberries. It may be used at the rate of 60 pounds to the acre, an amount that may be supplied by 200 pounds of ammonium nitrate, 400 pounds of nitrate of soda or appropriate amounts of other nitrogenous fertilizers. The fertilizer should be applied in early spring before growth starts. Stable and poultry manures are excellent for Raspberries, but they should be used with caution as they may cause too vigorous growth, which is susceptible to winter injury.

Pruning. Raspberry canes are biennial; they grow one season, fruit the next and then die. In the spring the Red Raspberry canes which grew the previous season are headed back (pruned back) by removing about one fourth of their length, and the weaker canes are cut out entirely. The remaining vigorous canes are thinned out to a spacing of 6 in. apart, in rows about 1 ft. wide.

With the Black Raspberry the pruning begins as soon as the new shoots are 18 in. high. At this height the top is pinched off to make the canes branch. They then become sturdier and easier to manage. If unchecked, they make long, sprawling canes that interfere with cultivation and are easily broken. The new shoots of the Purple

Red Raspberries are pruned by removing surplus canes and cutting the tips off those that remain.

After pruning, the young canes retained are tied to wires or other supports.

Raspberries are pruned by having their tops cut off at a height of about 2 ft. The following spring, before growth starts, the branches of Black Raspberries are cut back to 6-8 buds and the Purple varieties to 10-12 buds. The weaker canes are removed.

After the crop is harvested, the canes which bore it are removed and burned, although this operation is often delayed until the spring pruning.

Harvesting. Raspberries should be picked every 2-3 days and handled carefully, as they are very perishable. As soon as possible, they should be removed from the field to the shade, or a cool storage place. Overripe berries should be discarded when picked.

Red Raspberry varieties include the following:

Amber: Amber in color, of high quality, late.

Chief: Small, very hardy, early. Suitable for the upper Mississippi Valley.

Red Raspberries are one of the most satisfactory fruit crops for home gardens. They may be grown in rows spaced 6-7 ft. apart.

Cuthbert: Highest quality, but being replaced by others.

Latham: Large, late, heavy-yielding; one of the hardier varieties; a standard kind.

Milton: Large, firm, good, productive; escapes mosaic disease.

Newburgh: Large, firm, midseason, productive; a standard kind.

Sunrise: Small, very early; suitable for the region south of Washington. D.C.

Surprise: Best variety for southern California.

Taylor: Large, productive, good, late.

Van Fleet: Small, soft; for southern states only.

Viking: Medium-sized, productive, good. Grown chiefly in Ontario.

Washington: Medium-sized, good, productive. Replacing Cuthbert in Washington.

Willamette: Large, dark, firm; one of the best for freezing and canning.

Autumn-fruiting or so-called Everbearing varieties include:

Ranere: Small, early, heat-resistant. Useful south of Washington, D.C.

Durham: Early, suitable for short-season locations in the North.

September: Best autumn-fruiting variety.

Indian Summer: Latest autumn-fruiting variety. Suitable for the latitude of southern New England. This variety is being replaced by September, described above.

Black Raspberry varieties include:

Logan: Early.

Bristol: Midseason, productive.

Cumberland: Late, high quality.

Dundee: Late, productive, good quality.

Morrison: Late, large.

Munger: Popular in Oregon and Washington.

Purple Raspberry varieties have large, tart fruits and the plants are very productive. They are excellent for canning, jam and freezing. Marion and Sodus are the principal varieties.

RAT. See Pests and Diseases.

RATAMA. Parkinsonia aculeata, which see.

RATSTRIPPER. Pachistima Canbyi, which see.

RATTAIL CACTUS. Aporocactus flagelliformis, which see.

RATTLESNAKE MASTER. Eryngium aquaticum, which see.

RATTLESNAKE PLANTAIN. See Goodyera.

RATTLESNAKE ROOT. Prenanthes, which see.

RAVENALA — *Traveler's-Tree* (Ravena'la). Tender evergreen plants which are cultivated outdoors in frost-free and nearly frost-free climates and in greenhouses for their ornamental, banana-like leaves. They are found growing wild in Madagascar and in parts of South America, where they attain a height of 30 ft. or more and are very conspicuous. They form stout, cylindrical trunks, the lower parts of which are surrounded by the sheaths of the leafstalks, the leafblades having fallen off.

The Traveler's-Tree, Ravenala madagascariensis, is cultivated outdoors in Florida and southern California.

Giant Fan Leaves. The leaves, which average 15 ft. in length, are arranged in fan formation at the tops of the trunks. They are lanceolate (lance-shaped) or elliptic, and have very long leafstalks, the bases of which sheathe the trunks. In these cuplike sheaths water is collected and is said to have been used by thirsty travelers— hence the common name Traveler's-Tree. The name Ravenala is the original native name of the plant in Madagascar.

These plants, which are grown out of doors in the far South and in California, and in greenhouses of the conservatory type found in public gardens, develop flowers similar in formation to those of the Banana. They belong to the family, Musaceae. The small whitish blooms are crowded into compact spikes which are surrounded by large, conspicuous bracts. The fruit is a woody capsule which contains the seeds in two rows, each seed having a blue or reddish aril (fleshy covering).

Suitable for a Large Hothouse. Owing to their vigorous growth when grown indoors, they are only suitable for cultivation in large hothouses, where the leaves have ample room for development. They need a sunny, well-lighted structure, and should be shaded only from the hottest rays of the sun. A minimum temperature of 55 degrees is necessary in the winter.

Hints on Management. For repotting, a rich compost is required; two parts of fibrous loam and equal parts of peat moss and well-decayed manure with coarse sand added freely, form an ideal soil mixture. After repotting, careful watering is necessary until the roots have entered the new compost, the best method being to allow the latter to become fairly dry before moistening it. When growing vigorously, however, the plants must be watered freely. When growth becomes less active in the autumn, and for the remainder of the year, the soil should only be moistened when it becomes quite dry.

The chief method of propagation is by suckers. These are removed at any time during the spring or summer and potted in small pots. To assist them in rooting quickly into the compost, the pots are plunged in a propagating case with a bottom heat of 70-75 degrees.

The only kind in cultivation is R. madagascar-iensis, which usually reaches a height of 30 ft.

RAY FLORETS. A botanical term used in describing the outer florets of many composite flowers, ones belonging to the Daisy family, Compositae. The inner or central part of the flower consists of disc florets. The ray and disc florets are clearly seen in Daisy, single Aster, single Chrysanthemum and numerous other composite flowers.

REBUTIA (Rebut'ia). Easy-to-grow small Cacti (family Cactaceae), chiefly from Argentina and Bolivia, forming round cushion-like plants with closely set tubercles arranged in spirals. For details of cultivation, see Cacti. They

Rebutia minuscula bears its red flowers freely.

begin to flower while quite young and, as they produce seeds freely, are easily increased by this means. They are sometimes increased by grafting side shoots on species of Mediocactus and Eriocereus, and offshoots can also be rooted. The genus is named after P. Rebut, a French Cactus specialist.

The most popular kinds include R. senilis, with white spines and red flowers; R. minuscula, with small scarlet flowers freely produced; and R. pygmea, flowers rose-purple.

RECHSTEINERIA. This name is applied by some botanists to the group of plants treated in this Encyclopedia under the name Corytholoma. One of the most beautiful is C. leucotricha (Rechsteineria leucotricha) which was recently introduced to American horticulture from Brazil by Mr. A. B. Graf, East Rutherford, N. J. C. leucotricha is distinguished by its beautiful silvery-white leaves and its pleasing salmon-red, tubular

Rechsteineria leucotricha has leaves covered with silvery-white hairs and tubular salmon-red flowers. It was recently introduced to cultivation by an American plant collector.

flowers. Care must be taken in cultivating it not to wet its foliage. The name Rechsteineria honors the Swiss botanist Pfarrer Reichsteiner.

RED BANEBERRY. See Actaea rubra.

RED BAY. Persea Borbonia, which see.

REDBIRD CACTUS. See Pedilanthus.

REDBUD. Cercis, which see.

RED CABBAGE. See Cabbage.

RED CAMPION. Lychnis dioica, which see.

RED CEDAR. Juniperus virginiana, which see.

RED CURRANT. See Currant.

RED HELLEBORINE. See Cephalanthera.

RED-HOT POKER. Kniphofia, which see.

RED LEAD. Red lead is a heavy bright red powder normally used for making paint. It is sometimes employed by gardeners to protect seeds from mice and other pests. The powder is insoluble in water; in order to get it to adhere to the seeds, oil or an oily fluid of some kind has to be used. The seeds (generally red lead is used for large seeds like those of Pea and Bean) are placed in a can; a little kerosene or other oil is added and the seeds are shaken, or stirred until they are thoroughly wetted. A little red lead is put into the tin; again the seeds are shaken and more red lead is added until the seeds are well coated over. They are sown immediately.

RED MAPLE. Acer rubrum, which see.

RED OAK. Quercus borealis, which see.

RED PEPPER. Capsicum frutescens, which see.

RED SANDALWOOD TREE. See Adenanthera pavonina.

REDTOP. Agrostis alba. See Agrostis and Lawns.

REDWOOD. Sequoia sempervirens, which see.

REED CANE. See Arundinaria.

REED, GIANT. See Arundo.

REED GRASS. Phragmites maxima, which see.

REED MACE. See Typha.

REED, NEW ZEALAND. See Arundo.

REGIONAL GARDENING: A SURVEY

A Guide to Gardening in the Various Geographic and Climatic Regions of the United States and Canada

Climate and soil. Of factors that affect the distribution and development of plants, whether they grow wild or in gardens, the most important are climate and soil. Each of these is, of course, enormously complex. Under climate, for example, must be considered rainfall and temperature and such attributes as length of day, duration of growing season, dates of early and late killing frost, annual and seasonal distribution of precipitation, humidity, brilliance of the sun's rays, snow cover and drying winds.

Since nearly all the higher plants have terrestrial roots, the physical constitution of the soil (its texture, structure and humus content), its chemical composition, its acidity or alkalinity, and the nature and quantity of soluble salts are extremely important in determining not only where, but how, plants grow.

Other factors that serve to influence the occurrence of plants are topography (altitude and exposure, for example) and competition with other plants and animals, including man.

Climate and soil, however, must be regarded as the most universally significant of those multiple forces that constitute the plant's environment.

From this it might be concluded that in any area in which climatic and soil factors are uniform, there exists a homogeneous vegetation. In general this is the case, but it does not imply that there is always a sameness in the kinds or species of plants found there. Usually there is considerable diversity in the species occurring in a given area, yet, because of similar natural factors, certain kinds of plants are dominant and the community may be designated by a collective term such as "Hardwood Forest," "Larch-Pine Forest," "Short-Grass Prairie" or "Desert-Scrub," for example.

If it were possible to ascend high enough by stratoplane to see all of North America, and if visibility were ideal, the continent below would appear to be composed of a number of zones or belts, some running east and west, others north and south. This mosaic effect is produced by vegetational regions of varying nature, some forest, some grassland, others desert or scrub.

High up in Arctic America is the great Tundra belt. This area, which is essentially treeless, is characterized by its seemingly limitless expanse of mosses, lichens, grasses and sedges intermixed with low shrubs and carpets of matted or cushion-like herbaceous plants.

Lying south of the Tundra is the Hudsonian Coniferous Forest composed largely of Fir or Balsam, Spruce, Larch and several species of Pine, chief among them the Jack Pine. Associated with these are a few kinds of deciduous (leaf-losing) trees such as Poplar, Birch and Willow; but the region is dominated by needle-bearing evergreens.

From the St. Lawrence Valley to southeastern Manitoba occurs the Canadian Coniferous Forest. This area embraces the Maritime Provinces, southern Quebec and Ontario, the region around the Great Lakes, most of New England and New York and portions of Pennsylvania and New Jersey. It resembles the Hudsonian Forest in that it consists primarily of evergreen trees, but differs in the component species. Here the White Pine was dominant, but after heavy lumbering it is not present in such numbers as

formerly. With it occur the Red Pine, the Hemlock and the Arborvitae or White Cedar. The Canadian Forest also boasts a liberal sprinkling of broad-leaved deciduous trees such as Elm, Sugar Maple and Mountain Ash. A narrow tongue of this boreal vegetation extends in a southwesterly direction along the higher Appalachian Mountains into the southern states. It exists also in modified form on the flanks of some of the western mountains.

The area embraced in the Hudsonian and Canadian Forests conforms in a general way to the region covered by the great ice sheets of Pleistocene time, and as a consequence its soils, especially in the southern portions, are largely sands, clays and gravels. The whole region has had to be repopulated by plants since the disappearance of the ice, which means that the present flora is of comparatively recent origin—in existence probably not more than 25,000 years.

South of the Canadian Forest, and occupying most of the eastern United States, is a broad area composed primarily of deciduous trees, including such familiar forms as Ironwood, Black and Yellow Birch, Hickory, Walnut, Oak, Beech, Ash, Maple, Linden and Tulip Tree. This region, which is the only important deciduous formation on the continent, owes its existence to relatively abundant and well-distributed rainfall and fertile soils that have never been disturbed by mass action of glacial ice.

The Atlantic Coastal Plain extends from New Jersey south to Florida, and westward through the Gulf States to eastern Texas. A region of low relief and mostly sandy soils, it is characterized superficially by the presence of Pines, which, however, differ in species from those of the northern coniferous belts. Here, for example, are the Pitch Pine, the Loblolly Pine, the Longleaf Pine, the Slash Pine (Pinus caribaea), the Sand Pine (Pinus clausa) and a number of others. Here also occur the Swamp or Bald Cypress, the Live Oak, the Sweet Gum and various Magnolias.

Stretching from Texas north to southern Saskatchewan and Alberta lies the Plains and Prairie Province. This is the great grass belt of central North America that has played such an important role in the development of agriculture. Actually it consists of two parallel north-to-south subdivisions: a narrow eastern strip, the long-grass Prairie, and a broader western strip, the short-grass Prairie. Except for a fringe of trees along some of the watercourses, this entire province is devoid of arboreal vegetation. It is a region of relatively low rainfall, most of which occurs in the spring. The result is flora of tall or short grass (such as Buffalo Grass) intermixed with a great variety of herbaceous and shrubby forms.

The plant life of the western third of North America is profoundly influenced by the presence of the two great mountain systems: the Rocky Mountains and the Pacific Mountains (Coast Range, Cascades, Sierra Nevadas and others). The vegetation of these two systems has much in common, due to the vagaries of altitudinal distribution, and to the fact that both ranges are affected by the moisture-laden winds blowing in from the Pacific. The latter factor makes for abundant rainfall on the western slopes and comparatively arid conditions to the east. Where rainfall is adequate the slopes of both systems are densely clothed with coniferous forests in which Hemlock, Arborvitae and Douglas Fir often predominate. Higher up, these give way to Lodgepole Pine (Pinus contorta variety latifolia), Fir and Spruce. Above the limits of dense forest growth, a limit that differs widely according to climatic conditions such as exposure and rainfall, are regions of Parkland and Alpine Meadow, the latter often supporting the most spectacularly brilliant assemblage of plants found on this continent. The floras of the two mountain ranges are far from being identical, but they are similar enough to warrant treating them collectively as typifying high mountain conditions.

Between the Rocky Mountains and the Pacific Coast System lies the intermontane plateau, a series of broad plateaus of varying altitudes and vegetational characteristics. Botanically this is extremely complex, but it must suffice here to state that the northern portions are well forested, and that the region becomes increasingly devoid of trees southward. The great sagebrush area of the southwest lies in the lower reaches of this plateau and gives way to the desert scrub which, originating in Southern California, Nevada and Arizona, extends far south into Mexico and Lower California.

Plants, Gardens, and Regions. In this very superficial analysis of the chief plant formations of Canada and the United States it has been necessary to omit various assemblages and to place emphasis on the major vegetational areas and the significant physical factors that conduce to their development. It now remains to be seen what correlation exists between the natural plant areas and the six great garden regions described in the following sections.

Practically no gardens flourish in the Tundra area and relatively few in the area of the Hudsonian Forest. The rigorous climate, combined with a short growing season, makes it difficult for all but a few hardy species to flourish. Nevertheless, with careful selection and attention it is possible to carry on gardening even within the Arctic Circle.

It is difficult to grow plants in certain of the desert or scrub areas of the South and Southwest. Although the soil throughout much of this region is very fertile, the annual rainfall is less than twenty inches, most of it occurring in the spring. Gardening therefore involves artificial irrigation.

While it is desirable for the gardener to know something of the characteristics of most of the other plant formations listed above, he need not be restricted by the natural limitations that have established their boundaries and determined their floras. For example, a glance at the states included in the great temperate area reveals that, as here defined, this region embraces not only all of the eastern Deciduous Forest, but also portions of the Canadian Coniferous Forest, the Coastal Plain and the Grass Belt. The reason for this is that by employing proper cultural practices many plants may be transposed from one natural area to another. Therefore, a knowledge of the individual plant, no matter where it may have originated, enables the gardener to attempt to reproduce those conditions in his garden.

Even within a single relatively uniform area there exist frequently significant variations in growing conditions. For example, temperature, rainfall, late and early frost, soil and moisture all are affected by topography. Mountain ranges, rolling hills, river valleys, flat lands, a particular type of soil, proximity to the sea or other bodies of water—all these and countless others produce their effect on the vegetation. Even within the confines of a single garden such considerations as a south-facing slope, protection by a wall, house or windbreak, exposure to northwest winter winds or to southwest drying summer winds may produce greater effect on growing plants than moving them hundreds of miles from their natural homes. Once the gardener is aware of these conditions he is in a position to work with them instead of against them.

A garden is an artificial habitat capable, within reasonable limits, of being modified at will. By proper manipulation of the soil it is possible to grow plants requiring acid conditions in close proximity to those adapted to a neutral or alkaline soil. Or by providing adequate winter protection, one may succeed as well with rather tender species as with hardy ones. It is not unusual in a single garden in the middle Atlantic states to see, growing almost side by side, plants from British Columbia, Newfoundland and Georgia, as well as from Europe and Asia.

The boundaries of the great garden areas here treated are arbitrary and tend to overlap. Nevertheless, like the natural formations already described, they constitute highly useful concepts and have much to teach concerning the normal requirements of plants. The gardener who studies them will understand that climate is not just a simple matter of getting colder from south to north or proceeding from sea level to mountain top. He will realize that in cultivating plants it is frequently possible, nay imperative, to provide compensation for the deficiencies of his own locality. This is not to say that he can ever make a Desert Palm from southwestern Arizona grow in Maine or Delaware, or cause the Tulip Tree of Alleghenian America to flourish in Nevada, but it does mean that the more closely one observes natural conditions, the better able he is to reproduce them in that most interesting of man-made habitats—the garden.

The Extreme Cold Area

Canada, Maine, New Hampshire, Vermont, Northern New York, Northern Michigan, Wisconsin, Minnesota, North and South Dakota

This vast area comprises more than half our continent and has wide diversity of soils, mean

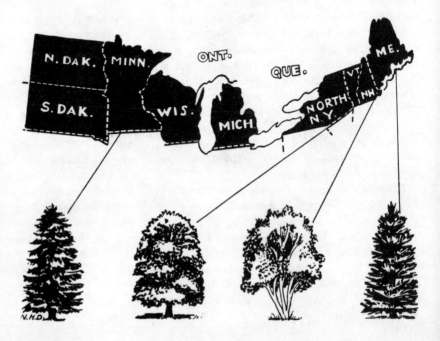

The extreme cold area. The cold winters, heavy snowfall and long summer days of the northern United States make this region especially suited to the growth of evergreens and the hardy strains of deciduous trees. Predominant throughout the entire area are (left to right) Fir, Maple, Birch and Spruce.

temperatures, length of frost-free periods, precipitation, wind movement, winter snow cover, evaporation and possibilities for plant cultivation.

Even in northern Canada, where settlement is sparse, the inhabitants nevertheless take keen pleasure in growing garden plants. Homemakers from Maine to the Yukon find gardening an appealing and successful activity. Home grounds are attractive with trees, shrubs, vines and flowers. Farm and home gardens produce bountiful crops of vegetables, fruits and cut flowers. The list of adapted plants narrows as the western prairie with its scant rainfall, and the northern territories with their severe winter temperatures and short growing seasons, are reached. Yet Dawson, in the Yukon territory, holds a very creditable garden show every August when vegetables, flowers and berry fruits are exhibited. The wild flowers of Alaska are so numerous and varied that visitors invariably are astonished.

Topography and Climate. Low winter temperatures, abundant snowfall and long days in summer mainly distinguish this area from others.

Except for the Rockies in the West and the ends of the Appalachian chain in New York, Vermont, New Hampshire and Maine, most of the cold region is less than 1,000 feet above sea level and is of smooth or rolling contour. Except for the mountains, it is a glaciated area with soil varying from extremely heavy clays to accumulations of gravel and rock. Many small areas, which appear uniform on the surface, may differ in the subsoil. Special forms of plant life may be restricted to areas especially suited to them, while a short distance away other forms take over. Some of the area is underlaid with granite, other sections with limestone. The soil reaction varies from extreme acid in the eastern end of the region and in the forest soils farther west, to highly alkaline in the Great Plains area of South Dakota, North Dakota and Manitoba.

The rainfall varies from 40 in. or more near the east coast, to 10 in. or less in the central west. The humidity of the air varies with the rainfall. Summer temperatures in the East are mostly cool day and night; temperatures in the West may exceed the 100 degrees F. mark during parts of the summer. Most of the rain in the more arid

regions comes during the growing season. This, with the comparatively short and cool growing season, reduces the danger from drought as compared to the more temperate regions. The long days increase the rapidity of growth during the summer. Some crops may be matured that might not be expected to do so if one were considering only the number of frost-free days.

For the most part, this section has a good cover of snow that provides a mulch throughout the winter season; and, because of this, plant life is not subject to such extremes of temperature as might be expected. Many of the plants native to this section are not hardy if the snow cover is removed. Experiments have proved them to be less hardy than the same species growing farther south, where continued winter snows cannot be depended on to prevent alternate freezing and thawing.

Native Woody Plants. The far North is the land of coniferous evergreens, and of Larch, Birch, Poplar, Willows and shrubs. There are many lakes. Countless areas of bogs have productive Blueberry and Cranberry patches. Streams are thickly flanked with Sweet Gale (Myrica Gale), which perfumes the air.

In most of the Great Plains area the principal trees are Poplars, Willows, Box Elder, Green Ash (Fraxinus pennsylvanica variety lanceolata), American Elm, Birch, Burr Oak (Quercus macrocarpa), Basswood, Hackberry, Mountain Ash, Jack Pine, Bull Pine (Pinus ponderosa variety scopulorum), White Spruce, Black Spruce, Red Cedar (Juniperus virginiana), Balsam (Abies balsamea) and Tamarack (Larix laricina). Prominent among the native shrubs are American Cranberry Bush, Wild Plum, Juneberry or Saskatoon (Amelanchier alnifolia), Buffalo Berry, Silverberry, Chokecherry, Sand Cherry, Hawthorn, Honeysuckle, Nanny Berry, Arrowwood, Smooth Sumac (Rhus glabra), Red Osier Dogwood, Cinquefoil (Potentilla fruticosa), Roses and Junipers. The chief vines are Wild Grape, Virginia Creeper, Bittersweet, Western Virgin's Bower (Clematis ligusticifolia), Honeysuckle and Moonseed (Menispermum canadense).

In addition, in the East there are evergreens such as White Pine, Hemlock and White Cedar and deciduous trees such as Sugar Maple,

Black Cherry, Beech, Red Oak and White Ash. The Cottonwoods decrease. Blueberry, Labrador Tea, Mountain Laurel, Red Raspberry, Flowering Raspberry, Blackberry, Buttonbush and deciduous Holly grow profusely.

Other than the limiting factors of growth, moisture and humidity that apply elsewhere, there are certain peculiarities about plant life in the far North. These depend on three principal factors: length of day, winter temperature and snow cover.

Plants tall enough to extend above the winter snow line must be able to endure a climate altogether different from the low-growing plants that are protected by the snow. The tall varieties must be limited to such trees and shrubs as can withstand temperatures of 20 degrees or more below zero. The gardener must not only know something about the species of plants, but he must look for unusually hardy geographic strains of these species. Only cold-resisting strains of Elm trees, for instance, can grow in the far North. Special attention, therefore, must be given to the factor of zonal source of stock.

While much of the cold area lies north of what is considered the Apple Belt, if the proper varieties of stock and scion are selected, trees may stand the winters several hundred miles north of the point at which they would grow otherwise. Thus in many cases they can be successfully grown with the proper selection of hardy strains within the species, whereas if no heed were given to this factor they would perish. Even such trees as Apricots and Pears, once excluded as being too tender, now may be grown successfully in this area if the nursery stock is restricted to a selection of hardy strains.

Hardy Rootstocks. In the case of grafted plants, precaution must be taken to see not only that the variety is hardy, but that the root on which it is grafted also is robustly winter hardy. A Plum variety grafted on a Peach root, which may be satisfactory further south, would be of no value in the cold region because the Peach root would be killed. Pears grown on Quince roots may be destroyed because the roots are killed by freezing. Rose bushes, Climbing Roses, Grapes and Raspberries, which, if left alone, might stand above the snow line, may be brought safely through the winter if the plants are laid flat on the ground and covered with soil in the autumn.

Herbaceous perennials and low-growing shrubs covered with snow during the winter months may thrive in far northern gardens, whereas 500 or more miles south they might perish because the lack of snow protection permits frost to penetrate into the soil. As one moves from the eastern humid area, where a blanket of snow may be depended upon, to the West, where snow may not come before the arrival of extreme cold, it is increasingly difficult to raise perennial flowers. Wherever snow does not provide a mulch, artificial mulching may be necessary and, being a practical method of plant insurance, it becomes a standard garden practice. All young plantings of herbaceous perennials should receive a protective mulch in November. Most commonly used is a 2-4 in. layer of clean wheat straw or corn stalks, evergreen boughs, or shrubbery branches to trap the early snowfall.

Hardy perennials that bloom in spring and early summer are best planted in late summer or autumn. Thus, Iris are planted in August; Peonies, Tulips, Scilla and Lilies in September and October. Phlox, Lupines, Columbines, Delphiniums, Hemerocallis, Dianthus, and Violas may be moved successfully in September in territory where snowfall comes early and persists until spring. In Manitoba, Phlox, Delphinium, Lupines and Hemerocallis usually are planted in April.

Trees and shrubs that reach above the snow line are best planted in the spring, but lower-growing shrubs are safely set in the fall and usually are better moved then. There is no reason why any garden need be deficient in perennial flowers, vines, shrubs and trees, with blooms from April to October in any section where a 100-day frost-free season is the rule.

With annual plants, both flowers and vegetables, the length of the growing season must be taken into consideration. If the plants require a considerable time to develop, then they must be started inside. It is common practice to provide protection for plants which are frost-tender in autumn. For instance, Watermelons and Muskmelons are planted in cold frames. When the first autumn frosts come, a night cover is put on

In the extreme cold area, any section may have perennial flowers, vines, shrubs and trees, with blooms from April to October, where a one-hundred-day frost free season is the rule. Mulching, natural or artificial, tides otherwise tender plants over the winter.

until the cool period is over, then removed for the crop to complete its growth in the warm part of the day.

A cold climate, provided it is in an area of good soil, need not be deficient in variety of plants which make for an abundant, pleasant

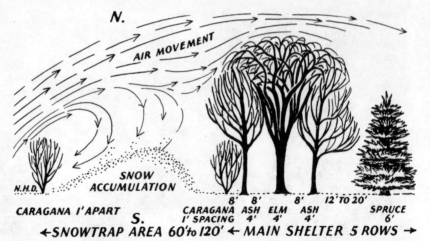

N.

AIR MOVEMENT

SNOW ACCUMULATION

N.H.D.

CARAGANA I'APART

S.

←SNOWTRAP AREA 60'to 120' ← MAIN SHELTER 5 ROWS →

CARAGANA ASH ELM ASH   8' 8' 8' 12' TO 20'
1' SPACING 4' 4' 4'   SPRUCE
                                              6'

A shelter belt of from three to five rows of trees is essential to a garden on the northern Great Plains. Planted on the north and west boundaries, it tempers and deflects the cold, dry winds. A snowtrap hedge of Caragana, planted 60-120 ft. farther out, is particularly beneficial to plantings of fruit trees; it provides space for the accumulation of snow which might otherwise pile on trees.

and satisfying life for the gardener who plans ahead.

The Great Plains. Dry, hot weather is a more limiting factor than cold, provided the growing season is sufficiently long for plants to mature.

In the areas of dry atmosphere and interior continental climate it is a distinct advantage to have plantations of fruit trees on an eastern slope. This affords protection from the predominantly westerly drying, chilling winds, thus lessening the tendency of the trunks to sunscald. If the slope rises above a large valley the advantage is even greater because the cold air settles down below the planting.

Drought and cold are the main limiting factors in gardening on the northern Great Plains, so alleviating measures must be sought. The first step is to establish a tree windbreak or shelter belt. Usually this entails planting 3-5 rows of trees on the north and west boundaries of the garden, with a snowtrap hedge 60-100 ft. farther out. This hedge most frequently is Caragana. Trees also are planted on the south boundary, partly to screen the sun and partly to deflect hot summer winds upward. Shelter on the east is less important. The snowtrap is a safeguard that prevents drifting snow from piling on the fruit trees and crushing them down during the spring thaw. Shelter belts benefit all types of prairie gardens by tempering the winds and lessening their drying and penetrating effect. They also help to avoid breakage during heavy storms.

In large garden areas another help is provided

by ploughing early snowfalls into ridges so that they remain to blanket the area during the winter cold, and to wet the soil during the spring thaw. This ridging resists drifting and in fact aids in catching snow that may drift in from adjoining fields. An artificial dugout made near the garden helps impound precious snow waters valuable for summer irrigation and for thorough watering in late October.

One advantage of gardening in the northern regions is that much of the land is deep and rich in nitrogen and other vital plant food, therefore the soil does not require the use of inorganic fertilizer.

In spots where the prairie soils carry alkali, gardening is narrowed to crops and plants that are relatively alkali-tolerant, such as the Russian Olive and Buffalo Berry. Plants sensitive to alkali, such as Amur Maple (Acer Ginnala), Rugosa Roses and Meadowsweet Spiræas, should not be planted.

Some parts of the western plains are affected by "chinook" winds, which, coming from the warm Japan current in the Pacific, cause pronounced winter thaws. These spells spur the plants to break their winter dormancy and frequently cause serious loss of flower buds.

New Plants. Siberian Elm and Nanking or Manchu Cherries from Central China are much less adaptable to far northern gardens than are the same species indigenous to northern Manchuria. Enterprising nurserymen are now featuring especially hardy strains of ornamental plants and fruits. In recent years an assortment of valuable hardy strains of trees, shrubs, and flowers has been made available through importation from Manchuria, Korea, Mongolia, Tibet, Turkestan, the mountains of western China, and northern Europe, including the rather dryland steppes of Russia. Some of the shrubs have a tendency to retain their fruits well into the winter.

Seed importations from the Orient, Africa and Europe have recently extended the range of vegetables such as Watermelons, Muskmelons, Eggplants, Cucumbers, Chinese Cabbage, and Soybeans, for northern gardens.

Flower gardens and borders have also benefited from such importations. Some fine-textured strains of Crested Wheat Grass from Russia are appreciated for lawns in the dry prairies when facilities for watering are not available. They are remarkably tolerant of dry conditions.

The extreme cold area is the domain of the plant breeder. It is he who should be credited with making horticulture the interesting avocation it is for so many thousands of home owners in the far North. Variety lists are constantly changing and the northern frontier for each species is steadily retreating toward the Arctic.

Evergreens and plants with bright twig color are especially suitable for adding cheerfulness to the winter scene. Among the evergreens are Junipers, Arborvitae, Spruce, Pines, Canada Yew (Taxus canadensis), Oregon Grape (Mahonia Aquifolium), Dwarf Euonymus (E. nanus), and Pachistima. Bark color in cheering tones is carried by several Dogwoods, the Amur Maple (Acer Ginnala), Sugar Maple (A. saccharum) and Mountain Maple (A. spicatum), Birches, Peking Lilac, Sand Cherry, Pin Cherry (Prunus pensylvanica), Prunus Maakii, Saskatoon (Amelanchier alnifolia), Lemoine Mock Orange (Philadelphus Lemoinei), Korean Bridal Wreath (Spiraea trichocarpa), Japanese Barberry, many Roses, Willows, some Viburnums and many other plants.

Excellence of Bloom. People from more southerly territory are impressed with the vigor and durability of flowers in northern gardens. The relatively cool, dewy nights permit the plants to refresh themselves against the heat of the warm summer days. The resulting excellence of the flowers helps to compensate for the shorter season of flowering herbaceous plants.

Many of the cool-weather flowers like Peonies, Sweet Peas, and various annuals have a much longer season in this area than when they are grown farther south. Delphinium, Monkshood, Lupine and Begonias excel in northern gardens. Bloom is available from April, when the Pasque Flower and the Siberian Squill usher in the season of flowers, until October, when Chrysanthemums and Asters falter and fade.

The Great Temperate Area

Massachusetts, Connecticut, Rhode Island, Central and Southern New York, New Jersey, Pennsylvania, Maryland, District of Columbia, Western Virginia, West Virginia, Western North Carolina, Northwestern Georgia, Tennessee, Kentucky, Ohio, Indiana, Michigan, Illinois, Arkansas, Missouri, Kansas, Iowa, Nebraska, Oklahoma

Many of the original settlers of these states came from homes that had gardens, and once their houses had been built in the new world, gardens followed very quickly. All along the eastern seaboard there is an old tradition of gardening, and when the pioneers began to push on to the Middle West they carried the tradition with them as well as the seeds and plants. The temperate climate makes it possible to grow a very wide variety of plants.

It is therefore natural that in this area there are more gardens and a keener horticultural interest than in any other. Here are the oldest horticultural societies, the largest number of garden clubs, garden centers and libraries, botanic gardens, arboretums, parks, nurseries, and horticultural schools. Both in public and in private life gardening has an important place.

Topography and Climate. The Appalachian Mountains run from northeast to southwest, from Canada to Georgia. They do not reach great altitudes, only a few of the highest peaks being over 6,000 ft. Most of the mountaintops are covered with trees, often dwarfed by the winds. Frequent showers and mists keep the hillsides green. Snow falls early, and especially on the north slopes remains late into the spring. In

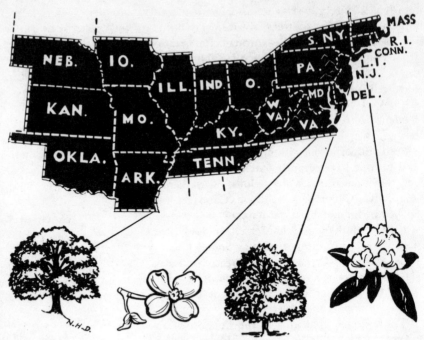

The great temperate area cuts across the middle of the continent. It varies widely in temperature, rainfall, soil and altitude, but a general lack of extremes in these factors produces vegetation similar in character throughout the area. Predominant plants of various parts of the area are the Oak of the middle western states, the Dogwood of Virginia and the Carolinas, the Maple of New England, and the Rhododendron of the Appalachian Mountains.

these mountains the soils are mostly acid, but there are many limestone ridges where a different flora persists.

Between the mountains and the fertile coastal plain lies the Piedmont, a rolling country with rich soil and abundant vegetation. Beyond the mountains to the west are the great rivers, the Ohio and the Tennessee flowing into the Mississippi, the typical prairies, and the corn and wheat fields of the plains states.

There is a wide range of temperature throughout the area. In Pennsylvania, New York and southern New England it may vary from zero to 100 degrees F., but in the Middle West the variation is greater. In Michigan, Nebraska and Iowa temperatures of 30 or 40 degrees below zero in winter and 105 degrees F. or more in summer are not unusual, while in Kansas and the southern part of the Middle West the range may be from zero to 110 or 120 degrees F.

The rainfall along the eastern coast is about 40 in. a year, and fog, which is of great benefit to plants, is prevalent. West of the Mississippi the rainfall decreases and the sunlight is more brilliant. Prevailing winds in summer are from the southwest. Many parts of the west are exceedingly dry. There is considerable snow, but

owing to the many periods of alternate thawing and freezing, snow coverage is not adequate for protection of plants, and they suffer much winter injury.

In most of the area the rainfall is abundant, but there is no part of it that may not suffer from severe droughts. This is especially true of those states as far west as Nebraska and as far south as Oklahoma, but even in the northern states of the Atlantic seaboard droughts can do much damage. Often plants weakened by lack of water during the growing season succumb to winter injury, so that winter hardiness often depends on the amount of summer and autumn rainfall.

Plants in this area do not grow so rapidly during the summer months as those to the north where the days are longer, but the growing season is more extended because spring comes earlier and autumn frosts are later. At the center of the area, in Pennsylvania for instance, spring planting may be done the first week in April or before, and tender plants may be set out by the middle of May. Killing frosts are not expected until late September or the middle of October. There are years when there are no heavy frosts until early November.

[10—8]
Rhododendron catawbiense album

[10—8a]
Rhododendron carolinianum

[10—9]
Moses-in-a-Boat
(Rhoeo discolor)

[10—9a]
Flowers of Moses-in-a-Boat
(Rhoeo discolor)

[10—9c]
Castor Bean
(Ricinus communis)

[10—9b]
Rondeletia odorata

The Great Temperate Area of North America is so big that climatic conditions differ greatly. In Boston, spring planting dates are about two weeks later than in eastern Pennsylvania, and autumn frosts come earlier. In the South there is a much earlier spring and longer autumn.

The southern section is especially susceptible to danger from late spring frosts. This is not because such frosts are especially severe, but because prolonged warm spells may start unseasonable growth that is nipped when normal winter weather returns. This happens not infrequently in Maryland, Virginia, Georgia, Tennessee or Kentucky. It may, of course, happen anywhere, but in New England and the Middle West, where it is colder, there is far less chance of spring growth starting so early that it may be caught by frost.

Soils differ greatly. Those of New England tend to be shallow and rocky. Property lines are marked by stone walls rather than by the post and rail fences of Pennsylvania and Virginia, or by the wire of the western plains. The rounded stones are evidence of the retreating glacier that covered most of New England some 30,000 years ago. The presence of stones does not necessarily mean infertility, but the vegetation growing in stony soil will suffer from drought and winds. Fortunately New England does not often have prolonged droughts or hurricanes, but when such violent weather does occur there is more damage than in an area where heavier, deeper soils produce stronger root systems.

The coastal plain has a sandy soil, acid in reaction. This area is newer land, geologically speaking, than that farther inland. Such soil produces certain excellent crops, as witness the truck farms and orchards in New Jersey and Maryland.

In the Piedmont the soil is richer due to the accumulation of decomposed vegetation on ground untouched by glaciation for many thousands of years. Except for steep, rocky slopes or where man has "mined" the soil, this section has good topsoil, but not so deep as farther west, where the rich, black soil may be ten feet deep or more.

Rainfall, temperature, soil and altitude, all of which directly affect plants, vary greatly in the different parts of this area. Yet from a gardening standpoint the general vegetation is the same. To the north of the area hardwood trees give place to evergreens; to the south there are first the Loblolly Pines (Pinus Taeda) and barren growth of the sandy coast, and beyond is the country where Magnolia grandiflora and Live Oaks thrive and tender plants grow outdoors.

Native Plant Material. Throughout the temperate area the predominant plants tend to be of the same general character. In the Appalachians the trees are mostly hardwoods: Oaks, Maples, Beech and some Birches, Hemlock and Pines. The fall coloring is deep red with scarlets and yellows. In places there are Rhododendron and Azalea in large quantities. Along the coastal plain, where the soil is acid and very sandy, Pitch Pine (Pinus rigida) abounds with White Cedar, Holly, Laurel, Sweet Gum, Azalea, Magnolia virginiana, Sweet Pepperbush and Bayberry. Both in the East and West the river valleys abound with Sycamore, Red Maple and many other deciduous trees. In the plains states from Indiana and Illinois to Iowa and Nebraska there are Hickories, Oaks, Elms, Box Elder and Buckeyes, and everywhere the natural prairie grasses.

The rolling country near and around the main rivers is alike and extremely picturesque in all parts of the area, but the plant material becomes richer as it nears the coast where typical plants are the Tulip Tree, Ash, Sweet Gum, Sour Gum, Dogwood, Cherry and Hickory, with Red and White Maples (Acer saccharinum) and Alders in the river bottoms.

The middle states along the eastern seaboard have a particularly large number of native plants because this is the meeting place of many northern and southern species that reach their limit in Pennsylvania and New Jersey. The humidity makes it possible to grow many plants that do not succeed farther inland, and the proximity of the sea tempers both the extreme cold and heat found west of the Alleghenies. The fact that there are both acid and alkaline soils is also responsible for a greater variety of plants than can be found in the Middle West, where practically all the soils are alkaline. Because of this combination of natural factors an extraordinary number of plants may be grown on the eastern seaboard.

Characteristic Usages of the Section. In communities that have been long settled, plant material unconsciously but inevitably reflects the general atmosphere of the countryside. Thus it is that in the rolling farm country of this area where the hills are softly rounded, trees such as Apple, Dogwood, and Cherry find a place. The hard, pointed forms of Spruce and Fir are an integral part of well-planted gardens where the background is steep and rocky. Good garden design fits the contours of the surrounding country. The 17th-century Italian garden was fitted to the rugged Italian hillsides but could not be adapted to the flat seashore of Holland. Just so do the gardens on a rocky Connecticut hillside differ from those in a level section of Indiana or New Jersey.

A hilly terrain produces gardens with different levels, while flat land can afford to emphasize horizontal rather than vertical lines. Rock gardens fit well into rough, stony country but seem artificial and out of place in flat, well-kept surroundings. Wild gardens are appropriate where they form a transition between the cultivated area around the house and natural country beyond. Rough stone steps and retaining walls are characteristic of southern New England and Pennsylvania. Brick and cut limestone terraces and walls are used father west. In the colder part of the region windbreaks are important, while in the warmer section shade trees are needed. Ponds or fountains are found in many gardens. Water is not only attractive, but also a practical aid in times of drought. The garden, an important part of the home, is closely connected with it in plan so that the owner may really live in his garden. A definite place to sit and dine in pleasant weather has become an integral feature of the gardens in this section.

Lawns are an important attraction. Except in the drier parts of the South and Southwest, grass can be grown without excessive difficulty.

Flowering shrubs are another attraction. Lilacs, Mock Oranges, Viburnums and innumerable others are used in endless combination and quantity. Good herbaceous borders are possible, although the hot summers prevent them from being as fine as the ones farther north. Spring bulbs such as Daffodils and Tulips and great quantities of annuals are used to supplement these borders. Annuals have a long season and do well, but they lack the brilliant colors of more northern gardens. There are many fine specialty gardens such as rock gardens, Peony gardens, Rose gardens and Iris gardens.

Many of the same plants that grow along the seacoast from Boston to Washington can also be seen throughout the middle west, northwest, and southwest boundaries of this great area, but as one travels from the sea the total number of varieties of plants that can be grown is very much less. Temperature is one great factor. The prevalence of lime is another, as this prohibits growing Rhododendron, Azaleas, Mountain Laurels, Blueberries and many other plants. However, the deeper soil of the West often results in finer individual specimens.

Garden practices are everywhere greatly affected by natural conditions. In the North spring planting is the rule. In the South, with its extreme heat and long summer drought, autumn planting is preferable. In most of this large temperate area both spring and autumn planting is possible, although fall planting requires mulching against the extremely cold winter. In most of the area autumn planting can be done in October and November, and even later south of Philadelphia.

From Illinois west many plants that flourish in the East are not reliably hardy, perhaps because they are weakened by long droughts and then, in their weakened condition, are winter-killed. At the Morton Arboretum near Chicago, for instance, evergreens cannot be grown as easily as they can east of the Alleghenies. In Nebraska many common eastern plants such as Dogwoods, Tulip Trees and Magnolias are reputed to be tender, yet occasionally they may be found in gardens. Sometimes this is because they are in sheltered places, but it is probably more often because the gardener has the familiar "green thumb" and has planted carefully and tended them affectionately for the first few years while they were getting established.

Gardeners in the more difficult areas are learning to grow more plants. The climate used to be a convenient excuse, but the comparative lack of plants probably was due more to the lack of garden traditions and the absence of local nurseries where interesting plants could be seen. These sections no longer look to the East for garden inspiration and material. The splendid agricultural and gardening schools of the various states are, to a large degree, responsible for this. Credit should also be given to the great numbers of active garden clubs, whose members, having visited fine gardens in other sections, went home determined to equal or surpass them.

The Middle West has been the home of great progress in Iris and in Peonies. The more conservative East has hesitated to plant the new varieties that the more progressive West has already adopted. Many of the plants growing in the older gardens have been superseded by modern improvement and should be removed. The changes have been rapid, and in such quickly maturing groups as Iris, Dahlias and Gladiolus, for example, the developments have come so fast that it has been almost impossible for the ordinary gardener to keep up with them.

If the East Coast has the advantage of a greater number of plants it also suffers from a greater number of pests and weed infestations. It has been long settled, and "civilization" has done much to upset the balance of nature. Between Boston and Washington, and west to Pittsburgh and Cleveland are to be found many serious pests such as Gypsy and Brown-Tail Moths, the Corn Borer, Mexican Bean Beetle, Peach Yellows, and Fire Blight, and various diseases of Lilies, Tulips and Daffodils. All such pests follow the development of gardening and are made worse by the upset of natural conditions where birds are driven away, and beneficial insects are killed, and also perhaps by the weakening of plant constitutions through soil deficiencies or by too great stimulation from the use of fertilizers.

This area has gardening advantages and disadvantages peculiar to itself. Even the oldest and most experienced gardeners have much to learn about their own climate and the type of plants they may grow.

Gardening cannot stand still. Gardeners should endeavor to understand better the type of climate in which they live, and the type of soil in which they work. It is easier to have good gardens by working with nature and growing plants adapted to soil and climate than to fight nature by trying to grow those that cannot be made to thrive without the use of exceptional ability and energy.

The activities of gardeners are limited by nature. Within the limitation they can create fine gardens where many plants may be well grown.

Southern Atlantic and Gulf States

Tidewater Virginia, Eastern North Carolina, Eastern South Carolina, Eastern and Southern Georgia, Florida, Alabama, Mississippi, Louisiana

The great region referred to as the Coastal Plain borders the Atlantic Ocean and the Gulf of Mexico. It is, comparatively, a lowland area that does not begin to rise materially until a considerable distance inland. The area in Tidewater Virginia is narrow but it widens southward until a large part of Georgia and all of Florida are included. Gradually the region rises, first into rolling lands, then into the mountains and foothills on the west and north where both the native and cultivated plants are much the same as those in regions to the north. Along the Atlantic coast there are numerous low-lying islands a short distance off shore where the climate is milder than in adjacent areas of the mainland.

Topography and Climate. Rainfall, 50 in. or more annually, is ample for plant growth, but often it is poorly distributed, the greater amount falling during the summer months. There are in the region three localities where rainfall is particularly heavy. These are the North and South Carolina area where the boundary between the two states reaches the Atlantic, the Mobile region, and the general area where the Mississippi reaches the Gulf. In Florida the annual rainfall averages about 53 in. over the entire state and about three quarters of this falls between June and November. Humidity during the summer season is high. Winters in much of the region are relatively dry and gardeners find it necessary to supplement rainfall with irrigation water obtained from rivers, lakes, canals or wells.

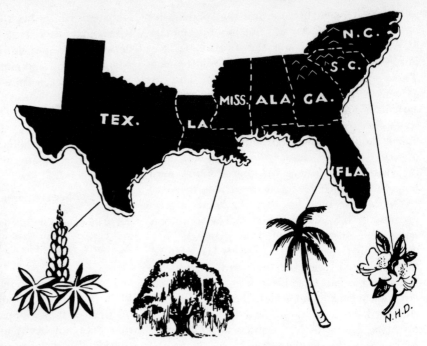

In the southern Atlantic and Gulf states the climate ranges from warm and temperate to tropical. The Lupine flourishes in the temperate climate of Texas; South Carolina is known for its Azalea gardens. Farther south there is more exotic vegetation: the moss-hung Live Oak and the Palm.

Throughout the area, summers are very warm although tempered by winds from Ocean and Gulf, and by frequent showers. In winter much of the area is subject to sudden drops in temperature caused by masses of cold air moving southward through the central states. The temperature may drop more than 50 degrees within a few hours. At varying intervals freezing temperatures are reached, particularly along the Gulf coast.

Soils for the most part are sandy, in some places to considerable depth, while in others they are underlaid with clay. There are also clay areas. While outcroppings of limestone are found here and there, acid soils predominate. There are also alluvial soils brought down from higher areas by the rivers that flow to Ocean or Gulf. The fertility of the lighter soils can be maintained with organic matter and the wise use of commercial fertilizer. Yields of garden crops are high and beautiful gardens have been developed and kept through the years.

Native Plant Material. Evergreen native growth predominates. Pines of several kinds, including Longleaf, Slash and Sand, are common throughout the region and are almost always a part of the landscape. Oaks of many species are abundant. Of these there are evergreen, nearly evergreen and deciduous kinds. Hollies in a number of forms are present. Bull Bay (Magnolia grandiflora), the finest broad-leaved American evergreen, is widely distributed. Loblolly Bay (Gordonia Lasianthus), Sweet Bay (Magnolia virginiana), Cherry Laurel, Wax Myrtle (Myrica cerifera) and others are native evergreens. The Camphor Tree, an introduced evergreen, is widely distributed in the more southerly sections.

There are many early spring- or late winter-flowering native trees such as the Plums, Silverbell, Dogwood, Crab Apple, Redbud and Fringe Tree, all of which are fine garden trees. There are a number of fine native flowering shrubs, Azaleas of several species (11 are native in Georgia), Viburnum, Illicium, Mountain Laurel and Titi (Cliftonia), to mention only a few. Palms of a few species are widely distributed, the most abundant and common being the Saw Palmetto and the Cabbage Palm. The number of varieties increases toward the south, and in Florida particularly there are fine Cabbage Palm forests of large extent. In lower Florida plant growth passes into a tropical phase, many of the native woody plants being closely related to or the same as those in the West Indies.

From northern Florida along the Gulf coast into eastern Texas, soils vary but climatic conditions are much the same. But from southeastern Virginia to extreme southern Florida the climatic zones run from warm and temperate through subtropical to tropical, with attendant variations in native plants as well as in those used for garden making. It is just as essential for all temperate-climate garden perennials, both woody and herbaceous, to be chilled or even frozen in winter, as it is for tropical and near-tropical plants to be kept warm during the same season. Consequently cool- or cold-climate plants, for the most part, are not suited to regions far south. Such plants as Peony, perennial Phlox, Forsythia, Weigela, Gooseberry, Raspberry, Horseradish and Rhubarb are not suited to regions of warm winters. There are some plants, such as the evergreen thick-leaved Ligustrum and Pittosporum, that are adaptable to both the northern and southern sections of the region, but the number is limited. On the other hand annual flowers and vegetables of many kinds, like Lettuce, Spinach and Cabbage, adapted to the summers of colder sections, may be grown in subtropical regions because they come to maturity in a brief period and can be fitted into a cool season of the year. If they were longer lived and took a longer time to mature, however, they could not be grown.

Planting Seasons. For seasonal handling, annual flower and vegetable plants are divided into two groups, those grown in winter and those grown in summer. Far south the differences are not so distinctly drawn as they are farther north in the southern and southeastern region. For instance, in latitude 30 degrees N. Zinnias and Marigolds are flowered in summer, while in the lower parts of Florida plants are set out in fall and early winter to come into flower and fruit in winter and early spring. In northern Florida, Tomatoes are a spring crop. The young plants produced in frames or greenhouses are set out about the middle of March. In Florida summer vegetables are limited almost entirely to Field Peas (Cowpeas), Okra, Sweet Potatoes

and New Zealand Spinach. Throughout most of the area, Collard, a loose-leaf Cabbage, is grown the year around. Cucumber and Watermelon are spring or early summer crops. In much of the region two crops of Beans may be grown, one in autumn before frost, the other in spring before hot, humid weather sets in; and far south they are grown throughout the winter. Lettuce, Endive, Cabbage, Pansies and Calendulas are grown in winter, not in the heat of summer. They must be fitted into a comparatively short season suited to their needs. Anyone interested in gardening, but new to the region, will do well to consult local gardeners on the time of planting for any given locality.

Temperatures and season largely control the time of planting but the kinds of plants, whether deciduous or evergreen, and the manner in which they are grown also must be considered. For deciduous trees and shrubs, Dogwood, Redbud, Plum, French Mulberry and native Azaleas, the planting season extends throughout the period when they are leafless, which in most of the area is from the middle of November to the first of March. Preference should always be given to the early part of this period so that the root growth may begin and become partly established before the normal season for top growth begins. Moreover, the spring season frequently is dry and if root growth has started in advance of it, the chances for successful outcome are greatly increased. Evergreen woody plants are sometimes set out after spring growth has hardened, but far greater numbers of them are set out in winter. Many evergreens are grown in pots, or are balled and burlapped. This method of growing or handling them extends the transplanting season greatly. If set out during the warmer season of late spring and early summer months, strict attention must be given to watering and it is best that they be shaded temporarily.

Mulches. Mulching is a very valuable cultural practice in southern gardens and should be adopted wherever possible. It can be put into practice beneath shrubbery borders, foundation plantings, among Strawberry plants and in vegetable gardens. It is essential to the welfare of Azalea and Camellia plantings. In this section where rainfall is variable there are protracted dry periods, and a mulch is a great help in maintaining an even supply of moisture in the soil. It keeps the soil cooler in summer, and in winter warmer than the air above. It adds to the organic content of the soil and as it decays it supplies acid for the many plants that require an acid soil. Leaves, bark, peat and sawdust are among the most important materials used for mulching.

Lawn Care. Fine lawns can be made and maintained throughout the region, but they require careful attention. Grasses most commonly used are Bermuda, Centipede and Saint Augustine. For extended areas where a green covering of coarser grasses will answer, Bahia and Carpet Grasses are satisfactory. Any of these, when well fertilized, watered and tended, produce attractive lawns. Sometimes these grasses, all of which are commonly established with cuttings, are grown in pure stands. At other times they are mixed.

In winter, lawns turn brown. The grass dies down and looks dead although the roots remain alive. However, a fine, fresh green lawn can be maintained all year by sowing Italian Rye Grass seed in autumn, and by fertilizing, watering and caring for it throughout the winter. With the coming of early summer the Rye Grass dies out and the other grasses come up for the summer, leaving no break in the green appearance of the lawn. For places where ground cover, other than grass, is needed, there is a large number of plants from which to select. Three of the best are Hedera canariensis, Ophiopogon japonicus and Liriope spicata. The last two are very dark green and grasslike in appearance.

In the southern Atlantic and Gulf states, the change in plant types from north to south is gradual. It goes on slowly, until finally the transformation to tropical and near-tropical plants, such as the Poinsettia, grown in Florida, is quite complete. Plants there are evergreen for the most part.

Adaptability of Plant Material. Soils and soil reaction, rainfall, drainage, temperature, length of day, all have their effect upon the kind and quantity of native vegetation in any particular region. Through the ages plants of many kinds have become adjusted to conditions in the southern Atlantic and Gulf states. Exotic plants, many of which have come from the Orient, must fit into these same conditions, else they cannot grow and thrive. It is here, in contrast to more northerly sections where the number is limited, that broad-leaved evergreen trees and shrubs may be used in large numbers and in wide variety.

The total number of all kinds of plants that can be used in making gardens in this region is very great, although many common in northern gardens cannot be used. There are plants adapted to every possible use in garden plantings: trees, shrubs, herbaceous plants, bulbs, ground covers and grasses. They run from Apples and Lilacs in Tidewater Virginia, through the first Oranges in eastern South Carolina and parts of coastal Georgia, through the great Grapefruit and Orange plantings of Florida, to Mangos, Guavas and Crotons (Codiaeums) in the southerly parts of that state. Southward from southeastern Virginia to northern Florida, and westward through the Gulf country, there is much less variation in the woody plants used in garden making.

From the northerly edges of the area, where the plants used merge with those planted farther north, southward to Florida and westward to Texas, the shade trees usually used are natives. Among these, Live Oak, Laurel Oak, and other Oaks, Magnolias, Hickory, Sweet Gum and Red Maple are most common. In the garden picture Crape Myrtle, Podocarpus, Azalea, Camellia, Pittosporum, Privet, Japanese Box, Pyracantha, Spiræa, Crab Apple, oriental Magnolias, Thuja orientalis, Holly, Kalmia, Hydrangea, Dogwood, Wisteria, Honeysuckle, Carolina Jessamine, Liriope and Day Lily are seen.

These same plants are also adaptable some distance southward into Florida, but gradually their numbers are reduced, while others adaptable to warmer areas take their places in landscape plantings. The change is not abrupt but goes on slowly until finally the change-over to near-tropical and tropical plants is quite complete. There come into the garden picture Croton, Acalypha, Hibiscus, Plumbago, Schinus, Allamanda, Petrea, Bougainvillea, Solandra, Thunbergia, Jacaranda, Ficus of many kinds, Casuarina, Royal Poinciana, Palms in variety, and many, many more. For the most part all plants are evergreen, and in the general appearance of gardens from one season to another there is little change.

Within the area there are a number of fine gardens typical of the South. Some of them are very old. There are the gardens of the Charleston area (Magnolia, Middleton, Pinehurst), of Savannah (Wormsloe), of Jacksonville (Oriental Gardens), of Vero Beach (McKee Jungle Garden), and far to the south, of Miami (Fairchild Tropical Garden). Westward there are the Killearn Plantation near Tallahassee, Bellingrath near Mobile, and Jungle Gardens on Avery Island. In these gardens are to be found the plants adapted to different sections of the region; here, in a short time and limited space, visitors can see what may be grown. Their beauty is unsurpassed.

The Rocky Mountain States

Colorado, New Mexico, Wyoming, Montana, Idaho, Utah, Nevada

This area, known as the Rocky Mountain Empire, comprises about one fourth of the area of the United States and is almost as large geographically as the great temperate area. The centers of population and hence the homes and gardens are virtually all on the high plains (2,000-6,000 ft.) that border and flank the mountains, in the wide river valleys, on the broad plateaus, or in the grassy mountain parks (3,000-7,000 ft.) among and between the mountain ranges.

A temperate climate with bright, sunny days, light snow protection in winter, cool nights in summer, rainfall usually insufficient for gardens without irrigation, occasional high, dry winds and soils more or less on the alkaline side is characteristic of many parts of this region. With garden hose plus a little experience and some

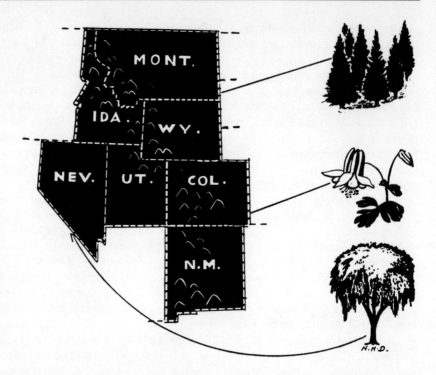

In the Rocky Mountain states, all climatic variations, from the temperate to the arctic, are reproduced as the altitude increases. In the high mountain regions are great evergreen forests. A popular tree in Nevada is the Siberian Elm. The Blue Columbine is Colorado's state flower.

common sense almost anything can be grown here that grows in the great temperate area. The centers of population, such as Denver and Salt Lake City, have trees, gardens and lawns unsurpassed anywhere and other cities and towns have or could have equally beautiful gardens. An ever-increasing number of garden clubs, horticultural societies, flower shows, arboretums and experiments by state agricultural colleges are stimulating better homes and gardens in this great inland empire extending from Canada to the Mexican border.

Topography and Climate. These states are traversed from north to south by mountain ranges, many with snow-capped peaks, covered with Pine and Aspen. Since high altitude corresponds to high latitude as far as plant growth is concerned, practically all climatic conditions, from the temperate to the arctic, are reproduced in the ascent from the plains to the peaks. Spring not only moves northward from the Mexican border to Canada, but it marches up the mountainsides as well. Spring bloom in mile-high Denver is at its peak from mid-April to mid-June. Only 40 miles west in the alpine meadows above the timber line on the Continental Di-

vide, spring does not arrive until July, when these alpine fields are blanketed with countless closely packed sky-blue Forget-me-nots, alpine Lilies, alpine Phlox, Rock Jasmine (Androsace Chamæjasme) and Moss Campion (Silene acaulis).

Of interest to gardeners is the effect of exposure and rainfall on mountain vegetation. On the sides of the foothills facing east, north and northeast where the soil does not dry out, Pine forests grow in Colorado and Wyoming with an average annual precipitation of only about 16 in. The sides of the foothills facing south and southwest get more sun and are often barren of timber. Higher up in the Spruce, Fir and Aspen forest country the annual precipitation is 20-30 in., and forests usually cover all sides of the mountains. Only a few areas have higher precipitation. Owing to the more extreme winter cold and the protection of the forest floor, the snow protects mountain plants against the freezing and thawing common to the high plains in winter.

With irrigation many attractive mountain plants grow well down on the plains. Colorado Spruce and Rocky Mountain Juniper (Juniperus scopulorum) are excellent for specimen garden evergreens. In mixed groups the Western Yellow, Foxtail and Limber Pines are used for large, bold groups and windbreaks. Piñon Pine is better for smaller scale material. Concolor Fir is beautiful either as a specimen or in groups. The native flowering shrubs, such as the rose-like Flowering Raspberry or Boulder Raspberry (Rubus deliciosus), are attractive in gardens. Perennials such as the Blue Columbine (state flower of Colorado) are popular. The Beardless Iris of high mountain meadows (Iris missouriensis) blooms in May with the Lilacs. The Mariposa or Sego Lily (state flower of Utah) varies from crimson and gold in New Mexico to white in Colorado; it will grow in plains gardens, but like the Indian Paintbrush (state flower of Wyoming), and Bitterroot (state flower of Montana), it is at its best in the mountains. Many rock gardeners experiment more or less successfully with natives and alpines, but the average plains gardener would do better to leave such things as the wild Orchids in their mountain homes.

Of more concern to most gardeners are the cultivated plants. These grow well in the well-watered high plains, plateaus and grassy parks that cover three fourths of the area. The normal rainfall is insufficient for growing gardens, but with additional watering by hose the gardens can be very beautiful. Every gardener should be aware of the importance of watering. The annual precipitation varies from 6 in. in New Mexico to about 10-17 in. on the eastern plains of Colorado, Wyoming and Montana. Most of it falls during the growing season. However, on the western side of the Rockies, in Utah, where the average is about 16 in., most of it falls in the winter months. In Idaho it varies from 6 to nearly 40 in.

The temperature ranges and extremes vary greatly. Yet many localities on the plains and in the valleys correspond closely to localities a bit farther north in the great temperate zone states, and in the Middle West and East. This area differs from the great temperate zone principally in the fact that it has more abundant sunshine, cooler summer nights, a shorter growing season, drier air and higher wind movements,

lighter rainfall in summer and, except in the mountains, less snow in winter.

The effect of climatic conditions can be best illustrated by the succession of bloom in a typical garden, and a brief outline of plants that are suited to the different states in this area.

Colorado. In Denver, with a little planning, something can be in bloom ten months of the year. The Snowdrops bloom in and between the light February snows. Warm spells come between the heavier March snowstorms and then Crocus, Scilla and Narcissus bloom. Daffodils in sunny, protected spots bloom weeks earlier than in more shaded positions. Location within the garden is important in advancing or holding back growth. A plant tender in one situation may be hardy in another spot within the same small garden. Intermittent spring snowstorms and cold waves usually end by mid-April. The warm spells bring into bloom Violets, Quinces (worth growing for forcing bloom indoors), the early dwarf Iris, flowering Almonds and Plums, Viburnum Carlesii, Hyacinths and Bleeding Heart, among others. Forsythia is beautiful when the buds and blossoms do not get caught by spring snowstorms. The April flowers continue into May and are joined by Tulips, Lilies of the Valley and Lilacs.

Nearly all Lilacs grow well almost all the way up to timber line. They like the rigorous winters, dry, warm summers and sunny skies. The bright sunshine of this area adds to the richness of the color. They bloom heavily three years out of four.

As the Lilacs pass their peak in May the Bechtel Double Crab Apple (Malus ionensis variety) comes into bloom. This and other late-flowering Crab Apples are safer than early-flowering varieties, which sometimes get caught by April frosts.

In late May in the Denver area the Rugosas and Scotch Roses that thrive without winter protection start off the Rose show that reaches its peak in June with the Hybrid Tea Roses. These latter need winter protection against alternate freezing and thawing. The Climbing Roses, which bloom on second-year wood, are spectacularly beautiful in some years and sparse-blooming in others, due to unpredictable and variable winters in that section of the country.

The Tall Bearded Irises bloom profusely in late May and early June. Flowers that reach their peak in this month include Mock Oranges, Delphinium and Peonies, which, like Lilacs, grow and bloom well almost all the way up to the timber line. The Large-flowering Clematis is fine once it is established.

In Denver gardens the June Roses and Delphinium are joined in July by the hardy long-lived Regal and Tiger Lilies. The Madonna Lily is shorter-lived. The Day Lily (Hemerocallis) blooms from June into August.

In August gardens Phlox is outstanding. Some of the world's finest varieties have been developed by Rocky Mountain horticulturists. Any August and September gaps can be filled with annuals, which bloom profusely under the bright, sunny skies. Dahlias are widely grown, and specialists of the region have developed many nationally known varieties.

Light frosts may arrive in Denver in September, but killing frosts severe enough to discourage the hardy Chrysanthemums usually do not come until late October or early November. The frost-resistant Chrysanthemums, especially the Koreans, make fine showings from September through October and sometimes up until Thanksgiving. Gardens farther north and higher should use the earliest and most frost-resistant varieties. At the end of the garden season additional color is supplied by the brilliant orange, rose and red autumn leaves of the Euonymus, the Sumac and the fruits of the Snowberries, Coral Berries and Viburnums.

Surveys of the Colorado Forestry and Horticulture Association show that the most useful large deciduous trees in the Denver area include the Silver Maple, Cut-Leaf Birch (Betula lenta variety laciniata), Hackberry, Green Ash, Honey Locust, Black Walnut, Western Broadleaf Cottonwood or Plains Poplar (Populus Sargentii), Bur Oak, American Linden and American Elm.

The most useful small deciduous trees include Hawthorns (Cratægus coloradensis, C. Crus-galli and C. mollis), Russian Olive, Bechtel's, Dolgo and Hopa Crab Apple, American Plum, European Mountain Ash and Tree Lilac (Syringa amuren-

sis variety japonica). The buds of early-flowering Crab Apples, Cherries and Peaches are liable to get caught by April frosts, although Sour Cherries and others do well, with attractive flowers and useful fruit. The Dogwood of the eastern states has not been successful, although one is growing well at Boulder, Colorado.

Boulder is closer to the mountains than Denver, more protected, with a less alkaline soil, and the following additional trees grow well there: Japanese Maple, Box Elder, Red Maple, Paper Birch, Sweet Birch, Yellow Birch, Hackberry, Dogwood, Hawthorn, Persimmon, American Beech, Purple Beech, Pignut Hickory (Carya glabra), Pecan, Shagbark Hickory, Cucumber Tree, Red Mulberry, Flowering Peach, Sweet Cherry, Pear, numerous varieties of Oak, and Linden, Tulip Tree, Sycamore, Maple, Varnish Tree (Kœlreuteria).

Farther south and in more sheltered areas are fine fruit orchards such as Apples, Peaches and Pears. For example, Grand Junction, in the Colorado River Valley on the western slope of the Rockies, is protected by tall valley walls that catch the early spring and late fall sun, and its growing season is about two weeks longer at the end of each of these seasons than Denver's. Grand Junction is famous for its Peaches, Pears, Apples and other fruits, and many trees doubtfully hardy in Denver are successful here. In less protected and more northern regions the lists have to be cut.

New Mexico. Santa Fe, Taos and Cimarron, in the higher northern areas of New Mexico, are favorable for Junipers, Pines, Firs and Spruce. At Albuquerque, in the central area, coniferous evergreens grow fairly well. Junipers and Ponderosa Pine are reliable. Colorado Blue Spruce does best when planted at altitudes, about a mile high or more. In southern New Mexico the native Arizona Cypress is popular. The flowering Peach is one of the first trees to bloom in the spring.

The following short list of trees widely grown in New Mexico under irrigated conditions is furnished by J. V. Enzie of the New Mexico College of Agriculture.

Deciduous: Arizona Ash, or Velvet Ash (Fraxinus velutina), thornless Honey Locust, Red

Mulberry, Mountain Cottonwood, or Lanceleaf Poplar (Populus acuminata), Balm of Gilead, Rio Grande Poplar (Populus Wislizenii) and other Poplars, Weeping Willow, Siberian Elm and Pecan.

Evergreen: Deodar, Arizona Cypress (Cupressus arizonica), Italian Cypress (Cupressus sempervirens), Jerusalem Pine (Pinus halepensis), Western Red Cedar (Juniperus scopulorum), Eastern Red Cedar (Juniperus virginiana).

Wyoming. W. C. Edmondson, of the University of Wyoming, furnishes the following list of some of the best and most useful plant materials suitable in the three typical areas of Cheyenne, Casper and Sheridan:

Trees: American Elm, Green Ash, Russian Olive, Hackberry and Honey Locust.

Shrubs: Honeysuckle, Cotoneaster, many Lilacs, Dogwood and Spiræa.

Vines: Woodbine, English Ivy, Purple Clematis.

Perennials: Shasta Daisy, Peony, Phlox, Chrysanthemums, Oriental Poppy, Iris, Delphinium. Most annuals grow satisfactorily.

Montana. Many of the finest ornamental plants suitable for the middle and southern Rocky Mountain states are hardy. Elevations are for the most part lower in Montana than in Colorado and Wyoming, which compensates to a large extent for its more northerly latitude. The following lists are recommended by V. E. Iverson, of the Agricultural Experiment Station, Bozeman, for average conditions in Montana, particularly the area around Missoula. In some sections, however, the climate is too severe to grow any except the hardiest trees in this list:

Deciduous: Green Ash, Paper Birch, American and European Mountain Ash, American Elm, Bolleana Poplar (Populus alba variety pyramidalis), Weeping Birch, Norway and Schwedler's Maple, Flowering Crab, Linden, Mountain Alder (Alnus tenuifolia) and Mountain Maple.

Evergreens: Colorado Spruce, Black Hill Spruce, Western Red Cedar (Juniper), Siberian Arborvitae, Pfitzer's Juniper.

Idaho. E. R. Bennet, Extension Horticulturist Emeritus, University of Idaho, states that practically all trees and shrubs that can be grown north of the Mason-Dixon Line can be grown in a large part of Idaho. There are probably 500 different species that can be grown; however, a few sections are too high for some of the best trees. He recommends especially the following small trees: European Hornbeam, Redbud, Yellowwood, Dogwood, Cratægus (50 species), purple-leaved Plum, European Mountain Ash.

Utah. The climates of Utah and Idaho are influenced by Pacific coast conditions, hence, except in local desert areas, are more moist and mild than the climates of Colorado and Wyoming. Laval S. Morris, Extension Landscape Architect, Utah Agricultural College, particularly recommends for high mountain valleys the native Aspen, Squawbush (Condalia spathulata), Mountain Maple and most of the evergreens.

For low valleys with a high alkaline soil he recommends Russian Olive, Green Ash, Lindens, Ailanthus, Golden Rain Tree. The French Tamarisk and Buffalo Berry are the most alkali-tolerant shrubs, but several others, especially among the natives, accept varying degrees of alkalinity.

Nevada. Prof. P. A. Lehenbauer, of the University of Nevada, Reno, reports that plants commonly used in ornamental planting in the northern half of Nevada include the following:

Trees: Siberian Elm, Green Ash, London Plane, Black Locust, Flowering Plums and Crab Apples, Rocky Mountain Spruce, Norway Spruce, Incense Cedar, Ponderosa Pine, Desert Juniper, Arborvitae.

Shrubs: Spiraeas, Honeysuckles, Forsythias, Lilacs, Barberry, Japanese Quince, Snowberry, Rugosa Rose, Mugho Pine, Junipers (Juniperus horizontalis, J. chinensis, J. chinensis variety Pfitzeriana and others).

Vines: Boston Ivy, English Ivy, Trumpet Vine, Clematis, Japanese Honeysuckle, Climbing Roses.

The Southwest

Arizona, Southern and Central California

The Southwest is a land of superlatives. The biggest canyon (the Grand Canyon of the Colorado River in Arizona), the highest mountain in the United States (Mt. Whitney, 14,495 ft., in the Sierra Nevadas of California), the lowest valley (Death Valley, 276 ft. below sea level,

The Southwest runs to extremes in climate and in altitude, and supports a wide variety of plant life. In California is found the giant Redwood, peculiar to the state, and such plants as the California Poppy. The Grape, although not a native, is grown successfully. The desert regions of Arizona produce many strange and beautiful varieties of the Cactus.

in California), the oldest, biggest living thing (the General Sherman Tree in Sequoia National Park) are all found within its boundaries.

Topography and Climate. The superlatives just mentioned mean extremes of climate. There is a band along the coast of relatively high humidity and comparatively even temperature between winter and summer. The width of this area depends on how close the mountains come to the shore line. The Santa Lucia Mountains south of Monterey rise to over 3,000 ft. sheer out of the ocean. These coast mountains catch the rainfall, and the interior valleys, in general, are drier. Many factors enter into the picture, such as altitude, in relation to mountains to the west, orientation of the mountains and valleys, prevailing winds and the flow of rivers. The whole area has a confusion of mountain chains running every which way. For example, at Santa Barbara the Coast Range, following the coast-line, runs east and west and gives to this area a warmer winter climate than the latitude would justify. Roughly, the farther from the coast, the drier the climate; the lower the altitude, the hotter the weather. The highest temperatures are in Death Valley and the Coachella Valley.

There are vast areas of desert. The Great American Desert is not barren sand exclusively. Every once in a while it can blossom unbeliev-ably. If there is rain in sufficient quantities and if the rain comes at the right time every square inch of barren soil may be covered with flowers. This phenomenon may occur only once in ten years. Besides the annuals and bulbs of the desert there are all sorts of Cacti, Yuccas, and strange shrubs that are difficult to transplant into gardens. The rocks, naked mountains, lava flows, dry lakes and Salton Sea make the desert plants seem weird and fantastic.

There are also vast areas covered with coni-fers. The Monterey Pine (Pinus radiata), the fastest-growing Pine, is found wild in a few small scattered colonies on the coast and on the channel islands. The Torrey Pine (Pinus Torre-yana) is found only in a very small area near San Diego and Santa Rosa Island. Abies ven-usta, the Santa Lucia Fir, is found only on the Santa Lucia Mountains. The Redwood (Sequoia sempervirens), found only on the California coast, is the tallest tree on the American con-tinent. The most celebrated of all, the Big Tree (Sequoiadendron giganteum), survives only in isolated groves on the western slopes of the Sierra Nevadas. Here, too, grow other conifers

The red, purple and gold desert dotted with Sahuaro, the Giant Cactus of Arizona (Carnegiea gigantea, Arizona's state flower). In this area most garden plants must be irrigated to assure good results.

with a wider range, such as Douglas Fir (Pseudotsuga taxifolia), Red Fir (Abies magnifica) and Incense Cedar (Libocedrus decurrens).

In between there are acres of land dotted with Oaks. There are plateaus where varieties of Juniperus californica, the California or Desert Juniper, is the predominant growth.

The high altitudes of the Southwest are not

In the desert areas garden design must be functional. Only plants that can stand heat will survive. Ground cover, to cut glare and add coolness, is essential. Naturalized among rocks, typical Cacti and succulents, such as these, lend interest to the need for the practical.

limited to single peaks. There are many square miles of country above 10,000 ft. These areas are covered with alpine plants. Throughout the entire Southwest the native flora is varied and exciting. There may be many species not yet discovered, and certainly there are many wild plants not yet reported.

The majority of gardeners, however, are cultivating the soil not on mountain peaks or desert wastes, but in well-irrigated subdivisions. These subdivisions are laid out in six general climatic zones:

The coastal area.

The comparatively frost-free area where Citrus can be grown.

Interior valleys.

Areas in which the native growth consists predominantly of evergreen coniferous trees.

Areas where native growth is predominantly Oak.

Desert too cold for Citrus.

Coastal Area. Coastal gardening is quite different from any other gardening in the Southwest. The high humidity encourages the growing of Begonias, Fuchsias, Cymbidiums, Ferns and a vast array of shrubs, trees, vines, annuals, perennials and bulbs from all over the world. The rainfall may be negligible in some years, but summer fog provides humidity and the hose will supply extra moisture. Garden design is more influenced by the high cost of water than by any other factor. The only tradition of gardening is the Spanish. Spaniards were not noted for horticultural progress, but from them

Californians have taken over and developed the idea of outdoor living.

Everything about coast gardening is experimental. There are new plants introduced every year. Each one has a different effect in the garden, and each one, as it grows, may change the entire garden picture. Contrasts impractical in other parts of the district are possible in the coastal area. Not only can the home owner have Palms and Pines, but he can hang the Pines with Orchids and Fuchsias and Begonias, and grow Sempervivums and Ivy Geraniums up the Palm trunks. Those who are homesick can grow the Roses, Abelia, Privet and Magnolia that they remember in the eastern gardens and, of course, all the annual flowers.

The planting season is the entire year for coast gardens. To be sure, bulbs and bare-root dormant plants are available only at certain seasons, but plants in pots or balled plants can be put in at any time.

It is well to remember that trees that grow a foot a month are going to change the garden picture in a short time and will need room. When the tree in question comes in a gallon can and is only a foot high it is difficult to allow for its future growth. Not all trees and shrubs are fast-growing. The best way to find out what a plant is going to do is to look at a well-established specimen in the neighborhood.

Citrus Belt. The Citrus Belt is not a well-defined area. Citrus are grown in the Salt River Valley of Arizona, and around Tucson and in the foothills of the Sierras in central California on the east side of the great central valley. Old plantings are seen near Riverside, the original home of the Navel Orange, and in the Coachella and Imperial Valleys. Citrus can even be grown among the Grapes in the famous Napa Valley northwest of San Francisco.

The Citrus Belt overlaps the Coastal area, but gardening in most of it is quite different. Many varieties of Citrus like less humidity than is found near the coast. The sweetest Oranges and Grapefruit are found in the very hot valleys.

Where the temperatures rise to over 100 degrees F. day after day the emphasis in the garden is on shade. Pergolas, lath houses and roofed-over garden shelters are found in infinite

variation. Most of the temperate garden plants are grown successfully here, and all the sub-tropical plants that will tolerate low humidity flourish. Notable are the Oleanders, Olives, the Bottle Brushes (Callistemon and Melaleuca species), Elæagnus, and so forth. Plant specialists have chosen the Citrus Belt for their gardens, and new Iris, Day Lilies, Roses and Narcissus are introduced each year. Gardens of the area reflect the background and the interest of the owners. Gardens here are not quite so exotic as those on the coast, but they are just as riotous in bloom. Most annuals thrive, and many that are subject to mildew near the coast do better here. Roses are very fine.

The remaining factors in determining what can be grown are soil and water. The soil can be changed to fit the plant, except in very large gardens where it is obviously impractical to make over the soil. There is no way of removing high alkali content permanently from water. For the average gardener acid-loving plants are too hard to grow.

All gardeners in the Citrus Belt should plan their gardens so that there is shelter from the hot, dry winds that occasionally blow. There must be an area that is shady in summer and another that is sunny in winter. The garden must be limited. Cultivated plants do not blend with the burnt-to-a-crisp natural landscape that predominates for the greater part of the year. The limits may be the orchard, a screen planting, the back of a building or a wall. Planting can be restrained and harmonious, all dark green foliage, or it can be a gay riot of color. Big soft leaves are subject to damage by drought and heat. It is impossible to achieve as great a contrast in foliage size in the dry areas as it is near the coast.

It is best to plant in the fall, winter and spring. Summer is often so hot and dry that plants not established dry out. In the areas that follow, the planting seasons are spring and fall.

Interior Valleys. In the interior valleys that are too cold for Citrus, the same general garden practices are followed as in other parts of the United States with similar climate. The only difference is that often in the Southwest the background of mountain peaks may call for a rather different treatment than the plains of the Middle West. Gardening with a view means making the most of that view. It becomes the feature of the garden and is far more satisfactory than a fountain or a figure. Make a foreground for the view; be sure that none of the garden trees or shrubs are going to cut it off; frame it so that the attention doesn't wander. The Texas Umbrella Tree (Melia Azedarach variety umbraculiformis) and Jerusalem Thorn (Parkinsonia aculeata) are about the extremes that are possible in trees for this region. The first is a veritable green umbrella offering dense shade in summer while the second gives the effect of a puff of green smoke, to which clings a swarm of little red and yellow butterflies. Before starting the garden, it is important to check on the minimum temperature and to select plants that can withstand it.

Coniferous Section. The Pine woods present quite a different gardening problem from other zones. The Pine needles produce an acid reaction and plenty of humus, and many kinds of plants that will not thrive in other parts of the Southwest can be grown here. The cultural aspects do not differ from those prevailing in other parts of the United States where Pines predominate, but the problem of design may differ greatly. A garden completely enclosed by Pine woods is the same anywhere. A garden in the Pine woods with a view out over a red, purple and gold desert dotted with Sahuaro, the Giant Cactus of Arizona (Carnegiea gigantea), is quite a different story. The potted Petunia here would look a little silly. It is necessary to use a more dramatic foreground, such as Adam's-Needle (Yucca filamentosa).

Oak Area. There are many square miles in the Southwest where Oak trees are the predominant native tree. The Oaks, whether evergreen or deciduous, occur singly or in clumps in most cases and give a parklike effect to the area. In parts of Arizona they are particularly effective because of their contrast with the adjacent highly colored rock formations and deserts sprinkled with Cactus. There is a species of Oak for every climate, from the California Live Oak (Quercus agrifolia), to the Valley Live Oak (Quercus Wislizenii) and the Maul Oak (Quercus chrysolepis) that grows wild only in the mountains.

The Colder Desert Area. Gardening in desert areas that are too cold for Citrus depends on the amount and chemical analysis of the water. Only plants that can stand heat will survive. The selection of trees and shrubs depends on their resistance to cold, according to the minimum temperature of each area. There are many varieties of Palms that can stand several degrees of frost.

Garden design in desert areas must be functional. There should be protection from the wind and drifting sand. There must be ground cover, to cut glare and add coolness. Shade is essential. In general, a formal design, not necessarily the old-type symmetrical Italian or French, looks more natural than a naturalistic design, because any irrigated plant in the desert looks and is put there by the hand of man.

Gardens of the Southwest should be the most exciting of any on the continent. There is every kind of climate, every type of terrain and every type of view. The flower fields of the great seed farms vie with the fields of wild flowers. Every kind of plant except the tropical can be grown somewhere in the area.

Gardeners in this section should study the plants recommended in other parts of this book for climates similar to their own; should visit the local nurseries and botanical gardens; should explore their neighborhood and note which plants they like and how these grow, and then plan their gardens.

The ingenuity of the individual is almost the only limiting factor in gardening in the Southwest, but what makes the gardens of this region famous is their living qualities—the great variety of plant material, the multitude of fragrant flowers, their adaptation to the often spectacular settings, their contrasts and their riotous bloom.

The Pacific Northwest

Oregon, Washington, British Columbia

The Pacific Northwest is one of the world's most favored garden regions. Its climate is much like that of the British Isles, so that a vast store of horticultural wisdom applicable to this kind of climate may be drawn upon freely, thus

[10—10]
Poison Ivy
(Rhus radicans)
in flower

[10—10a]
Poison Ivy
(Rhus radicans)
in fruit

[10—11] *Rock Garden at The New York Botanical Garden*

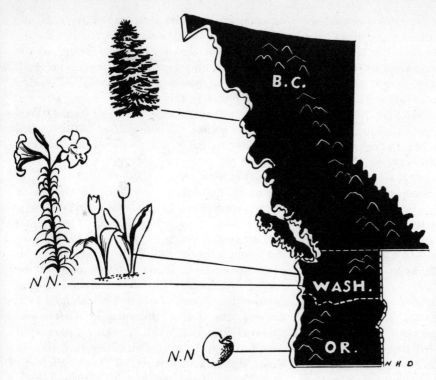

In the Pacific Northwest, the factors most influencing plant growth are mild winters, heavy rainfall, and extreme variations in altitude. Native to the region are the great Douglas Fir forests, and the favorable climate permits the cultivation of many introduced plants: Lilies, Tulips and other bulbs, the Apple and other fruits.

eliminating the expensive and time-consuming pioneering necessary in other parts of America.

This region has huge mountainous areas with snow-capped peaks. Conditions vary tremendously from the alpine meadows down to sea level, but as the vast majority of the population is found at lowland levels this section deals with the garden areas there.

The mild climate is due to the nearness of the Pacific Ocean and the warm Japan current. Winter temperature zones run east and west on the Atlantic coast but north and south on the Pacific coast. There are five natural north-south subdivisions: first, the seacoast; second and third, the east and west slopes of the coastal mountain ranges; fourth, the wide interior lowland, and fifth, the western slope of the Cascades. In southwestern Oregon the Cascade Range is connected by the Siskiyou Mountains to the Coast Range. Two great rivers, the Fraser and the Columbia, cut through the Cascade Mountains and expose the area to the extremes of the interior continental climate—hotter summers and colder winters.

The annual rainfall reaches the stupendous total of 260 in. a year on the west coast of Vancouver Island and about 140 in. a year on the western slopes of the Olympic Mountains. Only a few miles to the east there is the amazingly low average of 15 in. Other annual averages in this section are Victoria, B. C., with 27 in., Seattle with 33 in. and Portland with 48 in. The western mountain slopes have magnificent evergreen forests with Spruce and Hemlock predominating where the rainfall is more than 100 in., and Douglas Fir the predominant tree in the remainder of the area. Where the rainfall drops to 30 in. or less, the spectacularly beautiful broad-leaved evergreen, Arbutus Menziesii or Madrona, is found.

The most important characteristic of the rainfall is the marked division of wet and dry seasons. Over three quarters of the annual rainfall occurs in the six months between October and March. Gardeners offset a lack of summer rainfall by copious watering so that summer droughts seldom limit the choice of plant material. There is small difference between the average summer and winter temperatures in the greater part of the area, the least difference being on the seacoast. In the mildest coastal sections the summers are warmer and drier than they are in England. This weather is favorable for many woody plants that need to ripen their growth to be better able to stand winter cold. Many of the plants grown in full sun in England require at least partial shade here. The coastal regions not only have an exceptionally mild winter climate, but also relatively high humidity.

West, southwest, or southerly winds prevail, their greatest force being felt on the seacoast. Certain winds from the north and east, usually of short duration, bring extreme temperatures during the middle of summer and the middle of winter. A cold spell accompanied by such wind usually occurs about New Year's, and may sometimes be followed by as many as three others at intervals of several weeks. Shelter from this and from the summer wind is essential. The prevailing winds being northerly only during brief hot spells, and southerly in the cooler weather, maximum protection is needed from the south.

Late spring or early fall frosts do the most damage to plants. Fortunately they are not severe except in isolated low-lying sections or narrow interior valleys where the air drainage is poor. In the Puget Sound region especially, there are both large and small saucer-like depressions in the land. The soil in these depressions is frequently very fertile but there is always the serious menace of lack of air drainage. The selection of plants in such places must be confined to those least likely to be damaged by frosts.

The fertile soils contain ample available nitrogen but are generally deficient in phosphate and potash. Fertilizers with a high percentage of these two elements should be used. East of the Cascades the soil is predominately alkaline. West of the Cascades the soil is usually acid. One notable exception on the seacoast are the sites of old Indian clambakes, where large deposits of broken clam shells are mixed in the soil, making it necessary to limit the planting to lime-loving or lime-tolerant material.

Topography. In the narrow coastal belt west of the Coast Range the average January temperature ranges from 40-44 degrees F. and the average July temperature from 50-60 degrees F. Only occasionally does the temperature reach 90 degrees F. The rainfall ranges from 50-100 in., depending upon the nearness and height of the Coast Range, and there is little snow. The greatest wealth of native plant material of garden value is found in this locality. Gardens here can use the widest possible range of broad-leaved evergreen shrubs, including most of those used in California gardens a thousand miles farther south.

Southwestern Oregon and northwestern California have mild winters and summers with warm days and moderately cool nights. There is usually some snow every winter. The annual average in the valleys is from 7 to 19 in., with more in the mountains. This section is rich in plant material not found in other parts of the Pacific Northwest. The list includes Oregon Myrtle or California Laurel (Umbellularia californica), the Giant Chinquapin (Castanopsis chrysophylla), the Tanbark Oak (Lithocarpus densiflorus) and the comparatively rare Incense Cedar (Libocedrus decurrens). One of the most valuable of all conifers for the garden is Lawson Cypress (Chamæcyparis Lawsoniana), which has been in cultivation for many years and has yielded a multitude of horticultural forms.

The main interior lowland, although not quite so mild as the coastal strip, still has a warm temperate climate. The average January temperature ranges from 32-36 degrees F. and the average July temperature from 62-68 degrees F. The southern end of Puget Sound is a great gravelly glacial deposit and most of the ground has only a thin skin of black soil overlying beds of gravel. Considerable soil preparation is needed in this section to grow garden trees and shrubs. Farther south the winters are more severe and the summers hotter and drier due to the air drainage that follows the river valleys.

The great Douglas Fir forests have been removed from most of the area. Madrona and the native Dogwood, Cornus Nuttallii, are the two most striking native trees of garden value. The Oregon Oak (Quercus Garryana) is too slow-growing to be worth planting, but where it occurs it should be incorporated in the garden, for it is an excellent shade tree. Other plants of garden value include the Oregon Grapes (Mal-honia Aquifolium and M. nervosa), Salal (Gaul-theria Shallon), False Box (Pachistima Myrsi-nites), the handsome Giant Holly Fern (Poly-stichum munitum). Rhamnus Purshiana, source of the drug Cascara, is also native to this sec-tion.

The Pacific Northwest includes vast moun-tainous areas, wild and rugged, where many fascinating alpine plants highly valued by rock garden connoisseurs grow. In the Olympic Moun-tains are found several species that occur no-where else in the world. Among the most famous of these are Campanula Piperi, Senecio Web-steri, and Spiræa (Petrophytum) Hendersonii. The brilliant alpine and sub-alpine shrubby Penstemons are the joy and despair of English alpine enthusiasts. Aster, Erigeron, Aquilegia, Lewisia, Phlox and a host of other genera are all well represented.

Diversity of Plants. Throughout the Pacific Northwest the mild winter climate and the hu-midity of the atmosphere are sufficient to grow many choice broad-leaved evergreen shrubs. This humidity becomes dangerously low for short periods in the vicinity of the Columbia River but broad-leaved evergreen shrubs can be carried through these periods by sprinkling their foliage with a fine mistlike spray of water. The broad-leaved evergreens such as English Holly, the best new hybrid Rhododendrons, Camellias, Azaleas and Heaths form the most noteworthy single group of woody garden plant material. Also a multitude of bulbs, herbaceous perennials and hybrid Roses grow superbly here. The wid-est possible range of herbaceous plants can be grown, from tiny alpines like the Kabschia Saxi-frages (see Saxifraga) to the huge, exotic-looking waterside plants such as Gunnera mani-cata, and all the popular much-hybridized kinds such as Delphinium, Peonies, Bearded Irises, Michaelmas Daisies, Phlox, Columbine and Chrysanthemums.

Garden material has been drawn from all over the world. Western China has been especially generous in its contributions, most spectacular of which has been a veritable host of Rhodo-dendron species. Besides these a number of Bam-boos, Barberries, Cotoneasters, Hollies, Hyperi-cums, Viburnum, Irises, Lilies, Primroses and many others grace the gardens.

Japan has contributed broad-leaved evergreen shrubs and some of the most beautiful of all the deciduous flowering trees—Cherries, Apricots and Plums. Broad-leaved evergreen shrubs in-clude such well-known favorites as Aucuba, Camellia, Euonymus, Fatsia, Pieris (Androme-da), Raphiolepis and Skimmia. The southwest-ern tip of South America has given Berberis Darwinii and a number of other species, includ-ing B. buxifolia, B. empetrifolia, and the better-known hybrid, B. stenophylla, which has more than a dozen distinct named variations, all valuable garden shrubs. There are several species of Escallonia hailing from South Ameri-ca that make useful shrubs for coastal gardens, although they are not so well suited to inland valleys.

New Zealand has contributed from its moun-tain sections such shrubs as the Daisybush (Olea-ria Haastii). The Mediterranean regions of southern Europe and northern Africa have con-tributed the Laurus nobilis, Grecian Laurel or Sweet Bay, and Myrtus communis, the classic Myrtle; numerous Cistus, both species and hy-brids; the Brooms, Cytisus and Genista; the Gorses; the Cherry Laurel from southern Europe and Asia Minor, and its numerous varieties; Pyracantha coccinea, and the magnificent much-planted species of Cedrus, the Blue Atlas Cedar, the Cedar of Lebanon, and the Deodar. From the high mountains of Mexico comes the popu-lar drought-resistant Mexican Orange (Choisya ternata). Shrubs from New Zealand, Australia and the Mediterranean are especially valuable for planting in locations that are watered very little during the summer. They may be com-bined with American shrubs such as Manzanita (Arctostaphylos) and Ceanothus to cover hot, dry banks.

Garden Development. Rock gardens have been exceedingly popular, but their popularity is waning due to the high maintenance they re-quire. Heather gardens provide an interesting and useful low maintenance treatment and since the soils here are almost entirely acid, these and all other ericaceous shrubs are readily grown. For those who live in or on the fringes of the native conifer forests there are wonderful opportunities to develop woodland gardens, where many choice and delicate plants can be made perfectly at home. On the margins of lakes, streams and artificial pools, luxuriant vegetation can be extensively utilized to form charming water gardens.

The foundation planting of houses is most effectively accomplished with broad-leaved evergreens of appropriate sizes and shapes and foliage textures. The structure of the informal garden also depends largely on the groupings of broad-leaved evergreen shrubs accentuated by well-placed deciduous flowering trees. The "outdoor living room" so much publicized in horticultural literature is practical in the Pacific Northwest for summer use if the area can be sufficiently screened from the prevailing winds by hedge, wall or fence. It should face south and west with a large deciduous tree to temper the heat of the summer sun.

The strong naturalistic character of almost all sections of this region—forest, woodland, lake, stream, valley and hillside—all suggest informal garden treatment. Also, being free from traditions, less responsive to Old World influences, and with the freedom and vigor of the pioneer spirit still evident, there is a constant reaching out for new things and a willingness to experiment that is making horticultural history.

Garden Practices. The ground is open and free from frost during most of the winter, so deciduous plant material may be moved at any time during its dormant period, from November through February. Evergreens, both broad-leaved and coniferous, are best transplanted immediately after they start into active growth in March or early April. The next best time for evergreens is late September or October. Evergreen material that must be ordered from distant nurseries should be obtained in the early spring rather than in the fall. A plant set out in the fall may have been weakened by a long journey, and is more liable to succumb during a hard winter, especially if it is near the border line of hardiness.

Herbaceous perennials are best planted out or divided in March and April. Bedding plants should be put out between the middle of May and the end of June because, when they are planted earlier, they often are checked by cold nights. Hardy annuals such as Larkspur, Clarkia, Godetia, and so on, may be sown in the early fall or from mid-February on. The same is true of vegetables.

It is almost impossible to give trees and shrubs too much water in the late spring and early summer, but many gardeners injure their plants by too frequent watering at other seasons. An easy method of watering is to scratch shallow ditches three or four inches deep around and between the plants and allow the water from the hose to run in slowly for several hours.

This works well for deciduous trees and shrubs and herbaceous plants, but is not so satisfactory for evergreens, which respond better to overhead sprinkling. This should not be done when the hot summer sun is on the foliage. It is better to leave a sprinkler running for several hours at night.

The rain in late spring and early summer seldom comes in sufficient amounts to soak the soil thoroughly, and each rain is almost immediately followed by a southerly wind that evaporates the moisture. For this reason the first year a planting is becoming established it should be thoroughly soaked every ten days from April to late August. This may produce lush growth and less bloom, but strong growth is of paramount importance.

The second and third seasons the watering can be cut down considerably. Weeds should not be allowed to rob the soil of moisture. It is well to hoe the soil to check evaporation immediately after watering. A mulch of compost, leaf mold, or grass clippings helps to keep the ground cool and conserve moisture.

Lawns and flower areas require much more watering than shrubs, but thorough soaking once a week (or in the hottest weather twice a week) is all that is necessary. Sprinkler systems are often installed to water the entire garden indiscriminately, which is a great mistake. From the standpoint of practical garden maintenance, it does not pay to mix flowers liberally among the shrubs as it complicates the watering problem. However, bulbs may be planted in shrub areas to good advantage.

Certain deciduous flowering trees and shrubs, like the flowering Plums and Apricots, the hybrid flowering Quince, and vines like Wistaria, tend to make excessive soft, rank growth during the summer unless they are planted in very hot, dry locations. To combat this, summer pruning may be resorted to, and it is an especially needed operation in Pacific Northwest gardens. The purpose of summer pruning is to control and direct the creative energy of the plant in such a way as to form growth only where it is wanted and to encourage the production of flower and fruit. Summer pruning is concerned entirely with the new, unripened current season's growth.

The gardeners and garden lovers in this area can look forward to thrilling progress in the field of horticulture. Richly endowed with the most favorable conditions of climate and terrain and a wealth of native plant material, the Pacific Northwest is in a position to make the fullest possible use of a vast store of horticultural knowledge and the treasures of plant material garnered by plantsmen in other lands.

REHMANNIA (Rehman'nia). Tender herbaceous plants with large, foxglove-like flowers. They are suitable for growing in pots in a greenhouse or out of doors in sheltered localities. These attractive free-flowering plants are found wild in China and Japan. They belong to the Figwort family, Scrophulariceae, and the name commemorates Joseph Rehmann, a physician of Leningrad.

A Beautiful Flowering Plant. R. angulata is

The pink-flowered Rehmannia angulata, a showy herbaceous plant for the greenhouse, is sometimes used for summer bedding.

the principal kind in cultivation. This has fleshy roots and forms a large rosette of leaves close to the soil, from the center of which several flower spikes arise and attain a height of 3-4 ft., bearing flowers practically their full length. The blooms closely resemble the Foxglove in shape and coloring, but are larger, less regular in outline, and reddish-pink, the throats being dotted with orange. The leaves are lanceolate (lance-shaped), 4-6 in. in length, prominently veined, and have deeply divided edges.

When raised from seeds, the seedlings exhibit great diversity, the flowers varying in size, shape and coloring, so that when a good variety is obtained it is necessary to perpetuate it by cuttings, to keep the offspring true to type.

Suitable for a Cool Greenhouse. Rehmannia angulata is an ideal plant for cultivation in a greenhouse with a minimum winter temperature of 45 degrees. Although the plants can be grown for several years, the best results are obtained by raising new plants annually from seeds or cuttings.

Seeds are sown in midsummer to produce flowering plants in the following year. Well-drained pans filled with light, sandy soil are used and the seeds are scattered thinly on the surface. A layer of sifted soil is sprinkled over them and the pan is covered with a sheet of glass and set in a greenhouse or frame.

When the seedlings have developed the first pair of leaves, they are transplanted, 2 in. apart, into other pans or flats of light soil.

When large enough, they are potted separately in 3-in. and, later on, in 5-in. pots, in which they remain for the winter. In March they are repotted in 7-in. pots, in which they produce their flowers in early summer.

How to Take Cuttings. As soon as the flowers have faded, the spikes are cut down to encourage the formation of basal shoots, which form a ready means of propagation. These are detached and inserted around the edges of small, well-drained pots filled with sandy soil. They are watered, placed in a cold frame or greenhouse, and covered with a hand light until roots are formed, when they are treated as advised for the seedlings.

Root Cuttings. The plants will also produce plantlets from their roots. Stand the pot on an ash (or gravel) bed on the greenhouse bench and allow the roots to grow through the bottom of the pot; on being severed, the roots left in the bed will produce numerous plantlets.

Summer and Winter Management. From April until the flowers have faded these plants should be liberally supplied with water, and occasional applications of liquid fertilizers are beneficial when the flower spikes are forming. Less water is needed later and the plants should be placed in a cold frame while the basal shoots are developing. During the winter months watering must be done very carefully, for if the soil becomes waterlogged the roots will decay, resulting in the sudden collapse of the plants.

No attempt must be made to "coddle" them, as they are almost hardy and therefore require abundance of fresh air at all times. Very little shading is needed during the summer months, except during bright sunshine; for the remainder of the year full exposure to light is necessary.

Treatment of Plants Grown Out of Doors. In mild parts of North America, Rehmannia may be grown entirely out of doors. A warm, sheltered, well-drained spot is necessary and light rich soil is required. The plants are set out in April and liberally watered in dry weather. When well grown, they make a very imposing sight and continue to flower for several weeks.

New plants should be raised annually to replace those which die off or deteriorate in vigor.

The chief kind is R. angulata, pink, 3 ft. The variety Pink Perfection is superior to the type, having larger blooms of a deeper pink. Other kinds are R. glutinosa (chinensis), 2 ft., purplish; R. elata, similar to but larger than R. angulata, bright rose-purple, with yellow throat; and R. rupestris, 18 in., rose.

REINECKIA CARNEA (Reinec'kia). An herbaceous summer-flowering plant from China and Japan, suitable for outdoor cultivation in mild climates and for pots. It was introduced into Europe in 1792, but has never become a popular garden plant. From a thick creeping rootstock it throws up stems, 12-18 in. in height, which bear tubular pink flowers with six recurving lobes.

The long, narrow, strap-shaped leaves are in a large tuft and in the variety variegata they are striped with green and cream-white. This plant belongs to the Lily family, Liliaceae, and the name Reineckia commemorates J. Reinecke, a German horticulturist.

Reineckia is quite easy to cultivate and will flourish in ordinary garden soil. Positions may be found for it in the rock garden, in the perennial border, or the variegated kinds make an attractive edging. A sunny position is necessary. Planting is done in March or April and the soil must be kept moist by copious waterings in dry weather.

Every three or four years the plants are lifted, divided and replanted in freshly prepared soil, this being necessary to keep them growing vigorously and to prevent overcrowding. This method of division is the principal form of propagation.

REINWARDTIA INDICA — *Winter Flax* (Reinward'tia). An evergreen, sub-shrubby, winter-flowering plant for a warm greenhouse, which was introduced from India into Great Britain in 1779. It grows 2 ft. in height, forming a bushy shrub, clothed with obovate apple-green leaves, 2 in. long and 1 in. wide. The flowers are salver-shaped, bright yellow and an inch in diameter. They are freely produced during the winter months and are ornamental for several weeks. The individual flowers are very fleeting, but as they are produced in quick succession, a constant display of bloom is maintained. A closely related species, R. tetragyna, has pale

Reinwardtia indica, a showy greenhouse plant which bears yellow flowers in winter.

yellow flowers and requires the same culture.

Reinwardtia belongs to the Flax family, Linaceae, and the name commemorates Kaspar Reinwardt, a German scientist of the early eighteenth century.

Winter-flowering Greenhouse Plant. By repotting the plants in larger pots each year, bushy specimens 2 or 3 ft. in height are obtained; or they may be planted out in a prepared bed in the greenhouse or conservatory. The most popular method of cultivation, however, is to raise fresh plants annually, and finally to pot them in 7-in. pots; they provide bright groups of color in the greenhouse during the winter months, when flowers, especially of this color, are scarce.

Although generally regarded as a hothouse plant, Reinwardtia can be successfully grown in a greenhouse having a temperature of 50 degrees in winter.

Taking Cuttings. To ensure well-developed plants it is necessary to commence propagation in March. The best cuttings are provided by basal shoots which are obtained by cutting back the branches to two or three buds and syringing often to assist them to break into growth.

When 2 in. long, the shoots are taken off, trimmed and inserted in a well-packed bed of sand or sand and peat moss.

Provided they can be given a little bottom heat, roots form quickly, and in two or three weeks the cuttings are ready for potting.

Pinching the Shoots. When the plants are well rooted in 3-in. pots, the tips of the shoots are pinched out, and when the side shoots are half an inch in length, repotting is done, using 5-in. pots. The side shoots are pinched in a similar manner after the second potting, and finally the plants are set in 7-in. pots. The best compost for potting consists of equal parts of loam, leaf mold and peat moss with a scattering of sand, and, for the final potting, an equal portion of well-decayed manure should be added.

A moist atmosphere must be maintained at all times as this plant is very subject to red spider mites. In addition it is necessary to spray the leaves (especially the undersides) with insecticide regularly.

RENANTHERA (Renanther'a; Renanth'era). Attractive Orchids, found wild chiefly in the Far

East—in India, Burma and Cochin China. All are epiphytal (grow on other plants) and evergreen; the leaves are arranged on opposite sides of an ascending stem which sends out clinging roots. They have no pseudobulbs. All have brightly colored flowers, red or orange-red, usually on branching, many-flowered panicles produced principally in summer. The name is derived from *ren,* a kidney, and *anthera,* an anther, and refers to the kidney-shaped pollen masses.

Orchids for a Hothouse. These Orchids require a greenhouse with a tropical atmosphere during the greater part of the year, and in winter a temperature of 60 degrees by night and rather more by day. In cultivating R. pulchella and R. Imschootiana, the temperature may fall to 55 degrees without injury, but R. Storiei and R. matutina require a rather higher temperature than 60 degrees. Shading is necessary during summer. Water may be given liberally, and the foliage syringed freely in summer, provided the flowers are not open, but in winter the plants should receive much less water, the compost being allowed to get moderately dry before fresh supplies are given.

The best potting compost consists of two parts of osmunda fiber and two parts of sphagnum moss, well mixed, with broken crocks or pieces of broken brick and charcoal. Drainage must be free and the pots should be filled to at least one third with drainage material. Repotting should be done as soon as fresh roots are seen in spring. If a plant has become "leggy" (lost a number of its lowest leaves) the stem may be shortened by cutting off its top. The upper part that is cut off may be planted rather low in a new pot. This must only be done, however, if there are virile roots above the point where the stem is cut. A stake is usually required to support the plant.

R. Storiei and R. coccinea both cling to trees in their native habitats and attain considerable lengths. While small, they may be grown in pots, but as they gain size they become unwieldy, unless given the support of a stout stake.

The most useful of the comparatively dwarf-growing kinds are R. Imschootiana, with leaves 3-4 in. long and vermilion-red flowers, appearing in May or later; R. pulchella, with yellow and crimson flowers, usually opening in sum-

mer; and R. annamensis, with yellow flowers marked with crimson.

RENIFORM. A botanical term used in describing a leaf which is kidney-shaped. See Leaf.

REPENS. A Latin word meaning creeping, and used in the description of plants of creeping or prostrate growth, as in the name of Mitchella repens, the Partridge Berry.

RESEDA—*Mignonette* (Res'eda). Hardy annual or perennial plants which are found wild in Europe, northern Africa and the Canary Islands, and naturalized in North America. They belong to the Mignonette family, Resedaceae. The name, derived from *resodo,* to calm, refers to the supposed medicinal virtues of the plant.

Mignonette, Reseda odorata, a fragrant garden flower.

The favorite kind is Reseda odorata, which grows wild in North Africa. It is a very old garden plant, having been introduced into European gardens nearly 200 years ago. It is grown for the fragrance of its flowers, which, in the wild type, are small and greenish yellow, though considerable color variation is shown in the modern varieties which have been raised by continued selection throughout many years. For details of cultivation, see Mignonette.

RESERVE BORDER. That part of the garden which is set apart for the purpose of propagating and growing a supply of plants until they are large enough to be planted in the permanent places. It is also known as a nursery border. A reserve border is a nursery area and should be regarded as indispensable, for large numbers of trees, shrubs and plants can be raised there by sowing seeds or taking cuttings.

Plants raised under glass, in a frame or greenhouse, may be grown in the reserve border for a few weeks, or a few months, as may be necessary, until they are sufficiently well developed to be suitable for planting out where they are to remain.

The reserve border is invaluable for raising such biennials as Sweet William, Canterbury Bells and Forget-Me-Nots. Almost all the favorite hardy perennials can be raised from seeds sown out of doors in spring or early summer, and the only convenient way to manage them is to grow them in a reserve border or in a nursery bed.

Numerous flowering shrubs as well as bush fruits can be grown from cuttings, and they, too, must be planted in a reserve border until they are large enough to be set in their permanent positions.

The possession of a reserve border is an incentive to raising plants from seeds and cuttings, and these methods will be found very useful and economical in augmenting the supply of garden plants.

Flowers for Cutting. If flowers in the show beds and borders are cut for decorative purposes indoors the display is soon spoilt. Certain kinds of flowers are more suitable for cutting than others, and a few plants of each will provide a large supply of cut blooms. Among those that should be grown in the reserve border for this purpose are Spanish Iris, Shirley Poppy, Border Chrysanthemum, Shasta Daisy, Dahlia, perennial Sunflower, Columbine, Iceland Poppy, Sweet Peas, and Roses. Thus the reserve border doubles as a cutting garden.

REST HARROW. See Ononis.

RESTREPIA (Restre'pia). Dwarf, tufted, epiphytal Orchids found wild in Central America. They have no pseudobulbs, but short slender stems, each of which has a single evergreen leaf.

Though small, the flowers are attractive; they are borne singly on thin peduncles produced from the junction of the stem and leaf. The old growths often continue to bloom. The flowers are noticeable for the disproportionate sizes of the sepals and petals, the latter being reduced to mere threads. The upper sepal is narrow and tapered; the lower sepals are much enlarged and joined together, except at their tips. The labellums lie on the upper surface of the lower sepals and are almost indistinguishable at first sight. The plants seldom exceed 6 in. in height, and flower at various times, often in summer and again in winter.

The name Restrepia commemorates Joseph E. Restrep, a naturalist. These plants belong to the family Orchidaceae.

Orchids for a Warm Greenhouse. Restrepias are of easy cultivation. They are grown in a greenhouse with a moist atmosphere and winter temperature of not less than 50 degrees. They must be shaded in the summer and kept moist throughout the year. Potting should be done in spring when the young growths appear, generally about March. The best compost consists of two parts of osmunda fiber and two parts of sphagnum moss with a little leaf mold. The pots used should be as small as possible and must be well drained. Propagation is effected by division.

The Chief Kinds. Several are known, but the best are R. antennifera, yellowish-white striped with red, and R. striata, smaller than the preceding, yellow with dark reddish-purple stripes. Other kinds are R. elegans, R. pandurata and R. trichoglossa.

RESURRECTION PLANT. Several plants are given this common name, the two chief kinds being Anastatica and Selaginella lepidophylla, which see.

RETARDING. A method of keeping plants and bulbs at rest, usually in a cool chamber, so that their season of flowering can be delayed. It is commonly practiced with Lily of the Valley, retarded crowns of which can be brought quickly into bloom at any time of the year. In the garden, flowering and fruiting can be retarded by planting in cooler locations, as against a north or east wall.

RETINOSPORA. A name previously given to varieties of Chamaecyparis and Thuyas which retain the juvenile type of leaves for a very long period or throughout life. These juvenile varieties look very different from the mature kinds or species and were at one time thought to represent a distinct genus.

REVOLUTE. With the margins (edges) or tip rolled backward or downward.

RHAMNUS—*Buckthorn* (Rham'nus). Usually leaf-losing, but sometimes evergreen, shrubs, a large number of which are widely distributed in the Northern Hemisphere, and some in South America and South Africa. Some have spiny branches; in others the wood is quite unarmed. The flowers are small, insignificant, and dull in color; they are followed by round fruits which in many cases are black when ripe. A few have attractive foliage, but the numerous kinds are rather uninteresting as garden shrubs. Rhamnus gives its name to the family Rhamnaceae; the name is said to be the old Greek name for one of the European kinds.

Propagation. Seeds form the most satisfactory means of propagating most kinds. They may be sown in pots or flats of sandy soil placed in a frame or greenhouse in spring. Varieties that cannot be raised true from seeds may be increased by means of cuttings of side shoots, 4 in. long, taken with a slight heel of old wood in July, and dibbled in a cold frame. No regular pruning is necessary but overgrown plants may be cut back in spring.

Shrubs with Variegated Leaves. A few of the more decorative foliage kinds are R. Alaternus, a vigorous evergreen bush, 8-10 ft. high, with glossy green leaves, 3/4-2 in. long and 1/2-1 in. wide. The variety aurea has golden-variegated leaves, but is not a really good variegated plant. The variety angustifolia has small, narrow leaves with toothed margins; argenteo-variegata, which has green and white leaves, is well worth growing. R. Alaternus and its varieties are hardy as far north as Washington, D. C.

R. californica, also an evergreen, grows 10-15 ft. high; its leaves are about 4 in. long. It is commonly called the Coffeeberry and is hardy in mild southern climates only. R. Purshiana is worth growing owing to its economic interest, as is also R. Frangula. Both are suitable for the wild garden. The former is hardy about as far north as Philadelphia. R. Frangula is hardy far north. Both R. Frangula and R. Purshiana are leaf-losing.

The Common Buckthorn. R. cathartica, the Common Buckthorn, is a very vigorous, spiny, leaf-losing shrub, native to Asia Minor and Europe, and naturalized in eastern North America. It is hardy far north. Although of no particular decorative value, it is useful in forming a protection belt where the soil is poor; and it may also be used as a hedge, for it withstands severe clipping. Syrup of Buckthorn is made from the juice of the berries.

Several of the leaf-losing kinds, although of little use in gardens, might be used for hedges, for they are of dense growth and appear to withstand severe pruning.

Provides Cascara Sagrada. Although the Buckthorns are of modest decorative value, several are of economic importance. The drug Cascara Sagrada is obtained from the bark of Rhamnus Purshiana, a large bush or small tree of western North America.

Rhamnus Frangula, the Alder Buckthorn, a European shrub which is naturalized in eastern North America, used to be in demand as a source of charcoal for use in the manufacture of high-class gunpowders.

RHAPIDOPHYLLUM HYSTRIX — *Needle Palm, Blue Palmetto* (Rhapidophyll' um). A stemless or nearly stemless Palm, family Palmaceae, that occurs as a native from South Carolina to Florida and Mississippi, usually occupying low, moist ground. The name is derived from *phyllon*, leaf, and Rhapis, a genus of Palms, and alludes to the fact that the leaves resemble those of Rhapis.

The Needle Palm is so called because the leaf sheaths are armed with sharp, erect, long needles that provide a formidable armor for the plant and protect the flowers and fruits that are borne down among them. The leaves are fan-shaped, 1 1/2-2 1/2 ft. across.

The Needle Palm Is Not Much Cultivated. It succeeds in a moist but well-drained soil and is propagated by seeds and by division in spring. In addition to being cultivated outdoors where winter conditions permit, it is easily grown in pots in a greenhouse. (See Palm.)

RHAPIS—*Lady Palms* (Rha'pis). Palms from China and Japan that are suitable for outdoor cultivation in southern California and southern Florida and for growing in pots and tubs indoors. They are quite distinct in appearance from other plants of the Palm family, Palmaceae. In general appearance they somewhat resemble Bamboos, for the stems are slender and reedlike and do not exceed 10 ft. in height. The leaves are fan-shaped and deeply divided into numerous segments. As these Palms produce suckers freely from the base, they eventually form very dense, bushy clumps.

Of the two kinds in cultivation, R. excelsa (flabelliformis) is the taller; it reaches a height of 10 ft. and the deeply cleft leaves have five to seven pendulous segments. In the smaller kind, R. humilis, the leaves have seven to ten segments. By these characters the two kinds are easily distinguished.

Rhapis is closely allied to Chamaerops, and is only slightly less hardy. The name Rhapis is derived from *rhapis,* a needle, and refers to the sharp awns of the corolla or to the needle-like leaf segments.

Palms for a Greenhouse. As these Palms are hardier than most, they are excellent for a greenhouse or conservatory with a minimum winter temperature of 45 degrees. They also may be used for decorating private homes as well as public buildings.

Their principal requirements are shade from bright sunlight, protection from frost, and abundance of water during the summer. Much less watering is required in winter, as the plants are then at rest and need only sufficient moisture at the roots to keep the leaves from shriveling.

Large plants are grown in well-drained, wooden tubs; they should be top-dressed annually in spring with fresh compost, and weak applications of liquid fertilizer should be given in summer.

Smaller plants are repotted in March or April, when they are transferred to clean, well-drained pots, two sizes larger. The best potting compost consists of two parts of loam, one of leaf mold, and a scattering of sand. Until established, they are watered moderately, the soil being allowed to become fairly dry before it is moistened. A moist atmosphere is maintained by dampening the floor and benches, and the foliage is syringed morning and evening during the summer months. Plants standing in rooms should be taken out of doors and syringed with water once each week to clean and freshen their foliage.

Propagation. Young plants can be raised by sowing seeds in pans of finely sifted soil plunged in a propagating case having a bottom heat of 75-80 degrees in spring or summer. As this Palm produces suckers freely, however, the best method of propagation is to detach the suckers and pot them in small pots.

The chief kind, R. excelsa, grows 10 ft. high, and there is also a form, foliis-variegatis, with green leaves striped with white. R. humilis is more dwarf than the above, and has more finely divided leaves.

RHEKTOPHYLLUM MIRABILE (Rhektophyll'um). A western African member of the Arum family, Araceae, that is grown in tropical greenhouses and sometimes as a foliage plant for decorating large rooms. It is a tall climber that attaches itself to its supports by means of roots that emerge from the nodes (joints) on the stems. Under favorable circumstances it attains a height of at least 30 ft. The name is derived from *rechtos,* torn, and *phyllon,* leaf, and refers to the perforations and slits that characterize the leaves.

The leaves of this noble aroid are arrow-shaped. In mature plants they grow to 6 ft. long by one third as broad, but in young plants, such as are ordinarily grown in pots or tubs, they are considerably smaller.

This plant is sometimes grown under the name Nephthytis picturata. It requires the same culture as Philodendron, which see.

RHEUM—*Ornamental Rhubarb* (Rhe'um). Herbaceous perennial plants which are grown for their handsome foliage and flowers. They belong to the Buckwheat or Knotweed family, Polygonaceae, and are found wild in China, Siberia and the Himalayas.

The principal characteristics of these plants are thick rootstocks, large palmate leaves and massive flower spikes. According to some authorities, the name Rheum is derived from *rha,* the ancient name for Rhubarb; others say that it is from the Greek word *rheo,* to flow, and refers to the plant's medicinal properties.

Plants with Ornamental Leaves. As they attain such huge dimensions, the ornamental kinds are most suitable for large gardens or public parks.

The ornamental Rhubarbs are handsome subjects for moist positions. Here is a plant of Rheum palmatum in bloom.

They have bold and striking foliage and the flower spikes are most impressive. They are particularly suited for grouping by the margin of a lake or stream, and look best against evergreen trees.

The cultivation of Ornamental Rhubarb is extremely simple. The ground is deeply dug and well manured, and the clumps are set in position, 4-6 ft. apart, in early fall or in spring. After planting, no further attention is required, but they benefit from an annual mulch of decayed manure and copious waterings in dry weather. In the North, winter protection, in the form of a covering of evergreen branches or of salt hay or dry leaves, is desirable. Propagation is by lifting and separating the plants into rooted pieces in autumn or early spring.

The best kinds are R. palmatum, 5 ft., leaves pale green, palmate, flowers crimson; R. emodi, 6-10 ft., leaves bronze-green, flowers purple; and R. Alexandrae, 4 ft., leaves glossy green, pale yellow bracts.

Details of the cultivation of Rhubarb (Rheum Rhaponticum) will be found under the heading of Rhubarb.

RHEXIA — *Meadow Beauty, Deer Grass* (Rhex′ia). Dwarf hardy herbaceous perennial flowering plants of North America, which belong to the family Melastomaceae. The principal kind, R. virginica, grows wild in boggy ground. It has tuberous roots, slender stems clothed with ovate leaves, 1½ in. long, and bears loose clusters of small purple flowers having four petals and conspicuous stamens. The name Rhexia is derived from *rhexio,* rupture, and refers to the plant's supposed value in curing ruptures.

Plants for Damp Soil. Rhexias require an open, sunny position and boggy or moist soil. They may be planted in the bog garden or in damp places at the base of the rockery. Light sandy or peaty soil is the most suitable. Planting is done in October–November, or March–April, and as the plants resent being moved they must not be disturbed for several years, or until they show signs of deterioration.

When it is desired to increase the stock of plants the clumps are lifted in autumn or spring, carefully separated into small pieces and replanted in their permanent positions. Rhexias are also easily raised from seeds sown in sandy, peaty soil.

The chief kind is R. virginica, 12-18 in., purplish-crimson, summer. R. mariana, a taller-growing kind, having reddish-purple flowers, requires somewhat drier conditions. R. ciliosa grows up to 18 in. tall, its simple stems being terminated by leafy clusters of purple flowers in late summer.

RHIPSALIS—*Mistletoe Cactus* (Rhip′salis). These greenhouse succulent plants, which belong to the Cactus family, Cactaceae, are found wild in South America and the West Indies. Several kinds are also found in Africa, Mauritius and Ceylon; these are, possibly, the only representatives of the Cactus which are natives of the Old World.

Rhipsalis are quite distinct from the majority of Cacti, and the various kinds exhibit great diversity of form in their branches. These vary in length from a few inches to 2 ft., and are either round, flat and jointed, triangular, or six-angled, knotted and leafless. The flowers are from ½-1 in. in diameter, star-shaped and rosy-white, or greenish-yellow, and are succeeded by white or pink mistletoe-like berries, from which resemblance the common name is derived.

The Latin name, Rhipsalis, is derived from *rhips,* wickerwork, and refers to the flexibility of the plant's interlaced branches.

Cacti for a Greenhouse. These plants flourish under the same treatment as most succulents. They are grown in a well-lighted greenhouse in which a minimum winter temperature of 45-50 degrees is maintained. Being chiefly of drooping growth, they are grown in pots or baskets suspended from the roof, or on a high shelf where the branches are allowed to hang downwards in a natural manner.

Repotting is done in April or May, and a porous compost, consisting of four parts of loam and equal parts of leaf mold, crushed brick and sand, is used. As good drainage is an important item, the pots should be filled to one third of their capacity with crocks, which in turn must be covered with rough siftings from the compost to prevent the soil from washing into the drainage.

Dry Conditions Necessary. After potting, it is best to allow the compost to become almost dry before it is watered, and to continue this treatment until the plants are well rooted. For the remainder of the summer the soil must be kept moist, although overwatering should be avoided; during winter the soil must be kept on the dry side, sufficient water being given, however, to prevent the stems from shriveling. No damping or syringing is required, and the greenhouse in which they are growing must be ventilated freely on all favorable occasions.

Unlike the majority of Cacti, Rhipsalis appreciate a little shade, and it is advisable to protect them from the fiercest rays of the sun in summer.

Propagation by Cuttings. New plants are easily raised by inserting pieces of shoots as cuttings. The cuttings, about 3 in. in length, are taken off and laid on a bench for twenty-four hours in order to allow a corky skin to form over the cut portion. They are then inserted in sand or sandy soil and are shaded from bright sunlight, and watered sparingly until roots are formed. Each plant is then set in a small pot and treated as advised for the larger plants.

Raising Seedlings. Seeds ripen freely, and these also form a ready means of propagation. Well-drained pots of sandy soil are used and the seeds are sown thinly on the surface in spring. They are covered with a thin layer of fine soil, well watered and placed in a temperature of 55-60 degrees. They germinate quickly and, when large enough to handle, the seedlings are transplanted, 1 in. apart, into a seed pan, and later on potted separately in small pots.

The dwarf kinds are very effective when grafted on slender stemmed Cereus. A piece of the stem of Rhipsalis is cut wedge-shaped at the base and inserted in a cleft in the top of the stock, where it is held in position with raffia or a large spine from another Cactus.

The chief kinds are R. capilliformis, stems slender, flowers cream-colored; R. cassutha, branches cordlike, flowers greenish-white; R. cereuscula, slender, flowers pinkish to white with a yellowish midrib, berries white; R. crispata, stems wide and flat, flowers cream, fruit white; R. pachyptera, stems flat, drooping, flowers yellowish, fruit red; R. paradoxa, branches hanging and producing many aerial roots, flowers large, white; R. pentaptera, stems 5- or 6-ribbed, flowers cream; R. rhombea, flowers cream-colored with a red spot inside; R. teres, stems cylindrical, erect, flowers pale yellow; R. trigona, flowers white or pinkish; and R. Warmingiana, drooping branches, flowers white.

RHIZOME. A surface-creeping or underground stem, bearing closely set scale-leaves and adventitious roots, and generally much thickened because of the storage of foodstuffs. It grows slowly in a horizontal direction, branching occasionally, and sending up every year one or more flowering shoots which die back in the autumn. The Flag Iris and Solomon's Seal are familiar examples of rhizomatous plants. Pieces containing buds may be broken off and planted separately. Some weeds, like the Couch Grass and Bindweed, bear numerous rhizomes, and every broken portion should be removed from the ground when weeding is done.

RHIZOPHORA — *Mangrove* (Rhizoph'ora). Rhizophora Mangle is the only representative of the Mangrove family, Rhizophoraceae, that occurs as a native in the United States. It is a tree that attains a height of 40-80 ft. and, like other members of the genus, it occupies tidal

Stilt roots of the Mangrove, Rhizophora Mangle.

shores and shoals and brackish marshes, where it serves the useful purpose of holding soil and preventing erosion.

It is an interesting tree and is noteworthy because its seeds begin to germinate before they fall from the parent plant. The seeds are more or less bomb-shaped and, when they fall, they bury themselves in the mud and begin to grow immediately.

The trees form great tangles of stilt roots (roots that develop from branches well above the ground and extend down into the soil, thus forming supporting props). Rhizophora Mangle is a native of southern Florida, the West Indies and Central and South America. Other species of this genus occur in tropical and subtropical regions throughout the world, always along shores. They form impenetrable thickets.

The name Rhizophora is derived from *rhiza*, root, and *phore*, to bear, and refers to the fact that the seeds germinate while yet attached to the plant if they touch the ground.

RHODANTHE. The dainty annual Everlasting Flowers commonly listed by seedsmen and cultivated under this name belong to the genus Helipterum, which see.

RHODE ISLAND, GARDENING IN. See Regional Gardening.

RHODOCHITON—*Purple Bell Vine* (Rhodoch'iton). A genus of only one species, R. volubile, or, as it is sometimes named, R. atrosanguineum. This free-flowering, graceful climber is a tender, Mexican species that belongs to the

Figwort family, Scrophulariaceae. It is of vigorous growth and is suitable for draping the roof or pillar in a large greenhouse or conservatory or for planting outdoors during the summer. Its name is derived from the Greek, *rhodo*, red, and *chiton*, a garment, and alludes to the large colored calyx.

The soft, slender shoots grow several feet high in one season; they are covered with roundish leaves, heart-shaped at the base and pointed at the tips.

The flowers, which are produced during the summer, are solitary (produced singly from the axils of the leaves), on slender, threadlike stalks 2 in. in length; they consist of a long, bell-shaped calyx which is red, and a tubular purple corolla; they are pendulous and are produced in succession on the young shoots. The name Rhodochiton is derived from *rhodo*, red, and *chiton*, cloak, and refers to the large red calyx.

A Climbing Plant. This plant climbs by means

Rhodochiton volubile, with red and purple pendent flowers, is a charming climber for the cool greenhouse.

of its leafstalks, which twist around any available support. It is suitable for covering arbors, trellises, pillars, etc. It requires the same culture as Maurandia, to which it is closely related. See Maurandia.

Propagation. New plants are easily raised from seeds or cuttings in spring. The seeds are sown in a well-drained pot filled with sandy soil. They germinate quickly in a warm greenhouse and when the seedlings are 2 in. high are potted singly in 3-in. pots. Before they become potbound, they are transferred to 5-in. pots, and from these they are planted out in the garden after the weather is warm and settled, or are potted on into larger pots or tubs if they are to be grown in the greenhouse.

RHODODENDRON: LOVELY EVERGREEN AND LEAF-LOSING SHRUBS

A Vast Race of Beauties for Gardens in the Northeast and the Pacific Northwest

Rhododendron (Rhododen'dron). This is a very important group of evergreen and leaf-losing trees and shrubs found wild in Europe, Asia, and North America. Several hundreds of wild kinds have been discovered and named, and many of them bear very handsome flowers. In addition to the wild kinds there are numerous hybrids, some of which are more widely grown in gardens than the species or wild types.

In the genus Rhododendron botanists now include Azalea and Rhodora, but gardeners usually regard these as being quite distinct from other kinds of Rhododendrons and retain for them their older names. This plan is followed in this Encyclopedia. See also Azalea and Rhodora.

Rhododendron belongs to the Heath family, Ericaceae, and the name is taken from the Greek *rhodon,* a rose, and *dendron,* a tree.

Remarkable Variation in Form and Size. Rhododendrons are very variable in habit. Some grow into trees of moderate size, others are prostrate shrubs, or little bushes, suitable for the rock garden, and there are many intermediates. It is the same with the foliage and flowers. Some

Rhododendrons are not excelled by any other flowering evergreen for beauty of foliage and flowers. This display of a variety of Rhododendron catawbiense is at The New York Botanical Garden.

kinds produce leaves up to 20 or 24 in. long, and 6-8 in. across, and at the other extreme there are plants with leaves little larger than those of Thyme. In some the flowers are tubular and like great Lilies in shape; in others they are like a saucer, 5 in. or more across, or they may resemble the flowers of a Campanula in form, or be quite flat when expanded.

The flowers are often in terminal bunches on the previous year's shoots. In a few instances they appear from the leaf axils. The bunches may be loose and contain very few flowers, or they may be 8 or 9 in. high, compact, and composed of a large number of blooms. Some are fragrant.

Long Flowering Season. The flowering period for the outdoor kinds varies according to locality; in favored climates a good selection of kinds will produce blooms from late winter until well into summer. After the flowers are over, seed capsules are formed which bear many seeds. Ripening takes place during the winter following flowering. When the seeds are ripe the fruits split and eject them.

Rock, Woodland, and Moorland Shrubs. In a state of nature Rhododendrons grow under many conditions. Some are found among the trees of mixed woods; others form thin woods or cover hillsides as the most prominent vegetation; some are epiphytes on the branches of other trees, others grow among rocks, and some cover hillsides and moorlands. At one time the Sikkim Himalayas were regarded as the headquarters of the Rhododendrons, but so many kinds have been discovered in western China and Tibet that the claim to being the chief home of the Rhododendrons must be awarded to that region.

There are now so many kinds of Rhododendrons that, to reduce them to some sort of order, experts have divided them into a number of groups or series, each series being named after a well-known kind.

The Chief Groups of Rhododendrons. These series are: Albiflorum, Anthopogon, Arboreum, Auriculatum, Azalea, Barbatum, Boothii, Camelliaflorum, Campanulatum, Campylogynum, Camtschaticum, Carolinianum, Cephalanthum, Cinnabarinum, Dauricum, Edgeworthii, Falconeri, Ferrugineum, Fortunei, Fulvum, Glaucum, Grande, Heliolepis, Irroratum, Lacteum, Lapponicum, Lepidotum, Maddenii, Micranthum, Moupinense, Neriiflorum, Ovatum, Ponticum, Saluenense, Scabrifolium, Stamineum, Taliense, Thomsonii, Trichocladum, Triflorum, Virgatum.

Climatic Requirements for Growing Rhododendrons. The climate of England, with its temperate winters and its moist, cloudy summers, is almost ideal for the culture of Rhododendrons. An influential Rhododendron Association there has classified this host of plants for hardiness and garden adaptability. It has encouraged hybridization and has given recognition to each worth-while introduction. England has been the storehouse from which American Rhododendron supplies of choicer and newer kinds have been chiefly drawn. The climate of the Pacific Northwest is similar to that of England, and Rhododendrons are accumulating in this region in increasing numbers. The American Rhododendron Society plays an important part in stimulating interest in Rhododendrons and Azaleas in North America.

Unfortunately, most Rhododendrons cannot be recommended for the large central portion of North America. The atmosphere is too dry and the winters too severe. Probably they will always be easiest to cultivate along the seaboard strips, from the western slopes of the Rockies and from the eastern slopes of the Appalachian Mountains to the coasts. Even within these latter regions, gardeners in the eastern states must be cautious about leaning too heavily upon English introductions. There are some which are excellent, but the climate of the East Coast is much more rigorous than that of England. The future of new Rhododendrons in this climate depends on the work of the plant breeders who are now striving to produce varieties that can withstand these colder, drier winters and hot summers.

Rhododendrons cannot generally be grown south of Washington, D. C., on the eastern coastal plain, but they can be cultivated considerably further south in the mountains.

Choosing Locations and Planting

For the best results, locations for Rhododendrons should be selected with some care. Consideration should be given to soil and exposure as well as to where they will look well in the landscape. They are grand shrubs for massing along boundaries, for planting as screens, for using in foundation plantings and for plantings as single specimens on lawns and elsewhere. The dwarfer kinds are handsome for planting in rock gardens and for using with other low evergreens.

They Need Shelter. Rhododendrons do not withstand exposure to sweeping winds well, particularly in winter. They should be planted where they are sheltered from such conditions. Hilltop locations and positions near the sea are generally unfavorable unless they are protected by windbreak plantings, fences or walls. Corners of buildings are often too drafty for Rhododendrons. Favorable locations are often found in the bottoms of valleys and dells and part way down hillsides. They may often be located advantageously some little distance in front of a planting of other evergreens, especially conifers, which provide shelter from wind, and at the same time a splendid dark green background against which the flowers and foliage of the Rhododendrons show their fullest beauty.

Rhododendrons Like a Little Shade. Although garden varieties of Rhododendron thrive in full sun, provided they do not suffer from dryness

Many nurseries sell plants of choice Rhododendrons of sizes small enough for the amateur to plant. Such plants should have a firm soil root ball wrapped tightly in burlap. The foliage should be ample and rich green in color.

at their roots, most kinds appreciate a little shade from strong sun, and in the case of the large-leaved kinds it is necessary or the leaves will be burned. For this reason it is wise to plant Rhododendrons in thin woodland, giving the large-leaved kinds the most shady places. North-facing and west-facing slopes are usually good locations for these plants. Varieties with brightly colored flowers, the reds and scarlets, should have the lightest places, the mauves and whites being reserved for the heavier shade.

For ordinary woodland planting it is difficult to find a better kind than R. catawbiense and its hybrids; they withstand both full light and shade and flower well, and the colors are very effective.

The north-facing sides of buildings afford good planting sites for Rhododendrons and so do northwest and even western exposures. Planting against south-facing, southeast-facing and east-facing walls is not usually satisfactory unless they are quite well shaded by evergreen trees such as Pines.

Exposure to strong direct sun in winter is even more harmful than in summer; it is in winter, especially late winter, that the most serious scorching of the leaves occurs as a result of

For planting on the north sides of buildings in acid soils Rhododendrons are especially well suited. The kind pictured here is the native American Rhododendron maximum.

excessive exposure to both the sun and wind.

The Soil. The soil for Rhododendrons should contain an abundance of organic matter—leaf mold, peat moss, rotted compost or very old and well-rotted manure. The soil should not be waterlogged or constantly saturated; on the other hand it should not dry out quickly. Good underdrainage and an ability to retain a fair amount of moisture are ideal.

With very few exceptions, Rhododendrons dislike lime, and will not thrive where lime is present in the soil in any appreciable quantity. R. hirsutum is an exception to the rule, for it is found growing on limestone formations.

Although it is often thought that peat is essential to the well-being of Rhododendrons, that is not so, for they grow quite well in moist loam, and even in heavy loam, provided it is somewhat acid or, at most, neutral in its reaction. It is always advisable to mix some peat moss or leaf mold in the soil that is packed about the roots when planting in loam, but it is a great mistake to excavate large holes, fill them with peat moss and set the plants in these. The peat is likely to become sour before the roots can penetrate it and the plants do not thrive.

How to Prepare the Sites. If the soil is acid or neutral, use the natural soil, spade it 2 ft. deep, and remove a little of the subsoil; in the top 12 or 15 in. mix a 3-6-in. layer of peat moss, leaf mold or good compost. Should the soil be very sandy, double or treble the amounts of these materials that are added.

If the original soil tests slightly alkaline, the location should be excavated to a depth of 18 in. and the beds filled with new soil prepared by mixing good topsoil, acid peat moss and leaf mold or commercial humus in equal (by bulk) proportions. This treatment is often advisable when planting against buildings where cement, plaster, lime and other alkaline materials may have been buried or mixed with the soil by builders.

If the soil is very alkaline (as the limestones of Virginia and over large areas of Ohio and the Middle West), new beds can be built on top of the existing soil surface. With adequate watering during dry periods, the plants may be persuaded to thrive in such beds. This is easier

A flat containing a variety of Rhododendrons raised from seeds.

Cuttings of Rhododendrons rooting in a cold frame outdoors.

Rhododendron cuttings must be shaded from direct sun. This structure shades a cold frame containing Rhododendron cuttings. It admits light only from the north.

than excavating and risking the danger of having the new soil impregnated with lime through lateral movement of rainwater, but, unless one is a connoisseur of plants, it is usually best not to attempt to grow Rhododendrons in areas where the natural soil is strongly alkaline.

If alkalinity of the soil is suspected, it is

always wise to have a test made and be guided accordingly. Changing the reaction of the soil by the use of such chemicals as aluminum sulphate and sulphur is sometimes recommended but is tricky to do effectively; the addition to the soil of liberal amounts of acid organic materials such as peat moss and leaf mold is more reliable.

Planting. Early fall and early spring are the best seasons for planting Rhododendrons, with the latter season preferred in regions of cold winters, but it is possible to move them at any season with the exception of June and July and the midwinter months.

The plants should be dug when the ground is moist or should be watered very thoroughly a few hours before digging. They should always be lifted with a good ball of soil attached to their roots, and this should be securely wrapped and tied in burlap. At no time during the planting operation should the roots be permitted to dry.

Holes of suitable depth and considerably wider than the root balls should be prepared for the reception of the plants. The plants should be set slightly deeper than they were previously, to allow a slight hollow over their roots to facilitate watering. Soil containing a generous amount of peat moss and leaf mold should be packed about the root ball, and when the operation is completed the newly set plants should be watered in very thoroughly, the water being applied as a fine spray.

A mulch of peat moss, leaf mold or compost should be spread around newly set out plants.

Care and Maintenance

Maintenance of Rhododendrons is less arduous than for many other groups of plants. They are shallow-rooted, and therefore do not need to have the surface of the ground stirred or cultivated. Digging among the roots is very harmful.

Rhododendrons seldom require weeding if they are provided each year with a mulch of old and very decayed manure, dead leaves, peat moss, pine needles or even hardwood sawdust.

Watering. During periods of dry weather, Rho-

dodendrons benefit greatly from being watered very thoroughly at weekly intervals. It is very important to attend to this if the weather is dry in late summer and fall because if they are allowed to suffer from lack of moisture at those times they are much more likely to suffer damage caused by sun and wind during winter.

Fertilizing is not necessary as long as the bushes make thrifty growth, but specimens that are old or have partly exhausted the soil of nutrients and are not growing vigorously benefit from an annual application of fertilizer made in spring. A mulch of really old manure is excellent; so is one of the complete fertilizers that are compounded especially for acid-soil plants.

Pruning. Young Rhododendrons that are inclined to become leggy should be cut back to induce dormant buds to grow and form a bushy foundation of branches. Once a good foundation is laid, no regular pruning is necessary. Except in the case of old straggly plants, the less pruning done to established Rhododendrons the better. If necessary, straggly branches may be cut back hard in spring just as the buds are beginning to open.

Specimens that have grown very tall and leggy may be rejuvenated and encouraged to grow into shapely bushes by pruning them drastically in spring before new growth begins. This rejuvenation pruning consists of cutting the entire bush down to within a foot of the ground. Following the cutting back, the soil should be fertilized and mulched, as described above, and throughout the entire summer special care must be taken to make sure that in dry weather the soil is soaked very thoroughly at weekly intervals.

Following such drastic pruning 2-3 years will pass before the cut-back bushes flower, but in the meantime, if they have space and light enough, they will grow into shapely specimens.

It is essential that a sharp lookout be kept for suckers that may develop from below the graft union on grafted plants or from below the bud union on budded specimens. If suckers are not removed as they appear, they grow vigorously and the grafted or budded variety gradually deteriorates until it is killed by starvation. It is for this reason that plants raised from layers,

It is beneficial to the plants to pick off the faded flower trusses of Rhododendrons before seeds are formed.

seedling stocks of R. ponticum or R. catawbiense or by cuttings or leaf cuttings.

How to Raise Rhododendrons from Seed. Seeds should be sown as soon as possible after they are ripe, in well-drained pots, pans or flats, which are then placed in a cool greenhouse or cold frame. A light sandy soil is necessary. This may be a mixture of loam, sand and leaf mold or a mixture of loam, sand and peat. Good results may also be had from sowing in sifted sphagnum moss.

Drain the pots or flats and fill them to within ½ in. of their tops with the soil or moss. Level this and press it lightly to ensure an even surface. Then water the soil thoroughly with a fine

cuttings or seeds are generally to be preferred to those that are grafted or budded.

Remove Faded Flower Heads. Rhododendrons benefit by the prompt removal of the faded flower heads. This should be done whenever possible before seed forms, unless, of course, seed is needed for propagation purposes.

Winter Protection. Some winter protection may be needed if the location is exposed, if the species is of doubtful hardiness, or if the garden is in a cold area. Winter protection should consist of shade and shelter against winter sun and drying winter winds. Cut pine boughs stuck in the ground around the plants, or burlap supported on stakes or chicken wire, serves this purpose. Tight-fitting barrels or boxes are to be avoided. The plants do not need to be kept warm. They need shade, but they also require good air circulation.

Rhododendron seedlings raised from seed sown in sphagnum moss ready for transplanting.

Propagation

Rhododendrons are propagated by seeds, cuttings, layering, grafting and budding. Some of the large-leaved species are very difficult to increase by cuttings, though many of those with slender shoots and small leaves root from cuttings quite readily. The hybrids should be propagated by layers, by budding or grafting on

Transplanted seedlings of Rhododendrons growing in a flat containing loam, peat moss and sand.

spray or by standing the pots or flats in water nearly to their rims and allowing the moisture to seep to the surface from below. Allow the pots or flats to drain, then sprinkle the seeds thinly over the soil or moss and press the seeds lightly into the compost. Scatter a little sand over the seeds, but do not attempt to cover them entirely. Cover the pots or flats with sheets of glass and shade them from bright sunlight. Water carefully, so that the fine seeds are not disturbed, taking care that the soil never becomes dry and yet is not maintained in a constantly saturated condition.

Germination will usually begin in 2-4 weeks. As the young plants develop, gradually admit air and light (but never expose them to direct, strong sunshine) and as soon as the seedlings are large enough to handle, transplant them into flats or pans, using one of the soil composts already mentioned and spacing the plants about 2 in. apart.

As soon as the leaves of adjacent plants meet, transplant the seedlings to a cold frame. Set them about 4 in. apart in a well-drained sandy soil that contains an abundance of leaf mold or peat moss and a little very well-decayed manure. Here allow them to grow for about a year, then transfer them to an outdoor nursery bed. Young plants must on no account be allowed to become dry at the roots. On all favorable occasions, while in the frame, they should be syringed morning and evening, and in mild weather the sash may be removed from the frame. At all stages they need shade from strong sunshine.

Should any of the young plants tend to become spindling or leggy the tips of the shoots should be removed to induce branching.

Seedling plants of the more vigorous kinds grow many years before they flower, possibly not less than ten, but seedlings of some of the small alpine kinds have been known to flower when less than two years old.

Cuttings of the small-leaved alpine kinds can be rooted in summer in a mixture of sand and peat moss in a close cold frame or under a bell jar. Those of the larger-leaved kinds, or at least some of them, including the hybrids of R. catawbiense, can be rooted in a mixture of sand and peat moss in a greenhouse propagating case, provided with a little bottom heat. They should be inserted in late summer. Cuttings made of single leaves (with a small hammer-like piece of stem attached at the base) may also be used to generate new plants. They should be inserted at the same time and under the same conditions as ordinary cuttings.

Cuttings of these large-leaved kinds are not easy to root. Before planting, they should be treated with a root-inducing hormone.

Layering may be carried out in spring, pegging the branches firmly into sandy soil, leaf mold or peat, or sandy loam mixed with peat or leaf mold. It is not necessary to notch the shoots, although that is sometimes done. A heap of a mixture of peat moss and sand placed over the layers where they are in contact with the ground will help to keep them moist. Roots are formed slowly, and it is wise to leave the layers undisturbed for two years. They should then be ready to remove with safety.

Grafting and budding should be carried out on healthy seedling understocks that are established in pots. Plants raised from layers should not be used for understocks, owing to their very decided tendency to produce suckers. Any seedlings that show a tendency to produce suckers should not be used either.

The plants to be used as understocks are taken into a warm greenhouse two or three weeks before they are to be grafted, in order that the flow of sap will be more advanced than that of the scions. Healthy shoots with good terminal buds—not flower buds—should be selected as scions, and the method called saddle grafting is the best technique to use. Plants raised by saddle grafting are more stable than those reared from side grafts. March or early April is a good time for the work. As soon as grafted, the plants are placed in a close and warm frame.

Budding may be carried out in a greenhouse in summer at a time when the bark separates easily from the stock—in June or July. It is a means of propagation used when large stocks of a new variety are wanted quickly. As soon as the union between stock and scion is complete, the plants must be removed from the propagating case and be gradually hardened off and placed in a cold frame until they can be planted in a nursery bed.

Hybrid Rhododendrons—Their Development Abroad

Many of the finest Rhododendrons grown in gardens are not natural species (that is to say, they do not occur as native wild plants in any part of the world) but are hybrids that have been raised by crossing various species and by crossbreeding between the resulting hybrids. Certain native American species, notably R. catawbiense, have played important parts as parents of many of these hybrids. The earliest breeding to produce Rhododendron hybrids was done in Europe, but more recently American hybridizers have turned their attentions to Rhododendrons and to the problems of raising varieties adaptable to the climatic conditions of the more favorable parts of North America. As a result, many splendid hybrids have been obtained and, as the breeding work is proceeding actively, we may expect many more improved

varieties to be raised and named in the years ahead.

The First Hybrids. It is probable that the first hybrid between evergreen Rhododendrons resulted from crossing R. catawbiense (an American species) and R. ponticum (a native of southern Europe and Asia Minor). This was effected in England in the early years of the nineteenth century. At that time R. caucasicum, a native of the Caucasus, was also grown in England and some hybridizing seems to have been carried on among all three species. However, the resulting progeny mostly had flowers of various shades of lilac or purple. Cultivators wished to introduce the reds of some of the more tender Himalayan species into the hardier Rhododendrons, therefore they began experimenting with them. Several hardy early-flowering red kinds were raised, but the earliest one that has maintained a prominent place in gardens is R. Nobleanum, a hybrid between R. arboreum and R. caucasicum raised in England about 1832.

This kind, however, flowers early and the blooms are often damaged by frost, therefore

Dexter hybrid Rhododendrons at The New York Botanical Garden.

Mr. Anthony Waterer of the Knap Hill nursery in England selected R. catawbiense as a seed-bearer, and carried out a very extensive series of crosses between this and various other kinds, the object being to raise varieties with R. arboreum "blood," that flowered late and produced shapely bunches of bloom. He was most successful, as were other raisers of the same period from the sixties onward of the last century; many varieties raised at that time are still great favorites in gardens in both Europe and America.

Less Hardy Kinds. While some breeders were giving their attention to raising hardy, fine-flowered varieties, others were concentrating upon the beautiful but more tender kinds, with a view to raising attractive hybrids for the milder parts of Great Britain. R. kewense was an early hybrid of this type. It was raised at Kew, presumably by crossing R. Griffithianum with R. Fortunei. The result is a very beautiful shrub, 12-15 ft. high, bearing large, fragrant, white, rose-flushed flowers in spring.

In Cornwall, England, many beautiful varieties of this type are grown out of doors, and these are adaptable for growing in parts of the Pacific Northwest. Among them are Beauty of Tremough, blush-pink; Ernest Gill, rose-carmine flowers; Gill's Crimson, deep crimson; Gill's Gloriosa, large pink flowers; Gill's Goliath, pink flowers up to 5½ in. in diameter; Gill's Triumph, large crimson flowers; Glory of Leonardslee, bright pink; Glory of Penjerrick, carmine; H. T. Gill, bright rose; Loder's White, large white flowers; Loderi, immense shapely truss or cluster of large white flowers; King George V, flowers as large as those of Loderi but flushed with pink; Manglesii, a hardy kind with large white flowers; Pink Delight, large flowers, white, shaded pink. These kinds can be expected to flourish only in the Pacific Northwest in North America.

Pink Pearl Rhododendron. There is also an extensive group of varieties raised by hybridizing R. Griffithianum and the hardy R. catawbiense varieties. Of this group one of the best-known is Pink Pearl. There are many others for example, Dulcie Daffarn, Daphne Daffarn, The King, and Kathleen M. Dallimore. They flower between March and June. These, too, are suitable for

Many of the Dexter hybrid Rhododendrons have delicately colored flowers which are fragrant.

growing in parts of the Pacific Northwest only.

Another very useful set of hybrid Rhododendrons has been raised by crossing the fragrant-flowered R. Fortunei with various garden hybrids. Most of them have fragrant pink flowers and bloom in May. A few raised in England are Mrs. Thiselton Dyer, Frances Thiselton Dyer, and Miss E. A. Boulton. Similar hybrids raised at Cape Cod, Massachusetts, are hardy in the milder parts of New England and are very beautiful. See The Dexter Hybrids, below.

Hybrid Rhododendrons in America

At the Century Exposition held at Philadelphia in 1876 the English nurseryman Anthony Waterer displayed 1,500 plants of the new Catawba hybrid Rhododendrons that he had raised. These, the first of the new hybrid Rhododendrons seen here, created a sensation and a demand.

The plants that Waterer brought over were sold, and many succeeding shipments were made from England. These specimens were mostly planted in gardens in New England, New York, Pennsylvania and Maryland, usually near coastal cities. A large collection was installed at the Arnold Arboretum near Boston, Massachusetts, and by the end of the century was the largest public collection of hybrid Rhododendrons in the United States.

Not all of the newcomers proved hardy in the Boston area, but a number of varieties did, and were later termed the "ironclads." These are still among the finest Rhododendrons for planting in northeastern America.

The "Ironclads." The hardiest hybrid Rhododendrons, based on observations made in the vicinity of Boston, Massachusetts, over a period of several decades, and supplemented by observations made in other parts of the Northeast, are: album elegans, lavender fading to white; album grandiflorum, good white; atrosanguineum, bright red; Boule de Neige, white; Caractacus, purple-crimson; catawbiense album, pure white; Charles Dickens, medium red; Everestianum, rosy-lilac, frilled; Henrietta Sargent, rose-pink; H. W. Sargent, crimson; Lady Armstrong,

rose, pale center; Mrs. Charles Sargent, rose-red; purpureum elegans, purple; purpureum grandiflorum, purple; roseum elegans, rosy-pink.

All of the above mentioned varieties are R. catawbiense hybrids except Boule de Neige, which is a R. caucasicum hybrid, and album elegans, which is a R. maximum hybrid.

The Dexter Hybrids. In the early years of the twentieth century, interest in the Catawba hybrid Rhododendrons waned in Great Britain as the wealth of new, but more tender, kinds from China and the Himalayas attracted the attention of planters and breeders. As a consequence, hybrids as hardy, or nearly as hardy, as the old "ironclads" were not produced. The new hybrids of the Asiatic kinds that were raised in Europe, especially in Great Britain, were brought to the United States but proved of little or no value in the East, for they would not survive the generally severe winters. They did thrive in favored parts of the West Coast, where the comparatively mild winters and the humid atmosphere are to their liking.

A notable milestone in the history of hybrid Rhododendrons in America occurred in 1922 when Charles O. Dexter of Sandwich, Massachusetts, formed the nucleus of what became

A superb specimen of a Dexter hybrid Rhododendron in full bloom in late May.

A Dexter hybrid. Rhododendron Fortunei is one of its parents.

the finest collection of Rhododendrons in eastern North America.

Sandwich, on Cape Cod, close to the ocean, has a climate that is cooled in summer and moderated in winter by the presence of the nearby sea. It was an ideal location for many Rhododendrons.

Mr. Dexter planted not only the old "ironclads" but as wide a variety of likely species as he could obtain from many sources. Among these were many seedlings of R. Fortunei which had been planted on Cape Cod by John Farquhar, who had obtained them from England.

Although not considered hardy in New England, these seedlings of R. Fortunei prospered in the comparatively mild climate of Cape Cod.

Encouraged by this success and stimulated by the interest of E. H. Wilson of the Arnold Arboretum, Mr. Dexter and his landscape architect, Paul Frost, sought out and obtained seeds of rare Rhododendrons from many sources. Seeds of the rarest kinds grown in England and Scotland and rare kinds received from China by the Arnold Arboretum found their way to Cape Cod.

At Sandwich, large numbers of Himalayan and Chinese Rhododendrons were tested. Many proved tender, but a surprising number thrived. These latter were used in an extensive breeding program initiated and carried out by Mr. Dexter. They were crossed among themselves and with the old "ironclads," and many thousands of hybrid plants were raised before Mr. Dexter's death in 1943.

Many of the Dexter hybrids are supremely beautiful and many are delicately fragrant.

Many of the best have been propagated, and the resulting plants established in both public and private gardens.

The test of time, several decades perhaps, will be needed to properly evaluate these American hybrids. It is unlikely that they will prove as hardy to cold as the old "ironclads," but where conditions are reasonably favorable they should grow well in the northeastern states and form a valuable addition to the rather limited list of broad-leaved evergreens that can be grown there.

The Dexter hybrids provide colors not found among the Catawba hybrids—apricots, peaches, salmons, etc.—as well as the more usual pinks and reds. They have immense trusses of bloom, they flower earlier than the Catawba hybrids, they grow rapidly, and many have the added virtue of fragrance. This group of plants is under study by a committee of the American Rhododendron Society.

More Noteworthy American Hybrids. Charles O. Dexter was by no means the only American breeder of Rhododendrons active during the second decade of the twentieth century and later. Another notable breeder is Joseph Gable of Stewartstown, Pennsylvania, who has devoted tremendous effort to breeding new varieties of Rhododendrons and Azaleas.

Of the many Rhododendron species he grew, he demonstrated by trial that R. Fortunei, R. discolor, R. adenopodum, R. auriculatum, R. longesquamatum, R. racemosum, R. Keiskii, R. Albrechtii, among others, had value as hybrid parents or as subjects for planting in eastern North America.

Among outstanding Rhododendrons that Gable raised and introduced are Disca, Cadis, William Montgomery, The Cardinal and Sir James.

Another pioneer American Rhododendron breeder of note is Guy Nearing of New Jersey. Among the superior kinds raised by Nearing are Beatrice, Pierce, Ramapo, Windbeam, Brandywine and Chesapeake.

Other American Rhododendron breeders have busied themselves in recent years in their efforts to raise superior varieties for American conditions. This work has been, and is being, carried out both in the Northeast and in the Northwest. Results are promising and there seems little doubt that the next decade or two will see notable additions to the list of fine American-raised Rhododendron hybrids.

Until the Federal Plant Quarantine No. 37 went into effect in 1919, very few American nurserymen propagated Rhododendrons and very few hybrids had been raised in the United States. Samuel Parsons, a nurseryman at Flushing, Long Island, New York, had raised several good seedlings, some of which are still in cultivation.

An attempt had been made by Paul Vossburg and Henry Hicks to raise new varieties on Long Island by crossing the finest Catawba hybrid kinds. Meadowbrook was the only one they produced that they considered worth naming and growing on.

Until Plant Quarantine No. 37 became law, it was the practice of nurserymen to import young plants of Rhododendrons from Holland and England and to resell them for planting. The establishment of the quarantine put a virtual end to this practice, and gradually American nurserymen took up the propagation of the choice hybrid Rhododendrons.

This practice has increased until now large numbers of fine plants are raised annually by skilled nurserymen both in the East and on the Pacific coast.

Most of the young plants are propagated by grafting, the favorite stock for this purpose being R. ponticum.

Cuttings and leaf cuttings are also used to some extent as commercial methods of propagating hybrid Rhododendrons.

Layering, a slower method of vegetative propagation, is carried out on a limited scale, mostly by amateurs. Recently air layering, using polyethylene film (see Air Layering) has proved a possible means of propagating hybrid Rhododendrons.

Native American Rhododendrons

The native Rhododendrons of North America include both deciduous (leaf-losing) and evergreen kinds. Most of the former are known as Azaleas, and are treated under that name in this Encyclopedia; one, R. canadense, is by some botanists named Rhodora. (See Rhodora.) Here are discussed the evergreen kinds that have thick, leathery leaves and that are popularly known as Rhododendrons rather than Azaleas.

Certain of the native American Rhododendrons are the hardiest of the evergreen kinds and have been widely used by hybridists to cross with other species to impart tolerance of low temperatures to the progeny.

In parts of North America where Rhododendrons can be grown, it is common practice to plant collected plants (plants taken from the wild) to produce landscape effects. Sometimes these plants are set directly in gardens, sometimes they are grown on in a nursery for a year or two and are then transplanted to gardens. Specimens handled in the last-mentioned way establish themselves with less setback and more surely than does newly collected stock.

These collected plants, or, for that matter, the same kinds raised from seeds or propagated from layers or cuttings, are mostly not nearly so fine as the better hybrid kinds. In many cases gardeners would find greater final satisfaction from setting out smaller specimens of choice hybrids (always choosing kinds hardy to the locality) than from planting larger collected plants.

The Catawba Rhododendron. A native of mountainous regions from Virginia to Georgia,

where it reaches elevations of 6,000 ft., R. catawbiense is one of the best-known of American kinds. It is sometimes called the Mountain Rose Bay.

Under favorable conditions this Rhododendron attains a height of 20 ft. but it is generally lower. It forms a shapely bush, broad and well-furnished with foliage to its base. Its flower clusters are of good size, although not extraordinarily large, and they are expanded before new growth develops sufficiently to hide them. Unfortunately, their color is not so good. In typical forms it is lilac-purple or reddish-purple, with leanings to vinous or magenta shades that in gardens are not considered particularly pleasing and that are difficult to associate with most reds and pinks.

R. catawbiense is hardy as far north as New England. In the North it suffers from damage in winter if it is exposed in a south-facing or east-facing position to strong winter sunshine or cold sweeping winds.

R. catawbiense has been much used by hybridizers, and some of its hybrid offspring are among the best Rhododendrons for planting in eastern North America.

White-flowered plants of R. catawbiense are sometimes found in the wild but they are usually less attractive than the plant commonly sold and

A native of the mountains of the southeastern United States, Rhododendron catawbiense has given rise to many splendid hybrid kinds.

grown as R. catawbiense album, which may be of hybrid origin. This last-named is a very fine variety.

The Hardiest Kind. R. maximum, the Great Laurel or Rose Bay, is the hardiest of all evergreen Rhododendrons. It occurs natively as far north as Nova Scotia, Quebec and Ontario and southwards to Alabama, being especially abundant through the Alleghenies. It is a most valuable evergreen for garden planting where few other broad-leaved evergreens will withstand the winter cold.

R. maximum attains a height of 30 ft. or more in the southern part of its range but not more than half this height in the northernmost parts. In gardens it usually ranges from 10-12 ft. tall. It has a rather loose habit of growth, and this may be accentuated if the plants are unduly crowded.

The flowers of R. maximum are borne late, after most Rhododendrons have finished blooming, and they are in disappointingly small heads. Usually they are partly hidden by the new growths. In color they are pale, rather washed-out pink, but are deeper colored in the bud stage. They are completely without the objectionable magenta-pink tones that characterize the flowers of R. catawbiense. R. maximum is

Hardiest of evergreen kinds, the native Rhododendron maximum has magnificent foliage but its blooms are comparatively small and less attractive than those of many other kinds.

usually less free-flowering than R. catawbiense.

This Rhododendron in nature inhabits damp, deep woods, ravines, river banks and the margins of bogs. In cultivation it needs a moist but not waterlogged soil, shade and shelter from winds. It will not stand open locations nor as much sunshine as R. catawbiense and it needs moister soil. In heavy shade it produces magnificent foliage but flowers more sparsely or not at all; this scarcely matters, however, for this is a shrub worth growing more for its foliage than for its bloom. Rhododendron maximum variety album is a white-flowered kind.

Kinds Native to the Southeast. One of the most lovely of the native American Rhododendrons is the Carolina Rhododendron, R. carolinianum. This species inhabits the Blue Ridge Mountains in North Carolina, South Carolina and Tennessee, growing profusely on mountain summits and in woodlands.

Ordinarily this shrub grows 3-6 ft. tall and is of compact growth. Specimens somewhat taller are not unusual and the variety foliatum, which is of looser habit, may attain a height of 15 ft.

The foliage is small and of neat appearance. The flower heads are borne in great abundance and are very handsome. They are less massive than those of R. catawbiense but the color is more attractive. The flower color varies from white (usually not a very good white) through soft pink, pale pink, rose and lavender-pink. Usually the buds are of a deeper color.

Rhododendron carolinianum and its varieties are about as hardy and require the same culture as R. catawbiense, with the one exception that they are more sensitive to dry conditions at the root. For their best development they must have a constantly moist, but well-drained soil.

Rhododendron minus is closely related to R. carolinianum and is similar in general appearance. It is of looser growth and it blooms considerably later than R. carolinianum. It is less attractive as a garden plant, but, as it grows naturally on the lower elevations of the Blue Ridge Mountains of North Carolina to Georgia and Alabama and of the adjacent inner Coastal Plain, it may have value in parts of the country that are unsuitable for the cultivation of its relatives.

The flowers of R. minus vary from purplish-rose through magenta-pink to bright magenta. They are more or less hidden by the young shoot and leaf growth. In cultivation it has proved equally as hardy as R. carolinianum. Records indicate that it has survived temperatures of 20 degrees below zero satisfactorily.

A Florida Native. R. Chapmanii is a rare species that occurs as a native in sandy pine lands near the Gulf Coast of Florida, a most unlikely place for a Rhododendron.

A plant of sea-level country, this species is most nearly related to R. carolinianum of the southern Appalachian Mountain region. It attains a height of 6 ft.

R. Chapmanii in general appearance resembles R. carolinianum; it is little known in cultivation. Its greatest value appears to be for planting in the far South and similar warm climates where most Rhododendrons will not grow, and as a parent of possible hybrids suitable for planting under similar conditions.

A West Coast Native. R. macrophyllum, sometimes called R. californicum, is the West Coast representative of R. catawbiense. It is considered to be a finer plant than its eastern relative but it is much less hardy. It does not thrive in the East; it cannot be expected to survive north of Philadelphia.

R. macrophyllum inhabits the mountains from California to British Columbia. It grows 6-12 ft. tall and bears rosy-purple or pink flowers that are spotted with yellow or brownish markings. In the bud stage the flowers are carmine.

This species is suitable for planting in gardens on parts of the Pacific coast but it is less decorative than many of the splendid hybrid kinds that can be grown there.

An Arctic Rhododendron. The Lapland Rhododendron, R. lapponicum, is a plant of the Arctic tundras and alpine tops of northern mountains. It occurs in Labrador and on Mount Washington in the eastern United States and also in northern Europe and northern Asia.

This beautiful plant grows a foot tall or less and bears bright purple blooms. It is notoriously difficult to cultivate and is unlikely to really succeed except where cool summers prevail and under the care of expert cultivators. It has been grown in gardens in the vicinity of New York City by skilled amateurs.

Natives of Europe and the Caucasus

A few cultivated Rhododendrons are natives of Europe and of the Caucasus. With the exception of R. ponticum, these are all reasonably hardy in the northeastern United States, and all can be grown in the Pacific Northwest. R. caucasicum, R. ponticum and R. Smirnowi have been used as parents in developing a group of hardy hybrid Rhododendrons. R. ponticum is used as an understock upon which to graft hybrids. R. lapponicum, described above under Native American Rhododendrons, also is a native of northern Europe.

R. caucasicum grows to a height of 2 ft. or less and has leaves that measure up to 4 in. long. Its flowers, which are borne in June or July, are pink or yellowish white spotted with green and are about 2 in. across.

R. ferrugineum, a native of the mountains of central Europe and called there the Alpine Rose (as also is the closely related R. hirsutum), grows 3-4 ft. high and forms a compact bush. Its flowers are deep pink or rose-scarlet and measure about ½ in. across. The leaves are shining green on their upper sides, rusty colored and scaly beneath. They are 1-1¾ in. long.

R. hirsutum is generally similar to R. ferrugineum and, like it, is called Alpine Rose in its native mountains of central Europe. It is one of the few Rhododendrons that will stand limey soils. In a wild state it is only found growing in limestone soil.

R. Kotschyi is a shrub of central Europe that attains a height of about 1½ ft. and that is sometimes called R. ferrugineum variety myrtifolium. Its flowers are clear rose pink and its leaves ¼-¾ in. long.

R. ponticum is a vigorous species that becomes a tall shrub or small tree and may range in height from 12 to 20 ft. It is a native of Spain and Portugal and of Asia Minor. Its flowers are purple, lavender-purple or pinkish purple, are spotted with brown and are in clusters that measure about 5 in. across. The leaves are 4-6 in. long and paler below than above.

R. Smirnowii is a very hardy kind that grows into a shrub 12-18 ft. high with leaves 4-6 in. long. It bears trusses of flowers that may vary in color from pale to deep rose-purple. The margins of the petals are distinctly frilled, and the individual flowers measure 2-3 in. wide. This kind, which blooms in May, is a native of the Caucasus.

R. Ungernii, of the Caucasus, attains a maximum height of 20 ft. in its native habitat but is considerably lower as known under cultivation. Its leaves are 4-7 in. long and its white or light rose-colored flowers are borne in trusses that measure about 6 in. across. It flowers late, usually in July.

Himalayan Rhododendrons

The travels of the English botanist Sir Joseph Dalton Hooker in the Sikkim Himalayas, about the middle of the last century, resulted in the introduction into England of many very beautiful kinds of Rhododendrons from that region. A few of these had been introduced previous to his visit, others arrived afterwards, but it was he who discovered many of these fine plants, and his descriptions of them led to their wide cultivation in England.

Suitable for Mild Localities. Soon after their introduction it was found that although these Himalayan shrubs were not hardy enough for general planting in the British Isles, they were excellent for the milder parts, and plants were sent to Cornwall for trial in sheltered gardens. They throve amazingly, and now some of the gardens are stocked with immense bushes of these handsome kinds. There are trees of R. arboreum over 30 ft. high which, in spring, are covered with bright red or pink flowers, and there are handsome bushes of R. grande and R. Falconeri that have been known to bear 500-1,000 heads of flowers each in a season. From Cornwall they were sent to other likely gardens and there are now many fine bushes in the warmer gardens of England, Wales, Scotland and Ireland.

More recently these kinds have been introduced into gardens in the Pacific Northwest, where, as in the milder parts of Great Britain, the climate favors their growth. The actual degree of hardiness of these Himalayan kinds varies considerably according to species; some are much more cold-resistant than others, but none can be expected to survive outdoors in regions of cold winters.

The Hardier Himalayan Species. Among the more cold-resistant are the kinds we shall now describe.

The beautiful R. arboreum may be a tree 30-40 ft. high, with a trunk a foot or more through, surmounted by a large, dense head of branches, or a shapely bush of large size, well-branched from the ground to the top. The dense flower heads in the best varieties of this species are made up of crimson or blood-red blossoms, but there are others with bright red, pink and white blossoms.

R. barbatum is another Himalayan bush. It can be distinguished by its deep red flowers in early spring and by the leafstalks' being armed with stiff bristles.

R. campanulatum, from the Sikkim Himalayas, is a large, dense bush, 6-12 ft. high with oblong leaves 3-5½ in. long and 1¼-2½ in. wide, dark green above and covered with dense brown or gray-brown feltlike hairs beneath. The flowers are in moderate-sized bunches and are purplish, rosy purple or lilac in color. It is one of the hardiest of the Himalayan Rhododendrons.

R. campylocarpum is the loveliest of the yellow-flowered evergreen Rhododendrons, growing up to 8 ft. tall and bearing, in May, clusters of bell-shaped, soft yellow flowers of waxy texture. Crossed with other species, it has given a race of very beautiful hybrids.

R. ciliatum is a shrub 4-5 ft. high with densely hairy leaves, and bearing very beautiful white, rose-flushed flowers in spring. In addition to being crossed with more tender kinds, R. ciliatum was also crossbred with a hardier one, and such excellent early-flowering Rhododendrons as R. praecox and R. Rosy Bell are partly the progeny of R. ciliatum.

R. Edgeworthii is an epiphytal species (kind that grows on other plants) from the Himalayas. It has rather straggling branches, dark-green leaves, the undersurface a mass of soft feltlike hairs, and it bears very beautiful, fragrant white flowers, 4 in. or more across, with prettily waved

Rhododendron Falconeri has huge leaves and terminal clusters of bell-shaped, creamy white flowers. It is one of the most handsome, both in foliage and bloom.

petals. It has been used in the production of a lovely group of hybrids.

R. Falconeri has leaves 6-12 in. long and 3-6 in. wide, and large, compact clusters of cream-white flowers; the clusters are 6-9 in. high, and as far through. The leaves are interesting by reason of their deep-green surface and the underside being covered with dense reddish brown feltlike hairs.

R. formosum, from Assam, bears fragrant rose-pink flowers on a bush that attains a height of 8-10 ft.

R. fulgens grows 6-12 ft. high and bears compact heads of crimson blooms.

R. grande is very attractive. It forms a very large bush or small tree with handsome leaves produced in whorls; the leaves, which are dark green above and silvery beneath, are 6-12 in. long and 3-5 in. wide. A considerable number of flowers, each 2-2½ in. long and wide, are borne together in dense heads, 8-9 in. long and wide. The flowers are cream-colored, often with a reddish blotch at the base of one petal. There is a form called roseum with reddish blooms.

Another very beautiful kind which grows into a large bush is R. Griffithianum. It forms a rather loose bush or small tree, with leaves 6-9 in. long and 3 in. wide, and bears loose heads of white, saucer-shaped, slightly fragrant flowers, which are 5-6 in. across. The calyx is also large and striking. R. Griffithianum variety Auklandii has larger flowers.

R. Hodgsonii is a large bush or small tree that bears leaves 6-18 in. long and has compact trusses or clusters of rosy lilac flowers. Its foliage is particularly handsome.

R. Kingianum is a vigorous plant of stiff habit, bearing dense heads of crimson flowers rather like those of R. arboreum. It is found in Manipur.

R. lepidotum, a native of the Himalayas, grows 2-4 ft. tall and in June bears its pale yellow, pink or dull purple flowers in trusses of two, four or occasionally six. It is a suitable shrub for cultivating in rock gardens.

R. Nuttallii forms long, straggling branches clothed with large leaves, and bears sulphur-colored or white, fragrant flowers, four to six together. The individual flowers are about 5 in. long and almost as wide across the mouth, giving the impression, at first sight, of a large Lily. It has, indeed, the largest flowers of any Rhododendron. Several hybrids have been raised between this and R. formosum, including R. Edinense and R. Tyermanni. Another very beautiful hybrid with fragrant tubular flowers, R. Victorianum, is the progeny of R. Nuttallii and R. Dalhousiae.

R. Thomsonii is another very attractive kind from Nepal and Sikkin, bearing blood-red flowers. In this case the individual blooms have longer tubes than those mentioned above, and they have also a large calyx.

R. Veitchianum is a white, fragrant-flowered plant of great beauty. It is a native of Burma and the flowers, which are borne several together, are 4-5 in. across. Beautiful crossbred varieties, which have been raised from the foregoing kinds, are Countess of Sefton, Mrs. James Shawe, forsterianum, fragrantissimum and sesterianum.

Tender Himalayan Kinds. A group of Himalayan kinds which are more tender than those mentioned consists of several very beautiful shrubs, some of which have long slender branches with large fragrant flowers. In a state of nature some of them live as epiphytes, growing on humus collected in the forks of trees. They respond very well, however, to ordinary methods of cultivation, but in most parts of the United States and in Canada they must be grown under glass during the cold months.

All are evergreen and many of them can be increased by cuttings of short side shoots set in pots of sandy peat placed in a warm propagating case. The cuttings should be taken as soon as the shoots are becoming a little firm. These kinds are little known in North America.

Chinese, Burmese and Tibetan Kinds

Chinese, Upper Burmese and Tibetan Rhododendrons of comparatively recent introduction are so numerous that it is impossible to do more than direct attention to them and to give a selection from among the several hundred kinds that have been brought into cultivation, chiefly during the present century.

Among these plants are many very beautiful kinds, although it is doubtful whether any of them are superior to the best of the older Himalayan Rhododendrons. Many are comparatively hardy, as far as winter cold is concerned, but they begin to grow early in spring and many bloom early in the year. Because of this it is not unusual for the young growth and flowers to be killed by late frosts, or crippled by cold winds. However, there are many that succeed quite well in sheltered locations where winters are not excessively severe. All or nearly all are likely to thrive in the Pacific Northwest, some few prosper in the Northeast at least as far north as Boston.

These plants grow best where they are screened from the early morning sun. An open wood of Oak or Pine makes an ideal location. They thrive near the sea, but great care must be taken that they are not planted in brackish ground, for even slightly salt water is harmful not only to these but to all kinds of Rhododendrons.

These Chinese, Burmese and Tibetan kinds show a very wide diversity of habit, from moderate-sized trees to dwarf alpine plants. Their leaves and flowers also vary greatly. Their flowering time is from late winter to late July, when the latest of all known Rhododendrons, R. auriculatum, opens its large white, fragrant blossoms. The collectors Wilson, Forrest, Farrer and Kingdon-Ward were chiefly responsible for the introduction of these kinds.

Low Kinds for Rock Gardens. In addition to

[10—12]
Genista and Basket of Gold
(Alyssum saxatile)

[10—13]

A rock bank planted with spring blooming plants

such older Rhododendrons as the Chinese R. racemosum, the Himalayan R. lepidotum and the European R. ferrugineum and R. hirsutum, many of the newer kinds from China, Tibet and upper Burma are suitable for rock gardens. Among the best low kinds for rock gardens are the ones we shall now describe.

R. racemosum usually does not exceed 3-4 ft. in height but sometimes it grows a foot or two taller. It has small leaves that are densely scaly on their undersurfaces. Its flowers are produced freely in clusters of 3 to 6. Each flower measures about 1 in. across and may be deep pink, pale pink or even white. R. racemosum is a spring-blooming kind that shows considerable variation in height, flower color and time of blooming.

R. calostrotum, from northeastern upper Burma, is a low or prostrate shrub with gray-green leaves and conspicuous rose-pink flowers. R. campylogynum, a small-leaved kind from Yunnan, of compact, cushionlike habit, has purplish flowers.

R. keleticum is a charming shrub, less than 1 ft. high, with slender branches, small leaves and solitary crimson or purplish-crimson flowers. R. saluenense, a slow-growing bush, 2 ft. high, from western China, produces small, sage-green leaves and violet flowers, and is one of the most charming of the dwarfs.

R. impeditum, 12-15 in. high, with small leaves and small, violet flowers, is a native of western China; it is a very neat and compact plant. Another very dainty little plant, 9-12 in. high, is R. intricatum; it is of compact habit, with small leaves and lavender-blue flowers produced in early spring. It is found wild in Szechuan. An allied kind is R. fastigiatum, a pigmy plant from Yunnan, with tiny leaves and conspicuous violet-colored flowers. This has been known to flower in 18 months from the time the seed is planted.

R. hippophaeoides grows 2-3 ft. high or sometimes taller; it may bear lavender, blue or pinkish flowers. It is a native of Yunnan and one of the best of its type. R. scintillans is another very beautiful dwarf, blue-flowered shrub from Yunnan. R. flavidum, from Szechuan, has small, yellow flowers; it blooms in April and forms a good contrast to the blue-flowered kinds.

R. Williamsianum is an extremely beautiful, very dwarf and sometimes prostrate shrub with slender branchlets, broadly ovate leaves and large rosy-pink flowers; it is from western Szechuan and is excellent for growing over low sandstone rocks. R. sperabile is a compact little plant from northeastern upper Burma, with small leaves which, together with the shoots, are densely woolly; the waxy-textured flowers are tubular and scarlet or crimson in color. R. orthocladum from western Yunnan, grows 1-1½ ft. high, bearing small leaves and small mauve flowers.

R. pubescens may eventually grow 2-3 ft. high but it develops slowly; the shoots and leaves are covered with soft hairs, the flowers small and pink. R. spinuliferum is a rather dense, erect shrub from Yunnan and western China; it has curious, tubular, brick-red or orange-red flowers.

R. repens is a tiny prostrate shrub, a few inches high, producing its leaves in small clusters; its tubular crimson flowers are borne singly. It is a typical rock plant, and was found in Yunnan and Tibet. R. sanguineum is another crimson-flowered plant that grows very slowly. R. Forrestii, which also has crimson flowers, is a very good rock-garden plant from southeastern Tibet and Yunnan, with creeping branches.

Some Taller Kinds. The following is a selection of the larger kinds of the newer Rhododendrons from China and Tibet:

R. discolor is a large spreading bush, 15 or more ft. high, native to central China. It has oblong, dark green leaves, 4-8 in. long and 1-2½ in. wide, and fragrant white or pink flushed flowers, 2½-3 in. across, in loose clusters. It is related to the older R Fortunei, and, like that plant, its flowers are composed of seven petals. It has been used by the hybridist, and a number of hybrid kinds have been raised. It is hardy in mild places in New England.

R. decorum is an allied shrub flowering in late June and July, although there are varieties that bloom both earlier and later. The fragrant flowers vary in color from white to pink. It is about as hardy as R. discolor and has been used by the hybridist.

R. praevernum is a free-growing, compact bush with handsome foliage; it reaches a height of at least 5-6 ft. and produces fine trusses of

The small-leaved, evergreen, early spring-flowering Rhododendron racemosum. Its flowers are in varying shades of pink.

large white, or white, pink-tinted flowers with a dark red blotch in the throat, early in spring. It is a native of China. R. sutchuenense is a very similar but larger bush that flowers at the same time. It grows 10 or more ft. high, and its larger leaves may be 9-10 in. long and 2½ in. wide. The flowers are very like those of R. praevernum. Both are hardy in sheltered places in the vicinity of New York City.

R. Griersonianum is a very distinct kind from western Yunnan. Growing 6-7 ft. high, with a similar spread, it is notable for its intensely hairy shoots and leaves, its long, bractlike bodies enclosing the buds, and its bright rose or red tubular flowers, which are 2-3 in. long with narrow tubes and about 1½ in. across the mouth. A large number of hybrids have already been raised with this as one parent.

A Beautiful Crimson-flowered Rhododendron. R. neriiflorum, which gives its name to a series, is a delightful shrub with rich crimson flowers, the large-lobed calyx being similar in color to the bell-shaped corolla. The dark-green leaves are white underneath. It grows 3-9 ft. high. It is found in western China and Tibet.

R. adenopodum belongs to the arboreum series. The deep green leaves are covered beneath with grayish feltlike hairs, the flowers are large and of a delicate shade of pink. It grows several feet high and is a native of China. R. argyrophyllum is an allied shrub which grows up to 20 ft. high and has long lance-shaped leaves covered beneath with white feltlike hairs. The rosy-pink flowers appear in May, but it does not appear to flower very freely.

Blooms When Very Small. R. callimorphum, from Yunnan, although eventually a shrub several feet high, is a particularly slow-growing

Rhododendron Fortunei, a fragrant-flowered kind from China, is the parent of many fine hybrids.

shrub when young. It bears pink flowers freely.

R. yunnanense was one of the earliest of the newer Chinese kinds to be introduced. At maturity it may be 10-12 ft. high and a large spreading bush, but it begins to flower when very small, and rarely misses flowering well. It has slender branches, rather small glossy green leaves, and blush-colored flowers with brown-crimson spots, produced in small clusters from the points of the shoots in May.

R. concinum belongs to the same triflorum series. It grows at least 6 ft. high, and is very striking when in flower in May by reason of its mass of purple-crimson flowers. The shade of the flowers, however, varies in different plants. R. Davidsonianum is, together with the last-named, a Chinese shrub of the triflorum series. The flowers are white, flushed pink, with crimson spots. It grows at least 5-6 ft. high, and is of rather slender growth.

Other desirable kinds in this series are R. chartophyllum, white or blush; R. ambiguum,

Rhododendron praevernum, a Chinese kind with white or blush-pink flowers, is one of the earliest to bloom.

yellow; R. chasmanthoides, rose-lavender; R. lutescens, lemon-yellow; and R. Augustinii, the Blue Rhododendron, a very beautiful kind with flowers varying from lilac to pale blue, of which several forms have been given variety names, such as Blue Diamond, Blue Tit, etc.

R. irroratum is a variable shrub which may be found between 6-30 ft. high in its native country, Yunnan. The flowers are in small clusters, and they may be from white to pink and deep crimson on different plants.

The Latest of All Rhododendrons to Bloom. A very late flowering kind is R. auriculatum, a large shrub or tree up to 30 ft. high, native to central China, with leaves 6-13 in. long and 2-5 in. wide, which bears very large, fragrant, white flowers in late July and August. The new growth is rarely made before late July. It was introduced into cultivation in 1900, and has been used as a parent by breeders.

This selection of the newer kinds directs attention to the wide variation in stature and habit, and in size, color and shape of flowers found among them.

Rhododendrons with Immense Leaves and Large Bunches of Flowers. There is a distinct group characterized by very large leaves and large heads of flowers—the Rhododendron grande series. We shall now describe some of the outstanding members of this group. They are adaptable only for conditions such as prevail in the Pacific Northwest.

R. sino-grande is a tree 30-35 ft. high, with dark green leaves 20-24 in. long and 8 in. wide, larger on a very vigorous plant. Leaves 3 ft. long and 1 ft. wide have been recorded. The large cream-colored, bell-shaped flowers are produced in very large heads in May. Each flower has a crimson blotch inside. This remarkable plant is a native of Yunnan.

An even more striking tree is R. giganteum. This grows 80-100 ft. in height in its native country, Yunnan, with a trunk 6 ft. or more in girth. The leaves are 12-14 in. long on old specimens, and the flower trusses are very large; the individual flowers are large and varying in shade from rose-pink to magenta-crimson, with a deep crimson blotch at the base.

R. praestans is another large-leaved bush or tree, 20-30 ft. high. It is allied to R. sino-grande, but has narrower leaves and rose-colored flowers, and seems to be of slower growth. R. protistum is another of this series, growing 20-30 ft. high, with large leaves slightly downy on both surfaces and heads of cream-white flowers flushed with rose. It is from northwestern Yunnan.

R. fictolacteum, which belongs to the R. Falconeri series, is characterized by very large leaves which are dark green above and covered by brownish feltlike hairs beneath. The leaves are 12-18 in. long and 4-5 in. wide. The white flowers are borne in fair-sized trusses, and there is a red blotch at the base of each.

Natives of Java and Malaya

The Javanese and Malayan Rhododendrons are too tender for cultivation out of doors except in mild climates. They may be grown in a greenhouse where a minimum winter temperature of 45-50 degrees F. can be maintained. They are easily raised from cuttings of young shoots, 4-5 in. long, inserted in sandy soil in a warm and close propagating frame. They may be grown in pots or planted in a border of soil in the greenhouse. The border should be raised a little above the paths and be well drained. A compost of light, sandy loam and peat, or sandy peat alone, placed among large pieces of sandstone, suits these plants well.

These Rhododendrons are of straggling habit and do not branch well after pruning. When they are grown in pots, the shoots are sometimes trained around stakes. There are many hybrids, in addition to the few species, and most of them have brightly colored, waxy-textured flowers. If a collection is grown, flowers may be found at almost any season of the year.

The species or wild types are R. jasminiflorum, from Java; R. javanicum, also from Java; and R. malayanum from Malaya.

Of varieties or hybrids the following is a good selection: Ajax, orange-red; Amabile, flesh-colored, tinged rose; Aphrodite, blush-pink; aureum, yellow; carneum, flesh-colored; Brilliant, scarlet; Mrs. Heal, white; President, buff-yellow, tinted rose; Triumphans, crimson-scarlet; Sybil, rosy-pink; Primrose, primrose-yellow; Taylori, bright pink, white tube. Balsaminiaeflorum album has double white flowers and Balsaminiaeflorum aureum has double yellow flowers.

These Javan and Malayan Rhododendrons and their hybrids are probably not in cultivation in America or, if so, are grown only by a few fanciers.

RHODOHYPOXIS BAUERI (Rhodohypox'is). A dainty little perennial herb, the only member of its genus, belonging to the family Amaryllidaceae, the Amaryllis family. The name is derived from *rhodon,* rose, and Hypoxis, another genus of plants, and refers to the flower color and botanical relationship of the plant. It is a native of South Africa and will survive the winter outdoors, in places where little frost is experienced, if planted in a sunny, well-drained position in light soil. It is also suitable for use as a pot subject for the alpine house.

Rhodohypoxis Baueri forms tufts of erect, narrow leaves about 4 in. tall and covered with silky hairs. The flowers are produced singly on 4-in. pedicels and are soft rose-red, paler beneath. A variety, R. Baueri platypetala, has white flowers.

RHODOMYRTUS (Rhodomyrt'us). Shrubs and trees of tropical and subtropical Asia and Australia, one kind of which is in cultivation. These plants belong to the Myrtle family, Myrtaceae. The name is from *rhodon,* rose, and *myrtos,* Myrtle.

Rhodomyrtus tomentosa, the Downy Myrtle or Hill Gooseberry, is an evergreen shrub that is a native of Ceylon, India, Malaya, Japan, China, and the Philippines. It bears large, purple, pleasantly flavored berries which may be used for making jellies, jams and pies.

This shrub grows without difficulty in a wide variety of soils. It withstands a few degrees of frost and is suitable for planting in the warmer parts of the South.

Propagation is effected by means of seed. The seeds should be sown in flats or in a frame or outdoor seedbed of light, well-drained soil. Sowing should be done soon after the seeds are removed from the fruits. The plants require ample water during their season of active growth.

The Downy Myrtle is a handsome plant in foliage, flower and fruit. Its flowers are pink and somewhat resemble single roses. The flowers are borne in spring, the fruits in early summer, the latter usually ripening over a period of several weeks.

RHODORA CANADENSIS—*Rhodora* (Rhodo'ra). The only cultivated member of a small genus of plants which by many botanists is now included in Rhododendron. It belongs in the Heath family, Ericaceae. The name is derived from the Greek *rhodon,* a Rose.

Rhodora canadensis occurs as a native of bogs and wet woods from Newfoundland and Quebec to Ontario and southwards to eastern Pennsylvania and southern New Jersey. It is a branched, leaf-losing (deciduous) shrub 2-3 ft. high with dark green leaves that are narrowly oblong to elliptic in shape and 1½-2 in. long. Its flowers appear in early spring at the same time as its leaves expand or slightly before. They are in terminal, few-flowered clusters and normally rose-purple in color, but they sometimes vary to white. Each flower measures about 2 in. across. When in bloom, this shrub is decidedly decorative.

As a garden plant Rhodora canadensis is useful for planting in moist or wet acid soil in slight shade or in sun. It is a good plant for wild gardens, bog gardens, rock gardens and similar informal plantings.

Propagation is effected by sowing seeds in the same manner as with Rhododendron and Azalea. See Rhododendron and Azalea.

RHODOSTACHYS (Rhodo'stachys; Rhodostach'ys). South American evergreen plants that belong to the Pineapple family, Bromeliaceae. The name is derived from *rhodon,* rose, and *stachys,* flower spike, and refers to the rose-colored flowers of some kinds. Their cultural requirements are the same as for Bromelia, which see.

Kinds are R. andina, leaves 1 ft. long, flowers rose-colored, a native of Chile; R. pitcairniifolia, leaves 1 ft. long, the inner ones of the rosette bright red at their bases, flowers blue, a native of Chile.

RHODOTHAMNUS CHAMAECISTUS — *Ground Cistus* (Rhodotham'nus). A charming little evergreen shrub, native to the European Alps and Siberia, allied to Rhododendron and

Rhodothamnus Chamaecistus, a dwarf evergreen shrub, closely related to Rhododendron, which bears clusters of rose-colored flowers in spring. It is a gem for the rock garden, but difficult to grow successfully.

belonging to the Heath family, Ericaceae, but differing from most of the other plants in that family by growing on limestone soil. It forms a low bush, 6-12 in. high, with narrow, oval leaves ¼-½ in. long, glossy green, edged with stiff short hairs. The rose-colored flowers, each 1-1¼ in. across, appear in April in clusters of two to four at the points of the shoots.

It is very difficult to cultivate and appears to do best when planted in a crevice between large stones in the rock garden. It is notoriously difficult to propagate by seeds, cuttings or layers.

Where it does thrive it should be left alone, for disturbance may mean the death of a plant and difficulty may be found in establishing another under what are apparently identical conditions.

The name Rhodothamnus is from the Greek *rhodon,* a rose, and *thamnos,* a shrub, and alludes to the rose-colored flowers.

RHODOTYPOS TETRAPETALA—*Jetbead* (Rhodoty′pos). A leaf-losing shrub, 4-6 ft. high, native to China, and often grown in gardens under the name of R. kerrioides. It has opposite leaves, and bears white flowers in May and June.

This plant is easily increased by seeds sown in the frame as soon as ripe, or in the following spring; or cuttings of half-ripe wood, 4 in. long, may be inserted in a frame in July.

Any good garden soil is suitable for this shrub, and it thrives in sun or part shade. Pruning takes the form of thinning out some of the older wood as soon as the flowers have faded. An occasional surface dressing of well-decayed manure or of good compost will be beneficial to this shrub.

The Jetbead has been in cultivation since 1866, and is allied to the golden-flowered Kerria japonica; it belongs to the Rose family, Rosaceae. The name Rhodotypos was taken from the Greek *rhodon,* a rose, and *typos,* type, and refers to the roselike type of bloom.

**RHOEO DISCOLOR — ***Moses-in-a-Boat*

Moses-in-a-Boat is the common name applied to Rhoeo discolor. It is often cultivated as a house plant.

(Rhoe'o). An evergreen perennial member of the Spiderwort family, Commelinaceae, that is a native of the West Indies and Mexico and is naturalized in southern Florida. It is popularly grown in pots as a house plant and greenhouse plant.

The common name Moses-in-a-Boat, by which this plant is sometimes known, alludes to the fact that the small, white flowers are surrounded by two conspicuous leafy organs called bracts, the two together forming a boat-shaped surrounding for the blooms. The flowers are not showy and each remains open for only a few hours, but they open, in succession, daily over a long period. The derivation of the botanical name Rhoeo (pronounced ree-oh) is unknown.

Rhoeo discolor, the only species, is of erect growth and has a stem that grows to an eventual height of 6-9 in. The leaves are attractive; they are fleshy, more or less erect, 1 ft. or rather less in length, dark olive-green above and purple beneath. The bracts and flowers nestle in the leaf axils against the stem.

This plant has the general appearance of an erect-growing Tradescantia, to which genus it is closely allied; in fact at one time it was called Tradescantia discolor.

In addition to the typical green-leaved kind there is a variety, R. discolor vittata, in which each leaf is striped lengthwise on the upper side with pale yellow.

The culture of Rhoeo presents no difficulties. It thrives in any reasonably good potting soil, preferring one that is rich and well supplied with leaf mold, rotted manure, humus or other decayed organic matter.

The pots should be well-drained and the soil should be kept moderately moist but not waterlogged. Well-rooted specimens benefit from regular applications of dilute liquid fertilizer.

Good light, but with some shade from the strongest summer sun, suits this plant best. A temperature of 60-70 degrees is satisfactory.

Propagation is very easily carried out by means of cuttings at any time. Spring is an especially favorable season for taking cuttings. They root readily in a greenhouse propagating case, in a terrarium, or under a Mason jar in a window. Sand, sand and peat moss, or vermiculite are good media in which to set the cuttings to root.

Seeds afford another easy method of securing increase. These should be sown in a pot of light soil in a temperature of 70-75 degrees. Spring is a good time to sow seeds.

RHOPALOSTYLIS—*Nikau Palm* (Rhopalos'-tylis). Uncommon Palms from New Zealand, Norfolk and Chatham Islands; in their native habitats they grow from 30-40 ft. in height, but small plants in pots are very ornamental. They have stout, treelike, cylindrical trunks, terminated by a cluster of large pinnate (feather-like) leaves; the leaflets are linear (long and narrow) and have prominent midribs. The name Rhopalostylis is from *rhopalon,* a club, and *stylos,* a pillar, and refers to the club-shaped spadix (flower spike). These Palms may be grown outdoors in Florida and in southern California. Rhopalostylis belongs to the family Palmaceae.

Palms for a Warm Greenhouse. The conditions necessary to success with these Palms, when they are grown indoors, are a minimum winter temperature of 50 degrees, a moist atmosphere and shade from strong sunlight. Small plants are repotted annually in March, using a compost of equal parts of loam and leaf mold, to which a liberal amount of sand is added.

When repotting, the roots are disturbed as little as possible. Well-drained pots are used and the compost is made firm with a potting stick.

Plants in large pots do not require repotting each year. It is sufficient to remove a little of the topsoil in March and replace it with fresh compost. During the summer months occasional applications of liquid fertilizer are necessary. During the summer months the soil is kept moist, but at other times water is applied only when it becomes moderately dry.

Raising Seedlings. Young plants are raised from seeds. They require a bottom heat of 75-85 degrees to cause them to germinate, and it is best to file them or soak them in warm water for a few days before sowing. They are set half an inch deep in pans of sandy soil, which are kept moist until the seedlings are 2 in. high, when they are potted separately in small pots and transferred to larger pots as becomes necessary.

The chief kinds are R. sapida, 30 ft., and R. Baueri, 40 ft. These Palms are included by some botanists in the genus Areca.

RHUBARB—*Pieplant.* The garden or edible Rhubarb is derived from varieties of Rheum Rhaponticum, a Siberian plant which was introduced into European gardens 300 years ago. The leafstalks form an article of diet. As it is in season in spring when fresh fruits are scarce, it was, and is, valued as a substitute for them.

Rhubarb thrives in ordinary soil but gives the best results in land which has been deeply prepared and well-manured.

Planting is done in early spring, the plants being set 4 ft. apart and the crowns or tops just covered with soil. After planting, the soil should be top-dressed with manure or rich compost. The flower spikes must be removed as they appear, for they rob the plants of food and prevent them from attaining their maximum development.

Keep the surface of the soil stirred with the hoe and water freely in dry weather. In the autumn, remove the dead leaves and apply a mulch of manure or compost, and in the following spring fork it in. In the first season the leaves must not be pulled heavily, but in subsequent years they can be pulled liberally until June.

How to Obtain Early Rhubarb. Plants which have been established for at least two years are selected for forcing. This may be done in the

The succulent leaf stalks of Pieplant or Rhubarb are used for stewing and for making pies.

open ground or in a heated greenhouse, shed or cellar. To prepare them for forcing, the clumps are lifted as soon as the leaves have died down, and are left on the surface of the ground for a few weeks. After exposure to frost they start into growth more readily.

The earliest supplies are obtained by placing the roots in boxes of soil in a warm greenhouse. If these are kept moist and dark, and syringed daily with water, an abundance of delicately blanched leafstalks will be obtained.

Later supplies are obtained by placing the clumps in a cellar or darkened shed and giving them the same treatment. The latest supply of forced Rhubarb is obtained by covering the roots in the open ground with large pots; drainpipes or deep boxes may also be used. To generate sufficient warmth to encourage growth, fresh manure is heaped around the pots or boxes.

Plants which have been forced are replanted in the open ground and are not used again for forcing until they have made two seasons' growth. Plants forced in the open ground will supply early produce in alternate years.

Propagation. The method of increasing Rhubarb plants is very simple. They are lifted in early spring and split into pieces, each piece containing one or more crowns (terminal buds), and replanted.

Young plants may also be raised from seeds. These are sown thinly in drills, 1 in. deep, in spring. The seedlings are thinned out or transplanted 12 in. apart, and planted permanently in the following spring at a distance of 4 ft. apart. Larger plants may be obtained in the first season by sowing the seeds in boxes of soil placed in a greenhouse in March. The seedlings are planted in the open ground when danger of frost has passed.

Some of the best varieties are Chipman's Canada Red, MacDonald, Myatt's Victoria and Valentine.

RHUS—*Sumac* (Rhus'). Leaf-losing and evergreen trees, shrubs and subshrubs, or sometimes climbing plants, which are widely distributed in temperate and subtropical regions of both hemispheres. Some have very decorative foliage that colors brilliantly in autumn. The individual flowers are small, but they are often arranged in large heads. The fruits of some kinds, however, are more showy than the flowers.

When the stems or roots of several kinds are injured, a thick, viscid sap is exuded. In a few kinds, particularly in R. radicans, R. diversiloba, R. vernix and R. verniciflua, this sap is very irritating and causes a serious eczema-like eruption to appear where it touches the skin. Even slight contact with the foliage or stems of these kinds may cause the rash and irritation to develop (see Poison Ivy). Rhus belongs to the Sumac family, Anacardiaceae, and the name is the ancient Greek name for the European kind.

Propagation by Seeds and Cuttings. Seeds form a satisfactory means of increasing most kinds. They should be sown in light, loamy soil in a frame in spring. Kinds with thin shoots can be increased by cuttings of half-ripe shoots, 4-5 in. long, inserted in a propagating case in a frame or greenhouse in summer. Those with strong shoots and long leaves, such as R. typhina, can be propagated by root cuttings. Sections of root, about as thick as a lead pencil, should be cut into lengths of 3-4 in. and set in flats of leaf mold in a greenhouse or in a well-drained border out of doors in spring.

Planting and Pruning. These shrubs should be planted in autumn or spring, in a sunny position in well-drained, loamy soil that is not overmanured. Very rich soil is liable to cause soft growth. The leaves of sappy shoots do not color well in autumn. Pruning consists of shaping the plants, and the work may be done in summer. However, there is no need for regular work of this kind.

The Staghorn Sumac. A very handsome shrub or small tree is the eastern North American Staghorn Sumac, R. typhina. It may grow 25-30 ft. high, but is often less than 15 ft. On ordinary bushes the leaves are 15 in. long, but on vigorous plants they may exceed 2½ ft.; they are made up of a large number of leaflets which, together with the shoots, are very hairy.

Leaves Color Brilliantly in Autumn. The leaves turn to red and orange shades before falling and the red fruits are in dense, erect heads. There is a variety, dissecta, in which the margins of the leaflets are very deeply cut. Both R. typhina and the variety can be grown for subtropical effect by cutting them to the ground line each year and restricting each plant to a single stem. In the course of the summer it will grow to a height of 4-5 ft. and produce leaves 3 ft. long. In order to obtain plants of this description rich ground is necessary, for cutting back and forcing the development of vigorous shoots is an exhausting process.

R. glabra, the Smooth Sumac, is a very similar

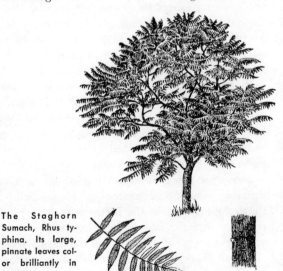

The Staghorn Sumach, Rhus typhina. Its large, pinnate leaves color brilliantly in autumn.

bush, but the leaves are not hairy. On normal plants they are 12-18 in. long. This also is a native of eastern North America. There is a cut-leaved variety named laciniata.

R. Potaninii (Henryi) is a leaf-losing tree, 15-20 ft. high, with a shapely head of branches having pinnate leaves, 9-16 in. long, made up of numerous leaflets. The small, greenish flowers are in good-sized clusters and are succeeded by red fruits. It is a native of China and was introduced into western gardens in 1888.

R. chinensis is a large shrub or small tree up to 20-25 ft. high, bearing handsome leaves, 12-15 in. long, or longer, on very vigorous plants, with large ovate, long-pointed leaflets connected by a leafy wing along the midrib. The yellowish-white flowers are borne in large terminal clusters in August, and are succeeded by small, orange-colored berries. It is a native of China and Japan, and is sometimes grown as R. Osbeckii or R. semialata. It is one of the most vigorous and decorative kinds.

Some Very Poisonous Kinds. Both in North America and in the Orient are found native species of Rhus that are highly poisonous to many people. Their effect is to cause a severe skin irritation and blistering as a result of contact with them; even wind-blown pollen and smoke from fires in which the plants are burned will produce this same effect. A frequent cause of infection is handling animals, such as dogs, which have been running where these plants grow. As noted below, the name Poison Oak is applied to more than one kind; Poison Ivy is R. radicans. See Poison Ivy.

R. radicans, known as Poison Ivy and Poison Oak, is the most widely distributed of the American species of poisonous species of Rhus. It occurs naturally over almost all of North America and is found also in Mexico and the West Indies. A plant of very variable habit and appearance, it exists in low-growing shrublike forms and as a tall-growing vine as well as intermediate stages. It grows abundantly both in woodlands and more open locations. R. radicans has leaves each composed of three rather pointed leaflets that are smooth-edged or shallowly toothed and that color brilliantly in the fall. The berry-like fruits are grayish-white.

R. Toxicodendron, also known as Poison Oak, differs from R. radicans in having leaves composed of three more bluntly ended leaflets which usually have 3-7 deep teeth or lobes along their margins. Their fruits are yellowish-white and are finely hairy (those of R. radicans are usually without hairs). R. Toxicodendron is a shrub, not a vine or climber. It attains a maximum height of about 3 ft. It grows in sandy woodlands and is native from New Jersey to Tennessee and Missouri and southward to Florida and Texas. This kind has also been known as R. quercifolia.

R. diversiloba is also known as Poison Oak. It is native from British Columbia to California, usually occurring as a shrub to 8 ft. or even more tall, but sometimes climbing. Its leaves are composed of three variously toothed or lobed leaflets. The fruits are whitish.

R. vernix, known as Poison Sumac, Swamp Sumac, Poison Elder and Poison Dogwood, is native from Maine to Minnesota and southward to Florida and Texas. The Poison Sumac is an inhabitant of swamps, usually in shade. It attains a height of 15-20 ft. and has leaves consisting of 7-13 leaflets. The fruits are grayish-white.

R. verniciflua, the Varnish Tree or Lacquer Tree, is a native of China and Japan. From this tree is obtained the lacquer used on woodwork for which the Orient is famous. Certain individuals who are especially susceptible to Rhus poisoning can actually be affected by handling lacquered articles. R. verniciflua is a tree to 60 ft. tall and has leaves consisting of 11-15 leaflets. Its flowers are whitish, its fruits yellowish.

R. trichocarpa is a small tree of Japan and China which grows 20-25 ft. high. The long leaves are composed of twelve to seventeen leaflets which turn to brilliant shades of orange and scarlet before they fall. The foliage is reported to be probably poisonous.

Economic Uses. Several kinds of Rhus have valuable commercial properties. R. coriaria, a shrub found wild in the Mediterranean region, is grown in Sicily and to some extent in Cyprus as a field crop. The shoots are cut down when about to flower and they furnish an important tanning substance. The roots of R. pentaphylla, the Tizra or Tizari, of North Africa, are used for a similar purpose.

Furnishes Japanese Lacquer. Japan wax, used for currying and finishing leather, is extracted from seeds of R. verniciflua, and the famous Japanese Lacquer is the sap of R. verniciflua. Great care is necessary in handling this sap. The woods of some subtropical Rhus trees are useful for cabinetwork.

RHYNCOSPERMUM JASMINOIDES. Trachelospermum jasminoides, which see.

RHYNCHOSTYLIS (Rhynchos'tylis). Orchids which are found wild in India, Burma, and Java. They are epiphytes, with evergreen leaves on rather woody stems; they have no pseudobulbs. The inflorescences spring from the axils of the leaves in the form of cylindrical, many-flowered racemes. The flowers are less than an inch in diameter, but the plants bloom freely. The sepals and petals are rounded or oval and the base of the short lip is in the form of a spur, the side lobes being very small. The flowers usually open in summer, from June to August. Rhynchostylis is derived from the Greek, *rhynchos,* a beak, and *stylos,* a pillar, and refers to the shape of the column.

Orchids for a Warm Greenhouse. A greenhouse with a warm tropical atmosphere is required, with abundance of atmospheric moisture. The plants need water at the root throughout the year, but never in excess. In summer the plants must be shaded, and when not in flower they may be freely syringed on warm days. In winter the night temperature should not fall below 60 degrees, and the day temperature should rise to 65 degrees, advantage being taken of sun warmth to bring it to 70 degrees.

The plants dislike root interference, and orchid baskets are therefore preferable to pots, as the compost can be partially removed and replenished when necessary. If the baskets become broken, it is better to patch them if possible, rather than tear the thick roots. The compost should be carefully looked over and renewed in February. The best compost consists of two parts of osmunda fiber and two parts of sphagnum moss, with an addition of broken crocks or small lumps of charcoal.

The Chief Kinds. The principal kind is R.

retusa, which has leaves about 12 in. long, and densely flowered, pendent or arching spikes, sometimes 2 ft. in length, of fragrant flowers; the petals and sepals are white, spotted with amethyst, and the lip is purple. R. Heathii, R. guttata, and R. praemorsa are now considered as varieties of R. retusa. R. coelestis, from Siam, has white flowers tipped with violet-blue; the spikes do not bear as many flowers as those of R. retusa.

RIBBON BUSH. See Homalocladium.

RIBBON GRASS. See Phalaris.

RIBES—*Currant and Gooseberry* (Ri'bes). Usually leaf-losing, occasionally evergreen, shrubs, natives of Europe, Asia from the Himalayas northwards, and North and South America. They vary a good deal in habit, some growing into bushes 5 or 6 ft. high, others having more or less prostrate branches. The branches of some are armed with formidable spines. The leaves are usually deeply lobed, but they have no special decorative characters, although in a few instances they color well in autumn.

Several kinds are very ornamental flowering shrubs and they can be grown with little trouble; in others the flowers have no special attraction.

Ribes is of chief interest from the fact that it provides us with several important bush fruits. The garden Gooseberries are selected and cultivated forms of R. hirtellum and R. Grossularia, the Red and White Currants are forms of R. sativum, and the Black Currants originated from R. nigrum.

Ribes belongs to the Saxifrage family, Saxifragaceae. Many kinds have been introduced, but comparatively few are sufficiently decorative to warrant their cultivation in other than botanical collections. Ribes takes its name from an Arabic name for Rheum, a plant with acid juice.

When to Take Cuttings. The species or wild types can be increased by seeds if necessary, but as cuttings of most kinds form roots easily, they are generally used. The best cuttings are those made from ripened wood. They should be made as soon as the leaves fall, and be 9-12 in. long. On bushes that will produce suckers, shoots from the base which are not wanted, cut out the lower buds when making the cuttings. In moderately mild climates they should be planted out of doors, with just their tips showing above the soil surface, about 3 in. apart in rows 12 in. from each other, and be left undisturbed for 12 months. They must then be taken up, trimmed, and the shoots shortened to within two or three buds of the base. If replanted immediately and kept in a nursery for another year, they will be large enough for their permanent places. Ordinary garden soil suits them.

Where severe winters are experienced, the cuttings, after being made in the fall, should be buried out of doors or in a cold frame under 6-8 in. of sand and there left for the winter. They may be laid horizontally in the sand or, better

still, butt ends up. In early spring they should be removed from the sand and be planted in nursery rows outdoors as recommended above for planting in the fall in milder climates.

Pruning is restricted to thinning out some of the old wood every few years to encourage the production of new branches. If plants show signs of deterioration, give a surface dressing of well-decayed manure, or an occasional application of liquid fertilizer.

The Mountain or Alpine Currant is Ribes alpinum, a native of Europe that grows to a height of 8 ft. and is cultivated as an ornamental. Its greenish-yellow flowers are followed by scarlet fruits. Varieties of this kind include aureum,

The Flowering Currant, Ribes sanguineum, one of the most decorative of deciduous shrubs. This native of western North America blooms in early spring.

with yellow foliage; laciniatum, with deeply divided leaves; pumilum, of dwarf growth habit.

This shrub bears its male and female flowers on separate plants and so it is necessary to have a percentage of male plants near the females to ensure fruiting. It is a shapely and desirable shrub of compact growth and is well suited for planting in shady places. It is hardy in the North.

The Flowering Currant of western North America, Ribes sanguineum, is a very beautiful spring-flowering shrub that is not hardy where winters are severe. The flowers appear in pendent racemes, just as the young leaves begin to unfold. They are rosy-red with a definite but not unpleasing scent, and last in good condition for a long period. The blue-black fruits ripen in summer, but have no special attractions. A number of varieties have been raised; they differ chiefly from the typical kind in the color of the flowers.

Good ones are Brocklebankii, pink flowers, yellow leaves; atrorubens and splendens, blood-red flowers; King Edward VIII, crimson flowers; albidum, white flowers with slight pink flush; carneum, pink flowers; flore-pleno, double flowers.

The Golden Currant. Ribes aureum, the Golden Currant, is another fine shrub, worthy of more attention from gardeners. Its golden flowers are somewhat fragrant and are produced freely in spring. There are several varieties. The fruits of this Currant are very dark purple. It is a native of western North America and is hardy into Canada.

Although a fine plant, the Golden Currant is less decorative and less fragrant than the next described kind, R. odoratum. Quite often the plant grown in gardens under the name R. aureum is the superior R. odoratum.

The Buffalo Currant, R. odoratum, is another fine golden-flowered kind that is quite hardy and that bears its fragrant flowers in early spring. It is even more showy in bloom than R. aureum. Occurring as a native from South Dakota to Texas, it attains a height of 5-6 ft.

The berries remain attractive all winter on R. fasciculatum, a native of Japan and Korea that is hardy in the North. The leaves also remain on these attractive plants until very late in the fall.

This handsome shrub grows to a height of about 4 ft. and has typically erect branches. Because male and female flowers are borne on separate plants it is necessary to have both sexes in a planting to ensure that the females bear fruit. The flowers have little decorative merit; they are greenish.

The Fuchsia-flowered Gooseberry, R. speciosum, is the most attractive shrub in the Gooseberry section of Ribes. A native of California, this evergreen kind grows 12 ft. high. The brownish shoots are armed with stout brown spines among which are numerous stiff brown bristles. The leaves resemble those of a Gooseberry, but the bright red, pendulous flowers are large and conspicuous, the stamens standing out well beyond the petals like those of the Fuchsia. It blooms very freely in spring. It is hardy in very mild climates only.

R. Menziesii is another western North American Gooseberry with attractive red and white flowers, but it is very coarse growing, and only suitable for semiwild places. It, too, is hardy only where winters are mild. R. Lobbii is more easily kept within bounds. It is a native from California to British Columbia and bears red flowers and purplish fruits covered with glandular bristles. R. pinetorum, from Arizona and Mexico, is a spiny shrub bearing orange-red flowers and purple fruits. It is hardy perhaps as far north as southern New England. R. leptanthum is a slender bush, 4-6 ft. high, bearing white, pink-tinged flowers. It is found in New Mexico, Utah and Colorado and is about as hardy as R. pinetorum.

The American Gooseberry, R. hirtellum, is native from Newfoundland to West Virginia and South Dakota. It grows about 3 ft. tall and has purplish or blackish fruits. It is the parent of garden varieties of American Gooseberries that are cultivated for their fruits.

The English Gooseberry, R. Grossularia, as a wild plant, differs very little from old neglected bushes of cultivated kinds. The fruits are less sweet than those of garden varieties. This shrub is the parent of the European Gooseberries and as a wild plant is widely distributed in Europe, northern Africa and the Caucasus.

Currants. Ribes sativum, from which the Red and White garden Currants are descended, is a widely distributed European shrub. Both Gooseberries and Currants thrive and fruit well in southern Lapland and other northerly countries. The Black Currants are the progeny of R. nigrum, a widely distributed bush in Europe and Siberia.

R. longiracemosum is a Currant introduced from western China in 1908. It grows into a large bush and bears its greenish flowers in long pendent racemes. The fruits are black, and racemes of ripe fruits 12-18 in. long have been recorded.

Evergreen Currants. Another unusual Currant is R. Gayanum. This is a bush, 3-5 ft. high, with evergreen leaves. It has bell-shaped, fragrant yellow flowers and is a native of Chile. It

The evergreen, white-flowered, laurel-leaved Flowering Currant, Ribes laurifolium.

is hardy perhaps as far north as Virginia. R. laurifolium is another curious evergreen shrub which was introduced from western China in 1908. Male and female flowers are on different plants; they are greenish-yellow and are not very attractive. This kind is about as hardy as R. Gayanum.

Other kinds of Currants are R. glaciale, from the Himalayas, central and western China; R. Gordonianum, a large shrub of hybrid origin, its parents being R. sanguineum and R. odoratum; R. cereum, an attractive western North American shrub with white or greenish-white flowers; R. bracteosum, the California Black Currant, native from Alaska to California; and R. americanum, the American Black Currant. The latter grows as a native from Nova Scotia to Virginia and Colorado.

RICE FLOWER. See Pimelea.

RICE-PAPER TREE. See Tetrapanax papyriferum.

RICE, WILD. See Zizania.

RICHARDIA. This name for the popular Arum Lily is now superseded by Zantedeschia, which see. The plant correctly named Richardia by botanists is sometimes grown as a cover crop in the South.

RICINUS—*Castor-Oil Plant, Castor Bean* (Ric'inus). A plant from tropical Africa which is grown as an annual for the sake of its handsome leaves. It belongs to the Spurge family, Euphorbiaceae. The name is derived from *ricinus,* a tick, owing to the supposed resemblance of the seeds to that insect.

Plants with Handsome Leaves. Only one species is known, Ricinus communis, the common Castor-Oil plant; a variety named Gibsonii, which has bronze-green leaves, is often grown in preference to the ordinary green-leaved kind. The variety sanguineus has reddish leaves, and those of cambodgensis are purple. Both the typical plant and its varieties are valued in gardens solely for their large, palmate (hand-shaped) leaves; they are used chiefly in subtropical

Foliage and fruits of the Castor Bean or Castor Oil Plant, Ricinus communis.

bedding—that is to say, in flower beds filled with tender plants of striking appearance which furnish a subtropical effect in the garden.

The seeds are sown in a greenhouse in March, or outdoors as soon as the ground is warm and the weather settled. Before being sown, the seeds are soaked in warm water for a night. When sown indoors, they should be set separately in small pots filled with a compost of loam, two thirds, and leaf mold, one third, and placed in a propagating case. The temperature of the greenhouse should be not less than 60 degrees.

When the seedlings show through the soil, the propagating case must be ventilated slightly, the amount of ventilation being increased every day until, at the end of a week, the seedlings can be placed on the benches of the greenhouse.

When well rooted in the small pots, the seedlings are repotted in 5- or 6-in. pots in a compost of loam, two thirds, and leaf mold and decayed manure, one third. They are kept in the greenhouse until all danger of frost has passed and are then placed in a cold frame to be hardened off, preparatory to being planted out of doors about the time it is safe to plant tomatoes out.

They should be set in deep, rich soil in a position sheltered from winds.

The seeds of the Castor Bean are very poisonous. Great care must be taken that children do not eat them.

RING-BARKING. This gardening operation is undertaken for the purpose of restricting the growth of fruit trees which are vigorous but do not bear satisfactory crops. See Bark-Ringing.

RINGING. This term describes a practice by means of which the leafy top of a bare-stemmed plant is induced to form fresh roots. It is carried out chiefly for the purpose of rejuvenating old specimens of such plants as Dracaena, and Rubber Plants which have become unsightly owing to the loss of all the lower leaves, thus exposing a considerable length of stem. When the top of the plant has been so treated that it possesses roots, it is cut off and potted, and thus forms a fresh plant well furnished with leaves to the base. Ringing is a form of Air Layering, which see.

How Ringing Is Carried Out. From that part of the stem immediately beneath the lowest healthy leaves, a ring of bark one half to one inch in width is cut off; the cut should not quite

Ringing is a form of air-layering. (1) A ring of bark is removed from around the stem. (2) Slightly moist sphagnum moss is wrapped around the point of operation. (3) The moss is wrapped with polyethylene film which is secured tightly around the stem. (4) When a good mass of roots has formed in the moss ball the film is removed and the rooted part is cut away from the parent plant.

extend completely around to encircle the stem.

The ringed portion of stem is then bound around with moss, and the plant is placed in a propagating case in a warm greenhouse. If the temperature of the greenhouse is maintained at about 60 degrees, it is not necessary to place the plant in a propagating case. It must, however, be kept warm and moist. In order to assure this latter condition, the moss should be wrapped around with polyethylene plastic film. This film admits air but prevents the escape of moisture.

Severing the Rooted Top of the Plant. When the roots show abundantly on the outside of the moss ball, the stem should be cut through just beneath the roots, and the top of the plant potted in a compost of loam, leaf mold and sand. After potting, the top should be placed in a propagating case, and kept warm and moist until the roots have penetrated the soil freely.

The propagating case is then ventilated, very little at first, but the ventilation is increased day by day until, at the end of a week or so, the plant is inured to the temperature of the greenhouse. It is then placed on the benches and will soon develop into a serviceable and attractive plant, well furnished with leaves to the base.

If a further supply of plants is wanted, the old plant, now consisting of bare stem only, is kept warm and moist; fresh shoots will soon develop on the old stem, and when they are 3 in. long they are taken off and inserted as cuttings in pots of sandy soil in a propagating case.

RIPE. As applied to fruits the word ripe technically means that they have reached that stage of maturity when their seeds are capable of germinating, but gardeners often employ the word to indicate that a crop is fit for gathering (ripe for picking) and is mature enough for eating; some crops reach this stage before their seeds are capable of germinating.

Ripe is also used to describe shoots of woody plants of the current year's development that have completed their growth, have formed woody tissues, and have hardened enough so that they normally break or snap when they are bent over.

The word ripe is also used to describe seeds that have attained maturity and are thus in a condition for sowing or for gathering and storing for sowing later.

RIVINA—*Rouge Plant, Bloodberry* (Rivi′na). Tender, subshrubby plants which are grown for their ornamental berries. They are natives of tropical and subtropical America and belong to the family Phytolaccaceae. The name Rivina commemorates Professor A. Q. Rivinus of Leipzig.

The only kind which is popular as a decorative plant is R. humilis. This grows 2 ft. in height, has slender, green, smooth, semiwoody stems, and ovate, pointed, light green leaves, 2 in. in length. The small, white four-petaled flowers are produced in slender racemes in the axils of the leaves throughout the summer and autumn. The flowers fertilize freely, and give rise to bright scarlet berries, about the size of Peas.

R. humilis is a common native of Florida and the Gulf states and in warm regions is grown outdoors for ornament. It is also cultivated as a greenhouse plant.

Attractive Plants with Scarlet Fruits. Well-grown potted plants are most attractive when laden with their numerous pendent "strings" of scarlet fruits. The racemes average 3 in. in length and each contains from twelve to twenty-four berries. Owing to the size and color of the berries, and the way they hang in "strings," Rivina is sometimes called the Red Currant Plant.

The berries commence to ripen in early

Rivina humilis has green foliage and bright red berries. It is a native of the southern United States.

[10—14]
Weeding in the rock garden

[10—14a]
Flowering shrubs used effectively in a rock garden

[10—15]
*Flowering Onion
(Allium Moly)*

[10—15a]
*Cobweb Houseleek
(Sempervivum arachnoideum)*

[10—15b]
*Spring Starflower
(Brodiaea uniflora)*

[10—15c]
*Yellow Rock Rose
(Helianthemum)
and blue Veronica*

summer, and others are formed and ripen in succession until autumn. They hang on the plants for many weeks afterward, and are most attractive in winter.

By growing the plants for several years, large specimens can be obtained, but as these become leggy and straggling it is better to raise fresh plants annually from seeds or cuttings. Although usually regarded as hothouse plants, they can be successfully cultivated in a greenhouse with a minimum winter temperature of 50 degrees. During the winter, when laden with berries, they remain attractive much longer than in a higher temperature.

When to Sow Seeds. The seeds, which ripen freely on the plants, are sown in a well-drained pot or pan of light sandy soil in March. The seedlings, when 1 in. high, are transplanted into a deep seed pan filled with a soil compost of equal parts of loam and leaf mold. This is sifted through a small mesh sieve, and pressed firmly into the pan. Before the seedlings become overcrowded they are potted singly in 3-in. pots, and, later on, in 5-in. pots.

After each repotting the plants are watered moderately, but when the final pots are well filled with roots the soil should not be allowed to become dry or the berries will drop. It is also beneficial to feed them occasionally with diluted liquid fertilizer.

From April to September the plants should be shaded from the fiercest rays of the sun, but for the remainder of the year full exposure to light is desirable. Very little syringing is required, as they are continually producing flowers, and it is therefore necessary to avoid wetting the pollen. The greenhouse may be damped down early in the morning and evening, but at midday it should be allowed to dry out to allow the flowers to fertilize.

When to Take Cuttings. Tips of young shoots, 2 in. in length, are taken off in spring and inserted in small well-drained pots of sandy soil. By plunging them in a close propagating case with slight bottom heat, roots are quickly formed. When rooted, they are potted separately, and treated as advised for the seedlings.

The chief kinds are R. humilis, scarlet, and R. braziliensis, purple (the colors refer to the berries). A variety of R. humilis with orange-colored berries is called variety aurantiaca.

ROBINIA—*Locust, False Acacia* (Robin'ia). Leaf-losing trees or shrubs, natives of the United States and Mexico; in some kinds the young wood is armed with prickles or stiff bristles. The pinnate leaves are made up of numerous leaflets and the base of the leafstalk encloses the dormant bud on the young shoot.

The pea-shaped flowers are attractive, usually white or rose, and produced in pendent racemes in May and June. Some kinds produce suckers freely and most ripen a profusion of seeds. The wood is hard and long-lasting even when in contact with the ground.

Robinia belongs to the Pea family, Leguminosae, and the name was given in commemoration of Jean Robin, herbalist to Henry IV of France.

Propagation of the tree kinds should be by seeds whenever possible, but suckers—shoots that grow through the soil—can be used. They are among the easiest of trees to raise from seeds. The seeds may be sown in a frame as soon as they are ripe, or stored until the following spring and be sown under glass in February, or out of doors in April, using sandy soil. It is better to sow the

A fine old specimen of the Black Locust, Robinia Pseudoacacia, in Connecticut.

seeds in autumn while they are fresh, for they may germinate slowly if stored until spring.

Varieties are usually grafted on stocks of the common R. Pseudoacacia. In some instances they are grafted low down; in others, as in the variety inermis, grafting is carried out on tall stems. Some kinds are grafted on sections of root of R. Pseudoacacia, and short sections of roots are used as cuttings.

The Robinia thrives in ordinary garden soil, but is most successful in well-drained loam. The branches are rather brittle; therefore, the trees should be pruned while young to make the branches develop as sturdily as possible.

Care must be taken to keep the tree kinds to a central trunk, for long, heavy branches are liable to break off during stormy weather.

The Black Locust Tree or False Acacia. R. Pseudoacacia, the Black Locust, Yellow Locust or False Acacia, is a tree 70-80 ft. high, with a trunk up to 10 ft. in girth with very coarse bark. The head is wide-spreading and composed of many strong, often contorted branches. The beautiful green leaves are 6-12 in. long and consist of eleven to twenty-three leaflets. The white, fragrant flowers are borne in dense racemes, 3-5 in. long, in May and June. This tree is a native of the eastern and central United States.

Young trees grow very rapidly and there is a definite tendency for long branches to be formed; they should, therefore, be pruned regularly to induce the formation of a moderately compact head. Poor soil has the effect of checking rampant growth. The wood of the Black Locust is very hard and durable and is highly valued for posts, gates and fences. It is one of the best woods for resisting decay when exposed to moist and wet conditions.

Some Distinct Varieties. A number of varieties of R. Pseudoacacia have been given names. The one called inermis is without spines; variety Decaisneana is a vigorous kind with handsome rose-colored flowers; variety unifoliola (monophylla) has its leaflets reduced in number to one or very few, and they are larger than the leaflets of the typical kind; variety erecta is a narrow tree, similar to the Lombardy Popular in habit and with each leaf consisting of one or few leaflets; variety Rehderi is a small, rounded tree with unarmed (thornless) branchlets; variety Bessoniana is also thornless and has decidedly slender branches; variety semperflorens continues to bear occasional inflorescences during summer; and variety pendula has weeping (drooping) branches; variety rectissima, the Shipmast Locust, is said to produce more durable wood, does not produce sucker growths from the roots, and has fewer flowers.

The Clammy Locust, R. viscosa, is a tree of moderate size, growing about 40 ft. high. The shoots and leafstalks are viscid and burs are often present on the trunk. The flowers are pinkish and produced in May or June.

The Rose Acacia. R. hispida, the Rose Acacia, is a shrub of the eastern United States that produces numerous suckers. The brownish branches are densely covered with stiff bristles, and the leaves and leaflets are generally larger than in R. Pseudoacacia. The rose-colored flowers are the size of those of the garden Pea and appear in small clusters in May.

This shrub is surpassed in usefulness and beauty by its variety macrophylla, which has unarmed shoots, large leaves, and larger flowers. This can be grafted on sections of root of the typical kind, or on stocks of R. Pseudoacacia. Heavy branches should be supported, for they are brittle.

R. Hartwigii is a shrub that grows to a height of about 12 ft. It occurs as a native from North Carolina to Alabama but is hardy in gardens as far north as New England. Its flowers vary in color from pinkish to rosy-purple.

The flowers of Robinia Hartwigii are white, pink or rosy-purple.

The pink-flowered Robinia Pseudo-acacia Decaisne-ana.

Beautiful Small Flowering Trees. R. Kelseyi is a very attractive tall shrub or small tree which is a native of North Carolina. It was introduced to commerce by Mr. H. P. Kelsey, a nurseryman of Boston, Massachusetts. It has small leaves and bears clusters of rose-colored flowers in early summer, smaller than those of R. hispida. Seed pods covered with reddish bristles are freely produced. It is usually grafted on the roots of R. Pseudoacacia.

R. Boyntonii is an allied pink-flowered shrub of the southeastern United States. R. Slavinii is a hybrid between R. Kelseyi and R. Pseudoacacia and bears rosy-pink flowers.

R. luxurians, native from Colorado to Utah and New Mexico, is a very vigorous tree when young, although at maturity it is only 30-35 ft. high. Shoots on young trees may grow to a length of 10-12 ft. in a single season. The leaves are 9-12 in. long and are made up of fifteen-twenty leaflets. The flowers are rose-colored and in short, dense clusters in late spring; a second crop often appear about the end of summer.

R. Elliottii is another shrubby kind, allied to R. hispida. It has rose-colored or rose-purple flowers. This kind is native to North Carolina and Georgia.

All the Robinias are useful garden and park trees, thriving both under city and country conditions. R. Pseudoacacia is useful for roadside planting.

ROCAMBOLE (Roc'ambole). A native of southern Europe, this hardy perennial Onion (Allium Scorodoprasum) is grown for its strongly flavored bulbs, which are used in the same way as Garlic. Increase is achieved by separating the "cloves" (bulblets) formed within the underground bulb, and by planting the bulbils produced in a cluster at the top of the stem.

They are planted in autumn or in very early spring, about an inch deep and 6 in. apart, in well-cultivated but not too rich ground in a sunny position. When the tops die off, the bulbs are lifted and dried thoroughly before storing in the same way as for Shallots.

ROCHEA (Ro'chea). A small group of succulent-leaved plants from South Africa, which belong to the family Crassulaceae.

Only one kind, R. coccinea, is in general cultivation. This grows 18 in. in height and has stiff upright stems, clothed with narrow, bright green leaves, closely set in four rows. During the summer months it develops large flat trusses of four-petaled, scarlet flowers. For details of cultivation, see Crassula.

These plants have been confused with Crassula and are often grown under that name. To add further to the confusion, the plant known to gardeners as Rochea falcata is classified by bot-

The scarlet-flowered Rochea coccinea, a good greenhouse and house plant.

anists as Crassula falcata. This has banana-shaped, thick, fleshy grayish leaves, and terminal, flat heads of small, reddish-yellow flowers in summer. The name Rochea commemorates a French botanist, François de la Roche.

ROCK BRAKE. Cryptogramma, which see.

ROCK CRESS. See Arabis.

ROCK CRESS, PURPLE. Aubrieta, which see.

ROCKET SALAD. See Eruca.

ROCKET, SWEET. See Hesperis.

ROCKFOIL. See Saxifraga.

ROCK GARDENING

How to Plan, Develop, Plant and Care for Rock Gardens

Rock gardening is that branch of horticulture which deals with the cultivation of alpine, rock-inhabiting and other selected plants in areas in which the chief landscape feature, other than plants, is rocks. The rocks may be natural to the location or may be brought in and arranged to afford appropriate backgrounds and suitable planting sites.

Rock gardening originated in attempts to grow plants that are natives of high mountain (alpine) regions and to accommodate them in settings reminiscent of their mountain homes. The art chiefly developed in Great Britain and has reached its greatest perfection there, where the climate is particularly favorable to the cultivation of alpines.

During the present century rock gardening has taken a firm hold in America and an active organization, the American Rock Garden Society, devotes itself to promoting the art in Canada and the United States.

As interest in this phase of gardening developed, its devotees ceased to restrict themselves to alpine plants and began to grow also plants that were natives of rocky areas at lower elevations and finally of certain lowland species not naturally associated with rocks.

Because of this, it is impossible to say with any degree of exactness what a rock-garden plant is. One expert has defined it as any plant that looks right in a rock garden, but we are then faced with deciding the question: looks right to whom? The plant that looks right to the layman or beginner may look completely out of place to experienced rock gardeners.

In the main, rock-garden plants are low and compact and some are very tiny indeed. Usually they are perennials. Most expert rock gardeners frown upon the use of annuals, although it would appear that from a standpoint of logic they are on weak ground here because annuals are not uncommon in mountain regions. Rock-garden

The Thompson Memorial Rock Garden at The New York Botanical Garden is a good example of a North American rock garden. It is partly natural and partly constructed. It contains many hundreds of different kinds of plants from mountain regions all over the world.

This rock cliff, by judicious planting, has been converted into a charming rock garden by its New Jersey owner.

plants should be winter-hardy in the region where they are grown. This restriction admits in some regions certain plants that are inadmissible in others. The majority of rock-garden plants are natural species (plants that occur wild somewhere in the world and have not been changed markedly by the plant breeder or selector) or are selections of wild species chosen because of improved color or habit of growth. However, not all belong in these classes, and each year sees an increasing tendency to admit more hybrids and improved garden varieties into lists of plants acceptable as rock-garden kinds.

And so, perhaps, the best definition of a rock-garden plant is any plant that looks right in a rock garden to an experienced rock gardener. This certainly precludes plants of distinctly gardenesque appearance such as Dahlias, Geraniums, Cockscombs and many others that are more reminiscent of formal flower beds and borders than natural scenery in a mountainous and rocky area.

Rock gardens may be classified into two types, those which result from the development and planting of naturally rocky land, perhaps after some rearrangement of the surface rocks and the baring of buried rocks, and those that are constructed from rocks introduced into the area from elsewhere and are then planted appropriately. The first type may be called natural rock gardens, the second constructed rock gardens.

Natural Rock Gardens

The development of a rock garden often provides a charming solution to the problem of how to landscape a piece of rocky ground that does not lend itself to more formal treatment. Frequently, it is more fitting as well as less expensive to develop a rock garden on such a site than to install flower beds, lawns and other more formal features.

Examine the Site. Before beginning such a development it is well to make a careful survey of the site and identify the plants growing naturally upon it. In most cases light shade is a distinct advantage, especially if this is provided by deep-rooting trees such as Oaks; therefore, any trees that will give shade for part of each day or shade all day should be carefully preserved. There may be, too, on the site, evergreens, bushes and native herbaceous perennials, such as Ferns, bulbs and other wildlings, that are suitable for retaining in the rock garden.

Clearing and Pruning. By deciding which plants, if any, are to be retained, the gardener automatically determines which are to be discarded. The work of clearing should then proceed. All unwanted growth, which includes all brush, coarse herbage and the like, should be dug out completely. Trees and shrubs that are retained should be pruned appropriately. All dead wood should be cut from them as well as any

This naturally rocky area has been converted into an attractive rock garden by judicious planting.

that is seriously diseased. A certain amount of thinning of crowded branches may be desirable. Quite often it is advantageous to "raise the heads" of trees by removing some of their lower branches. This permits side light to reach plants growing under them, to the great benefit of the latter.

Improving the Soil. Before planting, the soil should be made as agreeable as possible to the plants that are to be set out. This is done by mixing with it, to as great a depth as conveniently possible, decayed organic material such as leaf mold, peat moss and compost and, if the natural soil is clayey, some gritty material, such as coarse sand or fine coal cinders (but not fine ash).

There is usually no need to add fertilizer because the majority of rock-garden plants prefer a rather "lean" soil to one that is decidedly rich; however, the addition of a little bonemeal will certainly do no harm and is often helpful.

Narrow crevices should be raked out and filled with good soil, shallow ones deepened whenever practicable and then filled with good soil. The soil put in the crevices should be made reasonably firm by packing it with a stick.

Planting should not be attempted before the soil has settled and it is certain that it is free of

perennial weeds that might grow and choke out the plants that are wanted. To be sure of this it is advantageous to allow one whole summer after preparing the site and soil before setting out the rock-garden plants. This period gives the gardener an opportunity to dig out every scrap of unwanted growth that appears and assures a site free of obnoxious weeds at planting time.

Planting may be done in spring or fall. The plants should be set in groups and drifts and, occasionally, as solitary specimens or in twos or threes, in as natural a manner as possible. A planting of one kind of plant may follow a narrow crevice, a group of another may nestle under the base of a protecting rock, a drift of yet another kind may occupy a ledge on the face of a miniature cliff or be planted on a plateau on top of a cliff, with a few stragglers set near the bottom of the cliff as though they were chance plants that had developed from seeds dropped from the ledge or plateau above.

Inspiration for plantings of this type should be sought in the rocky areas in woods, mountains and hillsides. The final effect should be that of nature at her best or, at least, of an epitome of nature. The art of the gardener should be largely concealed. Plants should not be set in groups of formal shapes nor should the plants within a group of one kind be spaced evenly one from another. Here and there a few plants of a kind that is growing nearby may be planted among a group of another kind, as though they were chance seedlings that had developed on their own.

The Selection of Plants. In selecting plants for a natural rock garden the choice is usually more limited than for the best constructed rock gardens. This is because the site and soil are usually less diversified.

In general, it is well to rely largely on plants that are natives of the general region and on others that are known to thrive locally without too much pampering. They may include creeping plants that form ground covers and others of low stature, bulbs and dwarf evergreens. Many woodland plants are excellent for shaded areas. In places beside streams and ponds where the soil is naturally moist, bog and swamp plants may be planted with good effect. In dry, arid areas of North America Cacti and other succulents are excellent subjects for planting in natural rock gardens. See Hints on Planting the Rock Garden, below.

Constructed Rock Gardens

It has sometimes been suggested that a constructed rock garden is an unnecessary elaboration and that rock and alpine plants can be grown quite well in dry walls and in flower borders. Yet, in spite of such opinions, the man-made rock garden has taken a firm hold on the gardening public, no doubt because it has been proved in practice that a well-designed and well-constructed rock garden is the best and most appropriate place in which to grow the majority of low-growing rock and alpine plants, and because, when well made, such gardens are charming landscape features and can solve many landscaping problems, such as what to do with a steep slope or bank. See also Banks.

A good rock garden provides a wide variety of soils and locations and forms an ideal and more or less natural setting in which to show the plants. The fascination of rock gardening is great, and its strong appeal is no doubt due to the fact that garden lovers enjoy growing the small but brilliant flowers of the mountains and hills as well as of the lowlands in semi-wild conditions.

Various Kinds of Constructed Rock Gardens. Before setting out to make a rock garden the amateur should first consider the subject carefully, and decide just what his ideas are and what particular sort of rock garden he wishes to have. There are many types of rock garden. There is, for instance, the sort in which a mound of soil is covered with odd pieces of rock or stone with little or no regard to the way it is arranged. Such rock gardens are usually planted in a haphazard way with a miscellaneous lot of plants, most of which might be grown much better and more appropriately in an ordinary flower border.

The owners of such rock gardens are seldom satisfied with them, and it is hoped that the advice which follows may encourage and help them to better rock gardening.

Another type is the rockery in which everything is sacrificed to a theatrical rock effect, and in which plants are a secondary consideration, mere trimmings. The exponents of this type of rockwork rely on the use of gigantic stones and a sedulous aping of nature. Such rockeries have often been called rock gardens, but actually they have no more to do with gardening than the imitation ruins that were built by European landscape gardeners a hundred years or so ago.

A third type of rock garden is that in which the owner specializes in the cultivation of a large collection of alpine and rock plants, merely using rocks as a convenient means of providing a number of raised pockets, terraces and crevices for his plants, but making little or no attempt at producing a general effect of beauty.

Such a rock garden can be intensely interesting, and certainly gives opportunity to engage in real gardening. Its well-grown and often rare plants may be likened to a collection of precious stones arranged in the drawers and compartments of a museum cabinet.

Few people will be content for long with the first type of rock garden described, the rather ugly, haphazard affair. Few can afford, and few are so unwise as to want, the pretentious and theatrical rock scenery in which plants are merely tolerated. Many are content to grow rock and alpine plants purely for their own sake and to arrange them so that charming, unpretentious landscape effects are obtained.

Choice of Site. It has often been said that a rock garden should be as far away as possible from the house and other formal surroundings, but against this it may be argued that it is convenient to have the garden near the house, so that one may have it always at hand for personal attention and enjoyment.

With careful planning it is usually possible to screen the rock garden with evergreens or shrubbery from more formal areas, and it often is quite practicable to build the garden right near to or even against the house. When the latter plan is followed, the most important thing to do is to install the rockwork in such a manner that it appears as though the site on which the house was built was naturally rocky, and to avoid any suggestion that the area was naturally rockless and that the rock garden was constructed and imposed on the landscape.

Hillside Rock Gardens. A fairly long slope or hillside affords excellent opportunity for developing as a rock garden. Sometimes some grading is necessary to give interesting contours, to establish plateaus, miniature ravines and possibly a waterfall or stream. In appropriate places headlands and cliffs may be built up and provision for stepping-stone paths or other convenient means of access is necessary so that the plants may be examined and cared for with minimum effort. Plateaus, gentle slopes and crevices in cliff faces and outcropping rocks should be arranged to provide planting spaces.

Valley Rock Gardens. Any miniature valley or dell provides one of the happiest of all sites for the development of a rock garden. In effect such a location consists of two hillsides facing each other. Each may be treated in the manner suggested above under Hillside Rock Gardens. Because the slopes face in opposite directions a valley rock garden gives opportunity to grow a greater variety of plants than a garden sloped in one direction only.

If at all possible, a miniature stream should run along the floor of the valley. If this is not

Part of a hillside rock garden with an informal stepping-stone path leading up the slope.

possible, a reproduction of the bed of a dried-up stream may be constructed and planted sparsely near its margins to suggest that at certain seasons water flows in it.

On Level Sites. It is quite possible to build delightful rock gardens on flat sites by carefully contouring the land. Under such circumstances the best effects are usually secured by establishing what may be called a hill-and-dale rock garden.

The first thing to do is to decide on the main layout of the paths, for these will decide the shape and lay of the hills. It is convenient to mark out a main path running through the site, with one or more subsidiary paths branching off and subdividing the ground.

In order to create a hill-and-dale effect the main path should be dug out sloping down to a depth of a foot or two, or three feet at the lowest part. The subsidiary paths are also dug out in much the same way. The soil excavated from the paths may be thrown out so as to form low hills which will exaggerate the apparent depth of the valley paths between. The highest hills may rise up above the deepest parts of the paths; it should be remembered that too wide a path or valley will detract from the apparent height of the hills. Care should be taken in manipulating the soil and forming the main general contours of the ground, to keep the best soil on the surface, where it will be wanted.

Drainage Is Necessary on Clayey Land. If the soil or the subsoil is heavy or clayey, the drainage should be arranged at this juncture. Trenches may be cut through the hills and filled with rough stone rubble, or provided with agricultural tile drains. Care must also be taken that the lowest part of the valley path has some drainage outlet, either to lower ground, to a drain or into a sump hole (dry well). The sump hole should be dug several feet deep, if possible deep enough to reach down to a more porous soil. It must then be filled with coarse rubble or stones into which surplus water may drain and so eventually escape.

The Right Rock and Soil

Having selected the site, the next consideration will be the rock. Where cost has to be taken seriously into account, it is obvious that a source of supply should be found as near home as possible, for the transportation of rock is usually responsible for a large proportion of its cost.

It is well to remember that a porous rock is better than a hard one. It is more congenial to the plants and it weathers quickly and well. Granite is perhaps the least desirable of all rocks. It has a hard, cold, unyielding appearance, and it is so little porous that mosses, lichens and other growths find difficulty in existing on it.

The Best Kinds of Stone. Hard sandstones are good, and so is millstone grit. Most limestones are good, though some of those kinds which are very soluble have a bad effect on such lime-hating plants as Lithospermum diffusum, Epi-

gaea repens and many Rhododendrons, Heathers and other acid-soil plants.

One of the most beautiful of all types of rock is water-worn limestone. This is often blue-gray in color, and is to be had in an endless variety of interesting shapes which lend themselves well to picturesque and practical building.

It is not easy to obtain a convincing natural effect with boulders but this has been achieved at the Brooklyn Botanic Garden, New York.

Tufa Rock. Another form of limestone is tufa. This is soft and porous and eminently suited for growing many rare and difficult lime-loving alpines, especially the purely saxatile or cliff-dwelling sorts. It is possible to cut deep holes in tufa rocks with a chisel, fill them with soil, and plant Saxifrages, etc., in these holes. Tufa is comparatively rare and is somewhat expensive, but, being very light, a ton of it goes a long way.

Size of Rocks. The size of the rocks should bear some relation to the size of the rock garden; when only a ton or perhaps two tons of rock are to be used, it is a mistake to have such large rocks that only three or four of them go to make a ton. For a rock garden made with two tons of rock, a useful proportion would be to have five or six rocks weighing about 200 lb. each, nine or ten rocks weighing about 100 lb. each, and forty or so rocks weighing about 50 lb. each. This is merely intended as a rough guide, but rocks in approximately such proportions and sizes will be found to work out very conveniently. In every rock garden a few large rocks are valuable for making at least one extra bold feature.

Rocks of roughly 500-600 lb. are large enough for almost any purpose, though in big rock gardens in which 50-100 tons or more of rock are used it may be an advantage to use a few rocks of $\frac{1}{2}$ ton, 1 ton, or of even greater weight. For handling and placing rocks of moderate size the simplest apparatus will suffice. A couple of strong, intelligent men, using planks, a few wooden rollers and iron crowbars can handle rocks up to $\frac{1}{2}$ ton with comparative ease. For rocks over $\frac{1}{2}$ ton, "tackle" with ropes and pulleys is desirable.

The Most Suitable Soil for Rock Gardens. Soil is an extremely important factor in making the rock garden. If the natural soil on the site is a well-drained light loam, much trouble and expense will be saved for this may be used with merely the addition of sand, stone chips and leaf mold or peat here and there for the benefit of certain special plants. If the soil is a stiff, heavy loam or clay, then it is most important to prepare it thoroughly before building is begun, and it will be necessary to pay special attention to drainage.

How to Prepare Clayey Soil. A stiff, heavy soil may be improved by being thoroughly well broken up and mixed with such materials as sand, stone chips, leaf mold, grit, finely broken coal cinders, etc. It can also be enormously improved by burning. Garden refuse of all sorts may be made into bonfires, and on these as much of the soil as possible should be burned. Slow-burning bonfires will reduce large quantities of stiff loam or clay to a fine crumbly, red ashy condition, and the residue of such fires is invaluable for mixing with clayey soil.

How to Start Building

When the ground has been shaped to the desired contours the actual rock building may be begun. It is convenient to make a start at the lowest point, and begin by building up the most important headland or cliff. The object should be to construct a series of crevices and earth terraces, large and small, each suited for planting with various types of rock plants.

This bold outcrop of rock has been constructed from a number of small pieces. Note how carefully the rocks have been laid to simulate a single massive rock headland.

To form a bold headland the larger rocks will naturally be used, and here the slightly sloping and level terrace areas (called "pockets" by many rock gardeners) and crevices will be comparatively small. In this connection it is well to remember that, in planting, the smallest and choicest plants are most appropriate for putting among the largest rocks. Small plants such as rock Primulas and the compact-growing Saxifrages require large rocks to protect them from being encroached upon by stronger-growing sorts. Another good reason for putting small plants on the bold rockwork is that big, coarse plants would tend to dwarf the rocks, while small compact plants serve to emphasize their "bigness."

The arrangement of the rocks is intensely interesting work, and gives opportunity for endless ingenuity in devising cunning arrangements of the stones so as to form attractive and congenial homes for the plants. The builder should have formed a rough general idea of the effects he hopes to produce. He should work slowly, thoughtfully, deliberately, stopping now and again to study what he has done, and to consider what he is going to do next.

It is important to avoid a monotonous arrangement of the rocks. In some places the stone may be concentrated, as on the cliff or headland. Elsewhere, it may be spread out more sparsely, leaving wide open, meadow-like spaces and large sloping terrace areas, and then again it may come together into heavier building. Care should be taken not to use up all the best rock at the beginning, or the last stages will be weaker than they need be.

It should be noted that most types of rock have a grain or bed, or are more or less stratified, and that they should always be laid as they occurred in nature. In most rocks this grain or stratification should run throughout the rock formation, either in a horizontal position or else slightly tip-tilted. If this is done it gives a natural, restful effect, while if the rocks are laid, some with the lines of stratification horizontal, some tipped, and others perpendicular, it at once gives a chaotic appearance, and makes the rock garden look as though it were the result of an earthquake, or of casually dumping the rocks from a truck.

The rocks must always be bedded firmly. To achieve this it may be necessary to wedge them with smaller stones, as shown on the left. It is unnatural to have the whole of the rock face showing above ground. As a general rule about a third of it should be buried. As the rocks are set in position soil should be rammed firmly around them.

Bed the Rocks in Well. It is important, too, to pay most careful attention to bedding the rocks into the soil, so that the lower edge of each is at least an inch or two below the surface. A rock placed on the ground without having its base slightly buried in this way looks like nothing but what it is; but as soon as its base is slightly buried it assumes a solid, permanent air, and looks as though it were part of an underground rock bed cropping up through the soil. Every rock throughout the rock garden should be bedded in this way.

What to Aim At. The aim should be to arrange the stones in such a way that they look as though they were all part of one big buried rock system. It is often possible to give the illusion of a big rock by placing three or four carefully chosen, medium-sized ones close together. With care, practice and imagination this can often be undertaken with great success.

Planting in Rock Crevices. The narrow crevices between these rocks must be carefully filled in with soil, and planted with suitable small crevice-loving plants. This planting is important. The crevices are not only ideal for many choice and beautiful small plants whose roots will reach down deeply between the stones, but the plants go far in "pulling the rocks together" and making them look like one big rock which has been split and rent by frost.

During the building operations, care should be taken to put plenty of good soil under and between the rocks. Everywhere there should be a

Until the plants have grown over and partially covered the rocks a newly constructed rock garden is likely to appear quarrylike and barren.

depth of not less than 18 in. of soil, and if it is even deeper than this, so much the better. For the general run of easy-to-grow rock plants any light loam will do, but it may always with advantage be improved by working into it a proportion of sand, leaf mold or peat moss and stone chips.

Mixing Broken Stone with the Soil. If broken stone is available this may be mixed with the compost and buried, from small lumps and chips the size of hazel nuts, together with any smaller chips and dust which go with it, to lumps the size of half bricks and bricks. Such stone rubble has an excellent effect when incorporated with the soil, as it tends to keep it open, and also helps to retain moisture. The roots delight in running among the buried stones and seeking the moisture and coolness under and around them.

Packing the Soil Firmly. The greatest care must be taken while building, to see that the soil is packed fully and firmly under and behind the rocks. Air spaces must be most carefully avoided, as these can cause great harm to the plants. In building miniature cliffs this matter of packing the soil is particularly important. When one rock lies upon another below, the lower rock should be tilted slightly back towards the supporting soil behind it. Then the soil must be carefully packed in at the back of the rock.

Building Miniature Cliffs. A layer of good soil

must be spread upon the top of the rock, and the upper rock is bedded firmly on this soil bed, so that there is a sort of soil sandwich filling between the two stones. If the two rocks are tipped back at a slight angle, the soil between them will remain in place, but if they tip forward it will always have a tendency to wash and roll out. The narrow crevice between the upper and lower stones will form an ideal place to plant some cliff-loving Sempervivum, Fern or other rock-crevice plant.

Make Provision for Special Plants. It is during these building operations that provision can best be made for special plants requiring special soils. For instance, it may be wished to provide for a colony of Ramondas on part of a clifflike formation facing due north. As the rocks are built up it is an easy matter, instead of filling in with ordinary loam, to use instead a specially prepared compost of fibrous turf, leaf mold, sand and rough limestone rubble. This is the ideal soil for Ramondas, and it can be placed between and behind the rocks as they go into place.

It is easy to realize how much more satisfactorily it can be done in the first instance than if it be attempted, after building, to remove the ordinary soil from between and behind the rocks and replace it with the special compost. Peat moss may be put in during the building for peat lovers, lime or broken limestone (rubble) for plants that need a lime soil, and so forth.

The rock builder should be planning and providing for the future planting all the time.

Preparing for the Plants. Although the builder should aim at producing an arrangement that bears a reasonably convincing and pleasing resemblance to the sort of rock outcrop that might occur in nature, he should aim all the time at providing a series of homes for the plants he wishes to grow. He should never hesitate to take minor liberties with geological realism for the sake of making good crevices and other planting places.

Paths and Stepping Stones. The main layout should be such that the paths enable one to get to all parts of the rock garden with reasonable ease. There should be the main path leading through the garden for the convenience of visitors, and there should be smaller paths to take the owner and really interested visitors to all the other main features of the garden. For reaching outlying regions, recourse may be had to unobtrusive stepping stones so that the owner may get to any and all of his plants and enjoy them or attend to them in comfort. These stepping stones should be so placed that they are convenient for use, and yet appear to be part and parcel of the natural rockwork.

The Moraine or Scree. Many rock gardeners will wish to include a scree (or moraine, as it used to be called) in which to grow a number of the plants that enjoy, and even need, that particular type of soil compost, and it is a good thing to construct the scree at the time that the main rock garden is being built.

The best type of scree is to be made by choosing a larger or smaller slope of ground—a sloping gully, for instance—putting some rough stone rubble in the bottom for drainage and then filling in with a scree compost or mixture to a depth of 1 ft. or 18 in.

The scree compost is made by taking three or four parts of broken stone or stone chips and mixing with it one part of light loam, leaf mold, and sand in equal parts. It is really very simple and it is certainly most effective, for in a scree one may grow to perfection a number of beautiful alpine plants which are extremely difficult if not impossible in ordinary loam. Scree and moraine plants are found in nature in exactly such conditions, namely, broken stone, with only the smallest amount of humus.

A special feature of the scree in the rock garden is that it has the double quality of absorbing moisture quickly and retaining it long. A can of water poured into the scree soaks into it rapidly, and is then retained for a long period. Too often the screes made by enthusiastic rock gardeners are ugly, awkward affairs, put in as a sort of afterthought—square, oblong or oval beds which in no way fit into or harmonize with their surroundings. If the scree is made at the time of building the main rock garden, there is no excuse for this ugliness. It can be made to appear to be part of the whole scheme and as perfectly natural as it is in an alpine region. Its somewhat austere, stony, shaly aspect should add to the naturalness of the whole scene.

For the sake of harmonious effect it is best that the scree should be made of the same rock (broken up) as is used in building the rock garden. If necessary, however, in the event of such broken rock of the same sort being difficult or expensive to procure, it will do equally well if the whole of the underground scree compost be made of any other, more easily procured rock, the whole scree being surfaced with the desired rock chips to match the rest of the rock building.

The Alpine Lawn. Another attractive feature which may be introduced into the rock garden is the alpine lawn. This phase of rock gardening is well worth practicing, for it is a feature of extreme charm and beauty, and may be used not only for the sake of its own charm, but because it is the ideal way of growing the particular types of plants that are recommended for it.

It is, moreover, invaluable from the landscape point of view in affording contrast and relief from a too monotonous disposition of actual rocks and rock plants. Undulating sweeps of "alpine lawn," breaking up and separating the main rock outcrops, are one of the greatest assets we have in the production of picturesque and restful effects in the rock garden. For further details see Lawn, Alpine.

The introduction of water into the rock garden, if it can be done well, and in a natural way, adds considerably to the pictorial effect. A small pool may be all that can be managed, yet even there one or two of the pigmy Water Lilies may be grown, or other appropriate aquatic plants.

Making a Rock-Garden Pool. Concrete is perhaps the easiest means of making a small pond, but care must be taken to hide the cement edges with creeping plants. On no account attempt to hide the cement by placing rocks on the edges, for this device defeats its own end by emphasizing what it attempts to hide. If the rocks are pushed still farther forward on the concrete sides, the concrete is thereby advertised even more blatantly.

The better way is to keep the rocks—if any —at least an inch back from the concrete edge, and plant creeping plants which will grow forward and hide the cement. If water is available it is a simple matter to lay a pipe to feed the pond, and the feeding may be done by means of a simply constructed waterfall.

The overflow from the pond may be led away to form a bog garden, or to soak away among a planting of waterside Irises and Primulas. In making a cement pond it is a mistake to have it too shallow. If the water is deep enough to hide the bottom the effect is far better than a shallow pond which is entirely without the charm of mystery.

The cement may be colored with one of the coloring materials which are offered by the cement manufacturers, and a dark-brown or greenish tint is best. The stony gray of raw cement is unpleasing, while a dark tone enhances the apparent depth of the pool. A few fish will add still further interest to the pond, the interest of life and movement.

It is a mistake to plant small Water Lilies in too-deep water. If this is done they are slow in starting into growth and in coming into flower. They may be planted in boxes or baskets of turfy loam, and the basket or box can then be raised on a pillar of bricks so that the crowns of the plants are within a few inches of the surface of the water. Larger Water Lilies in extensive ponds may be planted proportionately more deeply under water.

Path Construction. Obviously it is a mistake to make paths of conspicuous materials, for these will look alien, and will clash with the tone of the rocks. The best of all path materials is the same stone that the rock garden is built of, broken to the fineness of gravel. This gives a charmingly natural effect.

A broad sweep of low-growing Thyme interspersed with spring-flowering bulbs makes an interesting alpine lawn and provides relief from the rocky areas.

Rock plants around a shallow pool, empty here to show construction, can create a garden of unusual appeal. The ideal rock plant is of low, slow, dwarf growth and of long life.

Here and there a flat rock or stone may be sunk in the path and will much improve the general effect.

Stepping Stones in the Alpine Lawn. Where a path has to cross the alpine lawn it is good practice to make it by placing a series of flat stones sunk flush with the soil, to act as stepping stones. Unless there is much traffic along such a lawn path, little or no harm will be done by walking on the Thymes and other plants which form the turf, but a flight of informal stepping stones will serve to indicate the line of the path, and will at the same time save the plants from too much wear and tear.

The actual placing of such stepping stones is not so simple a matter as it might at first appear. A common mistake, too often made by the unthinking, is not only to make the line of the path too straight and direct, but to place the stones one in front of another and all in line. A moment's thought or experiment will show that in walking the feet fall in zigzag pattern. Walking on stepping-stones laid in line is as uncomfortable and unnatural as walking on a curb.

A simple and effective way of placing the stepping stones exactly right for walking on, and of determining an easy natural line for the path to take between its extreme points is to stroll casually across the lawn from point to point. Then lay the stepping stones on the footprints left in the soil. It will be realized that exactly the right line has been found, neither dead straight nor taking artificial curves, and that the stones have taken just the right places for easy walking.

It is obvious that in the original walk, to determine the position for the stones, care must be used to take strides that are moderately normal.

The hints already given apply mainly to the making of small to medium rock gardens, of, say, from a ton or so of rock up to perhaps fifteen or twenty tons. The would-be rock gardener should not be discouraged because his means are slender or his garden is small. A gardener who is a true flower lover will obtain more real pleasure from a small rock garden than others may do from acres of pretentious rock landscape.

The best type of rock gardening is usually a compromise, a mixture; a technical exercise in cultivating what are sometimes difficult and exacting plants of great individuality and beauty, and creating for them a more or less realistic and natural setting. It is pleasant to try to recapture in the rock garden some of the spirit of the alpine scenes among which the rock plants grow when at home.

To those who have never visited alpine regions, this side of rock gardening must necessarily mean less than to those who have. Yet it is remarkable how many gardeners who have never seen alpine plants in their native haunts seem to grasp the spirit of the idea, and work as though they had known their alpines as intimately in the wild as they know them in cultivation.

Hints on Planting the Rock Garden

Having built the rock garden there follows the delightful task of planting it. It is assumed that much thought has been given to building in as natural a manner as possible, with a view to creating a beautiful and practical home for alpine and rock plants. It is desirable therefore to make the planting worthy of the building.

Wait Until the Rocks Have Settled. The builder-planter should not be in too great a hurry. It is a wise plan to wait a few weeks before starting to plant, to allow the rocks and the soil to settle. It is probable that here and there a rock will shift, and where this happens it is easier to put right if no planting has been done. Then, too, an unplanted rock garden is a sure test of the builder's skill; if he is content to wait a week or two before putting in the plants (which do so much to pull his work together, and cover his mistakes) he will have time to recognize any faults in rock placing that he may have made, and time also to put them right before the plants disguise them.

This waiting before planting is a counsel of perfection which few are likely to have the strength of mind to follow.

A few carefully placed pieces of rock . . . some well-drained soil between them, planted with Sempervivums and other rock plants . . . produce this charming natural effect.

(Left) Erythronium californicum *(Center)* Campanula Elatines garganica *(Right)* Anemone alpina.

A Basic Approach. Spring and early fall are favored seasons for setting out rock-garden plants, although pot-grown specimens can be successfully planted in summer. A good knowledge of the kind of growth that may be expected from each plant is necessary for the best results but it is not always possible to judge this, and even experienced planters make some mistakes. Fortunately, errors can usually be rectified by transplanting out-of-place items the following year.

Some few plants, in some few locations, look well when planted as solitary specimens, but usually the best effects are obtained by planting in naturalistic groups and drifts which suggest the manner in which plants most often are found when growing naturally.

Let the groups trail down gentle slopes, tumble down vertical crevices and hang over the tops of cliffs; let the plants that form them be planted closely together at one end of the group and gradually further apart at the other, as if the wind had scattered the seeds from which the plants developed. Let adjacent groups mingle somewhat at their margins or fringes and, above all, do not plant the groups in set, formal outlines.

Placing the Dwarf Trees and Shrubs. The planting should no more be rushed than the rock building. The wise planter will, during the interval between building and planting, do some more deliberate planning.

The most important phase of the planting is the placing of a selection of dwarf trees and shrubs, both deciduous and evergreen. A few well-placed shrubs and trees form a framework, giving character and point to the whole scene. They will prove especially important during the winter months, when there are few or no flowers, and when many of the alpines have retired below the soil and make no show at all.

Coniferous Evergreens. A fine selection of evergreens suitable for rock gardens is to be found among special varieties of the great cone-bearing group of trees that forms the botanical family Coniferae and among the closely related families Taxaceae (which includes the Yews) and Cupressaceae (which contains the Junipers, Chamaecyparis and Cupressus).

Some of the choicest of these are real pigmies that never grow more than a foot or two tall. A group of such tiny evergreen trees is an enchanting feature in a rock garden; they usually look best set on middle-distance slopes with nothing close to them other than very dwarf, creeping ground-cover plants such as Thymes.

(Left) The pink-flowered Aethionema Warley Rose, one of the showiest of all rock-garden plants. *(Right)* A free-flowering compact-growing variety of the dwarf Phlox Douglasii.

Alpine Campanula cochlearifolia.

Alpine Campanula variety Miranda.

Sedums thrive in the sunny crevices and rock faces.

planted in the rock garden. These may be used to form fine backgrounds for groups of flowering rock-garden plants; they may be set as screen plantings, and the trailing and prostrate types can be employed to carpet the ground and to provide relief from frailer-appearing types of plants. Always remember that golden-leaved and variegated Conifers should be used in the rock landscape with extreme caution, for they tend to

Nurseries that specialize in choice rock-garden plants usually offer a number of these treasures—extremely dwarf evergreen trees that grow slowly and never develop out of proportion to a miniature landscape.

In addition to very tiny and choice evergreen trees that so delight the connoisseur, there are many other dwarf and low-growing kinds that can with good purpose and excellent effect be

The free-blooming Cheddar Pink, Dianthus gratiano-politanus.

The pink, summer-flowering Saponaria ocymoides.

(Above) The blue spring-flowering Hepatica angulosa, which loves a cool, shady place in the rock garden. (Below) Another dainty little plant for a semishady position in the rock garden, the yellow-flowered Anemone ranunculoides.

give an artificial look, and may easily destroy the naturalistic alpine aspect which it is so desirable to preserve.

The dwarf Spruces are excellent rock-garden evergreens. Picea glauca variety Albertiana, the Alberta Spruce, is one of the best-known of these. It forms a tight, conical specimen that fits well with the alpine type of landscape. The Black Hills Spruce, P. glauca variety densata, is a very hardy, slow-growing kind, of compact, symmetrical habit, that is equally good. Many dwarf and handsome varieties of the Norway

A fine specimen of dwarf Spruce established in a rock garden.

Spruce, Picea Abies, are splendid for the type of planting we are discussing.

It is not always easy to identify these dwarf Spruces correctly according to variety but all are very worth while planting. Among varieties of Picea Abies that can be most confidently recommended are Clanbrasiliana, compacta, Gregoryana and Maxwellii.

There are dwarf varieties of many other evergreen trees, including Firs (Abies), Cedars (Cedrus), False Cypress (Chamaecyparis), Cryptomeria, Cypress (Cupressus), Larch (Larix), Douglas Fir (Pseudotsuga), Pine (Pinus), Arborvitae (Thuja) and Hemlock (Tsuga).

Notable among the Pines is Pinus Mugo, a dwarf mountain Pine which gives a fine somber alpine effect on the slopes, as also does its even dwarfer variety Mughus. Pinus Cembra, slow growing and alpine, makes a characteristic background. Another good Pine for the outskirts and background of the rock garden is Pinus parvi-

flora, with needle-like leaves curiously waved and twisted, and of blue-green color.

Yews and Junipers. In addition to the above-mentioned kinds there are available a number of dwarf and low-growing varieties of Yews and of Junipers. The Canadian Yew or Ground Hemlock, Taxus canadensis, is a particularly useful plant for shaded locations. Yet another good Yew that is popular for rock gardens is a hardy variety of the English Yew, Taxus baccata variety repandens. Taxus cuspidata variety densa is a slow-growing, compact variety of the Japanese Yew that can be used to good advantage in rock gardens. The last two named will stand some shade, but less than the Canadian Yew. They also grow well in sun.

The dwarf and prostrate Junipers, of which there are a great many different varieties, all need sun. Among the best is the Waukegan Juniper (Juniperus horizontalis variety Douglasii). This variety of a native American species is

Creeping and spreading Junipers are excellent low evergreens for planting in rock gardens.

quite prostrate and is effective for trailing down a bank or slope among rocks. Juniperus horizontalis procumbens is one of the dwarfest and choicest kinds. Juniperus Sabina tamariscifolia is bright green and has horizontally spreading branches. There are many more; it will pay the rock gardener to search out nurseries that offer a variety of these fine plants.

Other Evergreens. Besides evergreens that belong to the botanical families of the Coniferae, the Pinaceae, Taxaceae and Cupressaceae, there are other good kinds that are dwarf or low-growing and are most valuable plants for rock gardens. Many of these, unlike the evergreens previously mentioned, bloom in due season.

These non-coniferous or broad-leaved evergreens include the Heathers (Calluna) and the Heaths (Erica) as well as the Spike Heath (Bruckenthalia) and the Irish Heath (Daboecia). The Sand Myrtle (Leiophyllum) and the Broom Crowberry (Corema) belong here, as do several low-growing Daphnes, most popular of which is D. Cneorum. Varieties of Lavender (Lavendula), Germander (Teucrium) and Lavender Cotton (Santolina) are good low evergreens. In favored localities, such as the Pacific Northwest, many splendid dwarf Rhododendrons may be grown.

The dwarf Hollies, of which Ilex crenata variety Helleri and the variety known as Kingsville are examples, are useful for planting in rock gardens, and there are a few Barberries (Berberis), including the always delightful B. verruculosa, worth considering too.

Dwarf varieties of English Ivy, particularly Hedera Helix conglomerata and H. Helix minima, are valuable and effective evergreens for use in rock gardens.

Although not strictly evergreens, because in most cases it is their stems rather than their foliage that provide the "green" in winter, the low-growing Brooms (Cytissus and Genista) have all the advantages of being evergreen as well as glorious when in bloom.

Leaf-losing Trees and Shrubs. In addition to the evergreens, there are some leaf-losing or deciduous trees and shrubs of miniature or dwarf dimensions that can be used with good effect in rock gardens. Viburnum Opulus nanum is one of these; the varieties of the Fairy Rose, Rosa chinensis minima, are others. The dwarf flowering Forsythia named Forsythia viridissima bronxensis is also an attractive plant for setting in the rock garden; it blooms freely in spring and does not grow more than 1-2 ft. tall.

Among the shrubby Potentillas, varieties of P. fruticosa, such as parvifolia, Bowles' variety, Veitchii and Vilmoriniana, are to be found some very fine rock-garden deciduous shrubs, and there are a few dwarf Willows of value.

Some of the dwarf-growing Japanese Maples are extremely pretty, and their modest dimensions fit them admirably for the rock garden, but here caution must be used lest they give too exotic an air to the scene. For autumn leaf color they are unsurpassed.

Rock-Garden Color in Winter. A selection of dwarf shrubs and trees, both evergreen and leaf-losing, carefully chosen and cunningly disposed, will do marvels purely for the landscape effect in the rock garden, and they are especially valuable in winter, when color largely goes, and the scene depends more upon form. It is wise therefore to plant the little trees and shrubs first, so that one may best judge their effect as they will eventually be in winter.

How to Place Miniature Trees and Shrubs. It is important, in placing the shrubs and dwarf trees in the rock garden, to give them positions where they give point and character to the landscape, and it is essential to keep the taller alpine plants well away from them. It can easily be imagined that such a tiny tree as Juniperus communis compressa will be dwarfed and thrown out of scale if planted side by side with such a plant as Linum perenne, the 18-in. blue Flax, or a Geum as tall as the tree itself. The little trees should have nothing but dwarf, prostrate alpines, such as Thymes and creeping Achilleas, in their immediate neighborhood.

Evergreen Rock Plants. Next in importance in planting and building up the rock-garden picture, and especially for permanent winter effect, are such evergreen plants (many of which

are technically shrubby or subshrubby) as the perennial Candytuft. Iberis sempervirens, apart from its brilliant show of snow-white flowers in spring, forms a big cushion of lustrous evergreen foliage which is extremely welcome and satisfying in the dark days of winter.

The Rock Roses (Helianthemum) are brilliant in early summer with their myriads of satin-textured blooms that resemble little wild Roses in pink, crimson, orange, gold, sulphur-yellow, white, scarlet, salmon and terra cotta shades. Where the climate is not too severe, these plants are decorative, too, in winter, though in a quieter manner. They form big rounded knolls of evergreen foliage (which may be kept compact and within bounds by clipping them immediately after flowering), and, with foliage varying through every shade of green and silver, are among the most valuable of what may be called all-the-year-round rock plants.

The Silver Saxifrages. The Saxifrages are very useful for building up an all-the-year-round picture in the true alpine rock garden. Unfortunately most do not thrive in many parts of North America, but they are likely to prove successful in the Pacific Northwest and other places where cool summers prevail. The Silver Saxifrages are the most striking. Saxifraga Aizoon makes bold cushions of numerous leafy rosettes, each leaf edged with a white encrustation; the white flowers are in graceful, 6-9-in. sprays in May and June. The varieties rosea and lutea have pink and pale yellow flowers respectively. The three sorts, planted together in narrow soil ledges among the rocks, give a charming effect and, in favorable climates, the closely packed foliage soon grows into masses which are interesting and beautiful all through the year.

Other good silver Saxifrages for similar raised positions among larger rocks are S. lingulata, S. lingulata variety Albertii, S. Cotyledon, with flower sprays 2 ft. long, and S. Esther, with silver-blue leaves and sulphur-colored flower sprays. All of these make good decorations in sunny or half-sunny places.

The Mossy Saxifrages. For cooler, shadier rock-garden locations, in regions where cool summers prevail, the mossy Saxifrages are equally good, forming mounds of evergreen, mosslike foliage which are smothered in spring and early summer with airy sprays of pretty flowers, in crimson, pink or white.

Apart from this groundwork planting of trees, shrubs and evergreen plants, which is so important in forming a permanent picture in the rock garden, comes the equally important question of general planting.

The Pinks. The genus Dianthus includes a great many splendid rock-garden plants that are well adapted for sunny situations and well-drained soils. All of them appreciate lime in the soil. They form mounds or cushions of green or, more often, glaucous-blue foliage, and bear flowers of white, pink, red or, rarely, yellow in early summer after the chief spring display of other plants is over. The Dianthus, or Pinks as they are often called, range in size from tiny gems not more than 3 in. tall when in full bloom to kinds that have flower stems 1-2 ft. high. Most kinds have flowers that are deliciously fragrant.

The Bellflowers or Campanulas include a fine variety of low-growing kinds that are admirable rock-garden subjects and, like the Pinks, they bloom in early summer, rather later than the majority of rock-garden plants. Their flowers are either distinctly bell-shaped or are more open and saucer-shaped; they are white, lavender, blue or purple. Many of the Bellflowers endure or prefer light shade. Not all are evergreen; some die completely to the ground in winter.

The Thymes are mostly splendid creeping plants for carpeting broad areas and for planting over bulbs and for setting in chinks and crevices between stepping stones. A few are tiny bushlets that do not creep. All are aromatic, all need full sun and all prefer rather poor, well-drained soil. Their flowers are tiny but are usually borne in profusion; they are white or rosy-lavender.

The Stonecrops or Sedums are nearly all sun lovers, although a very small minority of them prefer partial shade. Most are carpeting plants and some are of quite vigorous growth; a few, such as S. sarmentosum, are so vigorous and invasive that one should hesitate to admit them to the rock garden. All thrive in poor soils that are porous. These are not moist-soil plants.

The Stonecrops vary in height from 1 in. to 1-2 ft. or more, and in color of foliage range from bright green to glaucous-blue and shades of copper and red. Their flowers are white, yellow, orange-yellow, pink, lavender-pink and red. No plants are generally easier to cultivate, although a few kinds, such as the western American S. spathulifolium and S. oreganum, do not usually grow well in gardens in the East.

The Primroses or Primulas are predominantly plants for moistish soils and partial shade; some are definitely wet-soil subjects and are likely candidates for locating beside a stream or pool. A limited number only are of comparatively simple culture, but these are all lovely and some should find a place in every rock garden where conditions suitable for their growth can be provided. They like soils that contain plenty of decayed leaves or other forms of humus.

Primroses vary in height from little ones that do not normally exceed 2-4 in., such as P. rosea and the P. Juliae hybrids, to tall-growing Candelabra types, such as P. japonica and P. pulverulenta, that are usually 2-3 ft. or even more tall. Their flower colors range from white through various pinks and reds to deepest crimson and include many shades of lavender, blue and purple, as well as yellows from palest tints to golden-yellow and orange-yellow.

The Houseleeks or Sempervivums are among the very easiest of plants to grow, and they are most excellent for planting in crevices in vertical rock faces and in other restricted quarters. They are sun lovers and stand the driest conditions, but despite this preference for sun they will grow and flourish in partial shade.

Although grown primarily for the beauty of their rosettes of leaves rather than their flowers, the Houseleeks do bloom, and some have quite pretty flowers in pink, red or yellow. Their foliage is green, bluish-green, bronze or red or combinations of these colors.

The Gentians. In the Pacific Northwest and in other favored climates a great many very choice Gentians can be grown. These add immense interest and great beauty to rock gardens, but in areas where summers are hot most Gentians are difficult and many are impossible to grow. A few offer no extraordinary difficulty to gardeners in northeastern America; among the surest are Gentiana septemfida and its varieties Lagodechiana and procumbens, which in summer bear handsome, upturned bells of blue. As a group, the Gentians dislike lime and appreciate peaty soils and broken shade.

Bulbs for the Rock Garden. Certainly no rock garden is complete unless it contains a representative selection of bulbs. Just which should be included depends upon the location of the garden, whether it is sunny or shady, moist or dry, and somewhat upon the type of soil and its depth.

The smaller bulbs, those kinds that have not been highly developed by the horticulturist and the plant breeder, are best for the rock garden. Garden varieties of Narcissi, Tulips, Hyacinths and even Crocuses should, in general, be avoided as being too reminiscent of the flower border, and this is true of other kinds that suggest formal gardening or sophisticated flower gardens.

There are bulbs for shade and bulbs for sun. Always they should be planted in naturalistic groups and drifts so that they appear to spring from chance seedlings that have developed where the seeds fell and from the natural increase of the seedlings. They should be spaced irregularly and in groups of no recognizable formal outline. Never should they be planted at even distances

Crocus speciosus is an attractive autumn-flowering species that is suitable for planting in rock gardens.

apart or in roundish, oval or other set patterns. Because most bulbs lose their foliage for a part of the year it is generally desirable to plant them where they can be covered with low ground covers that do not interfere with their growth.

For shaded or partly shaded places a selection of bulbs may be made from the following: Anemones, Rue Anemone, Hepaticas, Bloodroot, Trilliums, Uvularias, Dutchman's-Breeches (Dicentra Cucullaria), Squirrel Corn (Dicentra canadensis), Jack-in-the-Pulpit, Spring Beauty (Claytonia virginica), English and Spanish Bluebells (Scilla nonscripta and S. hispanica), and May Apple (Podophyllum). In places that receive sun for a part of the day and shade at other times the dwarf species (not the large-flowered hybrids) of Narcissi, Spring Snowflakes, Colchicums, Scillas in variety, Snowdrops, Winter Aconites, Puschkinias, Fritillarias and Hypoxis can be grown.

For sunny locations in the rock garden a wide selection of bulbs is available. Here may be used the species or "botanical" Tulips (but not the large-flowered garden varieties), Glory-of-the-Snow and Grape Hyacinth. Crocus species (but preferably not the garden varieties of the common so-called Dutch Crocus), Sternbergias, Calochortuses, Brodiaeas, Iris reticulata, Zephyranthes, Cooperias, and certain Alliums, notably A. Beesianum, A. caeruleum, A. cyaneum, A. flavum and A. pulchellum, all are worth planting.

Ground covers of low growth are especially valuable in the rock garden. By planting broad areas with these, relief is obtained from the "busy" appearance that often results when the entire garden is given over to rocks and a diversified collection of plants. Sweeps of low greenery give the eye an opportunity to rest and then to better appreciate the beauty of the other parts of the garden. Ground covers are also splendid for carpeting the soil above bulbous plants that die down during parts of the year and for using in sweeps up to the basis of small trees and shrubs and to rock cliffs, to emphasize their heights.

Splendid ground covers, some of which bloom charmingly in appropriate season, are to be found among the following: Bellium minutum,

Cotula squalida, Mazus reptans, Acaenas, Arabis procurrens, Houstonia serpyllifolia, Hypericum reptans, dwarf Veronicas including V. filiformis, V. repens and V. pectinata, Lotus corniculatus, Aubrietias, Nierembergia rivularis, Mentha Requienii, Chrysogonum virginianum, Ajuga, Phlox divaricata, P. procumbens, P. stolonifera and P. subulata, the Barrenworts or Epimediums, the little Meadow Rue, Thalictrum kiusianum, Partridgeberry, Potentilla tridentata, Cornus canadensis or Bunchberry, Douglasia Vitaliana, Arenarias, and the creeping Thymes.

Some Other Plants for Rock Gardens. In addition to the plants listed in the various categories mentioned above there are a great many other kinds that are suitable for setting in the rock garden, some of which are native American plants, others are natives of other lands. The following selection is by no means exhaustive.

For Shaded and Partially Shaded Locations: Violets of many kinds, Sweet Woodruff, Christmas Rose and Lenten Rose, Clintonia, the Foamflower (Tiarella), Columbines, Mertensia virginica, Wild Ginger, Pulmonarias, Synthyris, Silene caroliniana, S. virginica, Iris gracilipes, Androsace sarmentosa, Smilacinas, and many different kinds of Ferns, including the Maidenhair Fern (Adiantum pedatum), Polypodium Braunii and the Walking Fern (Camptosorus).

For Sunny Locations: Aethionemas, Achilleas, Talinum, Gypsophila repens and G. fratensis, Saponaria ocymoides, Arabis albida, Lychnis alpina, Globularias, Dwarf Penstemons, Armerias, Alyssums, and Phyteumas.

Care of Rock Gardens

The maintenance of rock gardens demands regular attention but, unlike some other phases of gardening, little or no heavy labor is required.

Spring Work. As soon as winter has passed and before spring growth is far advanced, the rock garden will need attention. The first task is the removal of the winter covering, which should be done gradually rather than all at one time, and on a dull, moist day rather than a sunny, windy one.

Following the removal of the covering, any plants that have been heaved out of the ground by frost should be carefully pushed back and dead foliage and weeds removed. Labels that are displaced should be pushed in firmly in the places where they belong.

The next task is top-dressing. To accomplish this, prepare a mixture of loam (good topsoil), leaf mold or peat moss and sand and modify this according to the needs of special plants. For areas where lime-loving plants are, mix in some limestone chips; for acid-soil plants, add more peat moss; for plants, such as some Primulas, that are known to like a richer soil, mix in some old rotted manure, and so on. Then, lightly stir the surface soil with a hand cultivator and carefully spread a layer of the top-dressing, about ½ in. deep, over the entire surface.

Early spring is a good time to attend to the lifting and dividing of many kinds of rock-garden plants. Many spring-blooming kinds, such as Arabis, Iberis and creeping Phlox, require shearing back as soon as they are through blooming.

Summer Care. The most important summer tasks in rock gardens are weeding, watering and the prompt removal of faded flowers (unless seeds are to be saved). Weeding in a rock garden needs special care. Some rock-garden plants self-sow and produce young plants that may be left in place to mature or may be transplanted to other parts of the garden. Careless weeding

Weeding is one of the most important summer chores in the rock garden.

A light covering of salt hay protects rock-garden plants from damage by alternate freezing and thawing.

may destroy these volunteers. The rule for watering is simple: if the ground is dry and the plants are in need of moisture, soak the soil thoroughly and then give no more until the soil again approaches dryness. Daily sprinklings are more harmful than helpful.

A careful watch should be kept for diseases and pests, although, in the main, rock-garden plants are remarkably free from these. In early summer a good many rock-garden plants may be propagated by means of cuttings inserted in a close cold frame that is kept shaded.

Fall Tasks. A general cleaning up of the rock garden, cutting back of rampant growth, etc., is needed in fall. The work may begin soon after the first killing frost.

Early fall is a good time to lift, divide and transplant many rock-garden plants and to attend to new construction work or revamping of old construction work, if any is to be done.

In harsh climates, it is wise to provide a protective winter covering of evergreen branches, salt hay or other material loose enough to allow free circulation of air and at the

same time guard the soil and plants against the effects of strong sunshine and drying winds.

It is a mistake to put the winter covering on too early or too thickly. The ground should be frozen to a depth of 2-3 in. before it is applied. Most rock-garden plants withstand cold well, but root breakage and displacement of the plants as a result of alternate freezing and thawing are very harmful. Exposure to strong sun and drying winds, without winter protection, is likely to damage the foliage of evergreen rock-garden plants.

Propagation. Not all rock-garden plants are naturally long-lived, and, for one reason and another, losses are liable to occur even among those kinds that normally do live for many years. It is therefore most desirable that the rock gardener engage in some propagating and keep a supply of young plants always coming along. In this way he can be reasonably sure of retaining his choicest items and he can have some surplus young plants to exchange or give away.

The methods of propagation employed vary with different kinds of plants and are discussed under the appropriate plant name entries in this Encyclopedia. Propagation is chiefly carried out in spring, early summer and early fall.

A Fascinating Hobby. The keen rock gardener will always be experimenting to find out the likes and dislikes of his plants. It is a fascinating hobby, full of difficulties and disappointments, yet packed with interest and triumphs. It is a hobby which maintains its interest the year through. The main floral glory is usually in spring and early summer, but, by careful planning, rock-garden flowers may be had in bloom throughout the season. There is no form of gardening so little dependent on space, and none in which so many lovely kinds of flowers can be grown in so small an area.

If the finest natural rocks are beyond the means of the rock gardener, he will find that his plants will do much to cover up geological defects and to distract attention from unattractive stones. Fine rocks are certainly desirable, but fine rocks with ill-grown plants are an affectation, while the poorest rocks may be the home of good plants.

ROCK JASMINE. See Androsace.

ROCK PURSLANE. See Calandrinia.

ROCK ROSE. See Cistus.

ROCK SPRAY. Cotoneaster horizontalis, which see.

RODGERSIA (Rodger'sia). A small group of more or less hardy, shade-loving herbaceous perennials which have handsome foliage and imposing flower spikes. About half a dozen kinds have been introduced into cultivation but only two appear to be grown today. They are natives of Japan and China and belong to the Saxifrage family, Saxifragaceae. The name commemorates Commodore Rodgers of the United States Navy.

Rodgersia podophylla, a herbaceous perennial with handsome foliage and large plumes of small white flowers in summer.

The best-known kind, R. podophylla, grows 3-4 ft. in height, and has a perennial fleshy rootstock. The leaves are large and palmate (shaped like a hand), with five spreading lobes. The young leaves are bright green, but as they mature they become bronze-colored, and are then most ornamental. In summer each shoot is terminated by a large inflorescence composed of small white flowers.

Another kind, R. pinnata, is similar to R. podophylla but less vigorous, and it has pinnate leaves. Other kinds are R. aesculifolia, with leaves 12-18 in. across (resembling those of the Aesculus or Horse Chestnut) and flat clusters of white flowers; and R. sambucifolia, which has small white flowers.

Ornamental-leaved Plants. These handsome foliage plants thrive best in deeply cultivated ground, in which a liberal dressing of peat moss or rich compost has been dug. They require a position shaded from the midday sun.

The spring months are the best months for planting. Rodgersia is most effective when planted in irregular groups by the waterside or in a large herbaceous border. In winter the plants should be protected by a covering of litter, salt hay or similar material.

Propagation is simple, as it consists of lifting the plants in spring, just before new growth begins, and splitting the clumps into several pieces, each of which is replanted into its permanent position.

RODRIGUEZIA (Rodrigue'zia). Orchids which grow wild in tropical America and are suitable for cultivation in a warm greenhouse. The flowers are very attractive and in many kinds are comparatively large for the size of the plants. All are epiphytes and have small pseudobulbs, which are often almost hidden by the evergreen leaves. The flower spikes, which arise at the base of the bulb, are generally arching and bear several flowers. The flowering season is usually in summer, but R. secunda and R. decora often bloom in early autumn. These plants were at one time known as Burlingtonia. Rodriguezia commemorates Emanuel Rodriguez, a Spanish botanist and physician.

Orchids for a Warm Greenhouse. These Orchids are grown in a greenhouse with a warm,

moist atmosphere. Moisture in the air is essential and the plants may be watered freely during the summer period of growth. In winter they must be watered far more carefully, the compost never being allowed to become either very dry or very wet. Shading must be given in the summer. The plants should be wintered in a minimum temperature of about 60 degrees.

The best compost consists of two parts of osmunda fiber and two parts of sphagnum moss. Flower pans are preferable to pots and should be as small as practicable. Fresh compost should be given in spring when the young roots are seen.

The Chief Kinds. R. venusta and R. pubescens bear a resemblance to each other, as each has white flowers flushed with yellow on the lip. R. secunda has smaller rose-colored flowers. R. decora should be placed on an Orchid raft as it is of creeping or ascending growth; the flowers are white, flushed and spotted with red. Other notable kinds are R. candida and R. maculata.

ROELLA—*African Harebell* (Roel'la). Tender evergreen shrubby plants which belong to the Bellflower family, Campanulaceae. These uncommon plants are found wild in South Africa. There are but few species, as many kinds which were formerly included in this genus are now classified as Wahlenbergia.

These dainty little plants, which do not exceed 12 in. in height, have woody upright stems densely covered with small, linear (narrow), rigid pointed leaves, and bear small Campanula-shaped white or blue flowers in summer. The name commemorates Professor W. Roell of Amsterdam.

For a Cool Greenhouse. These plants require careful handling to bring them to perfection, which no doubt accounts for their scarcity. A greenhouse in which a minimum winter temperature of 40 degrees can be maintained is required. No damping down or syringing is necessary because moisture which collects in the axils of the leaves is liable to set up decay. Watering must be done very carefully at all times. The best plan is to allow the soil to become quite dry before water is applied.

In winter sufficient moisture to prevent the leaves from shriveling is all that is required.

Summer and Winter Management. Repotting

is done annually in March or April, and a compost of equal parts of loam, peat and sand is used. The pots must be well drained and should be only slightly larger than those from which the plants were removed. Free ventilation is required in summer and on all favorable occasions during the winter; the ventilators should be closed only during severe weather.

During the summer months the plants need shade from strong sunlight, but for the remainder of the year no shading is required.

When to Take Cuttings. Young plants may be obtained by inserting shoots, 2 in. in length, in spring. The lower leaves are trimmed off and a cut is made below the lowest joint. The shoots are firmly inserted in small, well-drained pots filled with sandy peat, and plunged in a propagating case with slight bottom heat. As soon as well rooted, they are potted separately in small pots, and in larger pots as they become ready.

The Chief Kinds. R. ciliata, 12 in., white and purple; and R. elegans, 8 in., blue.

ROGUE. A term used to denote a plant which is not true to type. Thus, if in a row of red-flowered Sweet Peas several plants bear flowers of any other color, they are said to be rogues and are destroyed. Roguing is the removal of rogues or plants which are not true to type or strain.

ROHDEA JAPONICA (Roh'dea). One Japanese and Chinese evergreen herbaceous plant that is cultivated in numerous varieties in the Orient and that is sometimes grown as a pot plant or out of doors in mild climates in North America. Some of the varieties have prettily variegated leaves.

This plant belongs to the Lily family, Liliaceae. The name honors Michael Rohde, a botanist and physician of Bremen, Germany.

Rohdea japonica is hardy outdoors at Washington, D. C., and perhaps further north. When cultivated indoors it grows best in a fairly cool window or greenhouse in any good soil that is well drained. It stands partial shade and needs watering moderately.

Propagation is by division and by seeds. The plants grow slowly and do not reproduce by division speedily.

ROLLER. The garden roller is indispensable

A garden roller is used to make the surface firm after lawn grass seed is sown.

to the proper maintenance of lawns. The ordinary type consists of two or more revolving, weighted cylinders with frame and handle. Another type is the solid roller which is made of reinforced concrete.

Rolling the Lawn. The garden roller is often misused, especially on lawns on heavy, clayey soil. If these are rolled too frequently with a heavy roller the surface becomes impervious to air, with the result that the finer grasses perish. In dry summer weather, a lawn on heavy soil which has been rolled too frequently becomes very hard and cracks appear. A light roller is most suitable for use on a lawn on clayey soil.

During the spring, when the ground is moderately moist but not sodden, the use of a light roller on lawns on clayey soil will do good by keeping an even and fairly firm surface; if used excessively when the ground is very soft it will do more harm than good.

The Spiked Roller. The spiked roller is specially made for use on lawns to aerate them. Spikes are fitted to the cylinders and, as these revolve, the spikes pierce the ground and so let in the air and help to get rid of excessive surface moisture.

On lawns on light land a heavier roller may be used with advantage, for the soil is naturally loose, and rolling is required to ensure a firm surface, which is so necessary to the growth of the grasses and the maintenance of a good sward.

ROMAN HYACINTH. See Hyacinth.

ROMAN WORMWOOD. Artemisia pontica, which see.

ROMANZOFFIA (Romanzoff'ia). A small group of hardy perennial plants belonging to the family Hydrophyllaceae. The principal kind, R. sitchensis, native from Alaska to California, is of a dwarf, tufted habit and resembles a Saxifrage. It has a slender tuberous rootstock and small, lobed, heart-shaped leaves on long hairy stalks, and produces a raceme (loose spike) of small, white flowers. The flowers are funnel-shaped and spread out horizontally at the tips into five lobes. These plants, which average 4 in. in height, bloom in early summer. The name was given in honor of Count Nicholas Romanzoff.

For the Rock Garden. These dainty little plants require careful treatment. A sunny, well-drained position in the rock garden should be selected for them, and the soil in which they are planted should consist of 2 parts of loam, 1 part of leaf mold, 1 part of sand and a liberal quantity of stone chippings.

Romanzoffias should be planted 4 in. apart, in spring, and the soil must be kept moist by watering until they are established. Afterwards very little attention is required, with the exception of an annual top-dressing of fresh compost each spring.

When it is desired to increase these plants, the clumps are lifted in spring, and divided by pulling them apart. The pieces are then planted separately and treated as advised above.

The chief kind is R. sitchensis, 4 in., white, May and June.

ROMNEYA (Rom'neya). Striking and beautiful shrubby perennials which are natives of California and Mexico and belong to the Poppy family, Papaveraceae. There are two kinds only, Romneya Coulteri, the Matilija Poppy, and R. trichocalyx; the latter differs only in slight botanical characteristics from the former. The name Romneya commemorates the Reverend Dr. T. Romney Robinson, an astronomer.

Needs a Mild Climate. Romneya Coulteri, which reaches a height of from 4-8 ft., according to the conditions under which it is grown, has attractive, deeply divided, gray-green leaves and

A Matilija Poppy, Romneya Coulteri.

in summer bears large, white, poppy-like flowers of great beauty.

This plant is not very hardy but will live outdoors in the vicinity of New York City in a very sheltered place, as for instance at the foot of a wall facing south or southwest or in a corner formed by southwest and south walls, where the plant receives the maximum sunshine and is well protected from north and east. It is seen at its best, however, in climates where comparatively little frost is experienced.

The most suitable soil is well-drained, sandy loam. Ordinary garden soil should be prepared by deep spading and by mixing in leaf mold and decayed manure. If the soil is clayey, a hole 2 ft. wide and long, and 2 ft. deep, should be excavated, broken bricks or stones placed in the bottom for drainage, and the remaining space filled with good topsoil with which leaf mold and thoroughly decayed manure and sand have been mixed. It is useless to attempt the cultivation of Romneya in heavy land unless the site is prepared in this way.

In gardens the stems may be cut down annually in winter, but the woody rootstocks send up fresh strong shoots again in spring. In mild districts the stems of Romneya persist throughout the winter.

If the stems are killed by frost, they should be

cut down in spring; if they persist, it is only necessary to cut out any very weak ones and to cut back the remainder to sound, undamaged parts if necessary.

In Cold Regions. Where winters are fairly severe, the rootstock should be protected by a covering of old ashes before cold weather sets in, as a precaution against damage by frost.

The simplest method of propagation is by means of root cuttings. Pieces of root, 3 or 4 in. long, are cut off in spring and set in sandy soil; the pieces of root are laid horizontally and covered about ½ in. deep. If the roots are placed in a frame kept close, or in a slightly heated greenhouse, and the soil is moist, the root cuttings will start into growth. When growth is sufficiently advanced, they should be potted separately in 5-in. pots, and grown in a cold frame until they are large enough to be planted permanently.

This plant may also be raised from seeds sown in a slightly heated greenhouse in spring; they are sown in a pot or flat of sifted sandy, loamy soil, and kept moist and shaded until germination takes place. Subsequently they must be potted separately in small pots, and eventually in those 5 in. wide.

Romneya trichocalyx, which is very similar to R. Coulteri, needs the same treatment; it generally blooms more freely than the latter. Romneyas are sometimes known as Tree Poppies.

ROMULEA (Romule′a). Tender bulb plants which closely resemble the Crocus in appearance and growth. The chief difference is that they have shorter flower tubes and longer peduncles (flower stalks) than Crocus. Most kinds are natives of southern Europe, but a few are from South Africa. They belong to the Iris family, Iridaceae, and the name Romulea commemorates Romulus, who, according to mythology, was one of the founders of Rome.

Bulbous Plants for Mild Climates. The corms are ½ in. in diameter, and the narrow, grasslike leaves average 9 in. in length and usually protrude above the flowers, which are on long, slender stalks. They appear in May and June. They are 1 in. in diameter and funnel-shaped; with wide variety of color from white to greenish-yellow, yellow, rose, lilac and violet-purple.

In warm localities the plants may be cultivated out of doors, but in colder regions they must be grown in a cool greenhouse or frame, where they are protected from severe frosts. The flowers are displayed to their best advantage in sunshine when they are fully open.

The hardiest kinds for growing out of doors are R. Bulbocodium, R. ramiflora, and R. Columnae.

Cultivation Out of Doors. A sunny position and well-drained soil are required. If the soil is heavy, it must be replaced with light, sandy soil or made porous by the liberal addition of sand, cinders and leaf mold, compost or humus. The corms are planted in September and are placed 2 in. apart and 4 in. deep. After the foliage has died down, they are lifted, ripened off and replanted in the autumn.

Treatment as Pot Plants. Any of the kinds mentioned above may be grown in pots, as well as the more tender kinds from South Africa, R. Macowanii and R. rosea.

These are potted in October in well-drained pots filled with a light, porous compost, and the corms are set 1½ in. apart and 2 in. deep. After potting, they are set in a bed of ashes in a cold frame and covered to the depth of several inches with sphagnum moss or peat moss. When the shoots are an inch in length the plants are removed from the covering material and are exposed to full light. They are grown on in the frame, in a cool greenhouse or in a light, cool sunroom. A night temperature of 45-50 degrees is sufficient.

Until growth becomes active in spring, water must be given moderately, but afterwards the soil is kept moist until the flowers have faded. Then the bulbs are gradually dried off and rested until potting time.

Propagation. These plants are readily increased by the offsets which develop around the old corms; they are detached and planted, or potted as advised for the older corms.

The Chief Kinds. The hardiest: R. Bulbocodium, 6 in., yellow and violet, June; R. Columnae, 6 in., greenish-white, with purple streaks, May; and R. ramiflora, 6 in., yellow and lilac, May. More tender kinds: R. rosea, 6